COMPREHENSIVE APPROACH TO
HUMAN RELATIONS DEVELOPMENT
Advanced Human Relations Training Program

John C. Moracco, Ph.D.
Associate Professor and
   Program Coordinator
Counselor Education Department
Auburn University
Auburn, AL

Earl B. Higgins, Ed.D.
Assistant Vice President
   for Academic Affairs
Auburn University
Auburn, AL

COMPREHENSIVE APPROACH TO HUMAN RELATIONS DEVELOPMENT
ADVANCED HUMAN RELATIONS TRAINING PROGRAM

International Book Standard Number: 1-878907-38-7

Technical Development: Michelle Crowe
Tanya Dalton
Judy McWilliams
Sheila Sheward

Printed in U.S.A.

Reprinted with permission from the copyright holder by:

TechBooks
4012 Williamsburg Court
Fairfax, VA 22032
Phone: (703) 352-0001

DEDICATION

We dedicate this book to the memory of Pat Hollis. Though we knew Pat for only a short time, she made a major impact on our professional lives. Her faith in this book sustained us when we reached points of abandoning the project. Her encouragement, sometimes gentle, sometimes prodding, helped us to persevere. Her enthusiasm shone when we could see none. Her confidence in this book reassured us that despite the trouble it was going to be, it was worth the extra effort. For these things we are grateful. For these things we are going to miss her.

PREFACE

In recent years, American education has come under review by Federal and State departments of education, private commissions, and professional education organizations. One general conclusion drawn from these reports is that the American educational system is not serving its clientele well. Criticisms have centered on the pattern of declining standardized test scores, the lack of appropriate living skills of typical high school graduates, and the shortage of students prepared to enter highly technical fields.

Further, international comparisons of our students indicate that our educational system is not producing achievement in students comparable to other industrial nations. Implications have been drawn to the extent that if nothing is done about the status of education in America, we may very well become a second rate country.

The now famous report of the National Commission on Excellence in Education (1983) titled, *A Nation at Risk: The Imperative for Educational Reform* states: "If an unfriendly foreign power had attempted to impose on America the mediocre educational performance that exists today, we might well have viewed it as an act of war" (p. 5). Thus, poor education is perceived as an assault on our way of life and that students who do not learn essential skills will be effectively disenfranchised from participating fully in our society. These students then become a burden to society's institutions. In an age of diminishing resources, unnecessary burdens can be catastrophic.

The reaction to *A Nation at Risk: The Imperative for Educational Reform* has been overwhelming. Not since Sputnik has the focus on education been so intense. We believe that in most cases the reaction to the report has been healthy. Parents, business leaders, educators, and politicians have taken notice of the status of education in America. It has rekindled their interest in education and it has produced the kind of involvement by the community that is necessary for effective educational reform.

Ways of remediating the rising tide of mediorcrity range from increasing time spent in school to decreasing the number of frill courses. Better teachers and more subject matter offerings in math, science, and languages also have been suggested as means to upgrade our educational systems.

We have no quarrel with these suggestions. We support the five areas for change recommended in the Report: content, standards and expectations, time, teaching, and leadership and fiscal support. However, while these reforms are necessary, they will not ensure increased pupil achievement. Making the curriculum more rigorous in and of itself is not enough. Good human relations is necessary. We must not overlook the psychological component of achievement. The appropriate classroom atmosphere must be present for most students to achieve maximally. In our rush to change or reform education, we must not overlook the central component of the process, the student. We must remember that the student is a person who exists in a psychological environment which affects profoundly how he/she learns. If we fail to be supportive of the student's affective concerns, no amount of reform, regardless of money spent or time planned, will do much to increase achievement.

The encouraging aspect of attending to the student's affective concerns is that it is not necessary to add onto the curriculum. We do not have to increase the curriculum or spend more of our resources for it. What we have to do is to ensure that teachers respond to the total student and to recognize that the student has affective concerns.

The integration of human relations training by displaying good communication skills is possible for all teachers. It may require retraining and perhaps more importantly, rethinking. But since skills are typically acquired, it is possible to achieve communication skills by practice. This is essentially the focus of our text. That is the recognition that each of us is unique and that teaching and learning is a complex interaction based on the fundamental assumption that learning is enhanced in classroom environments which prizes good human relations.

John Moracco   Earl B. Higgins
January 1985

REFERENCE

A nation at risk: The imperative for educational reform (1983). The National Commission on Excellence. Washington, DC: U.S. Government Printing Office.

CONTENTS

4 PROBLEM-SOLVING MODEL STAGE I: EXPRESSING FEELINGS 89

5 PROBLEM-SOLVING MODEL STAGE II: DEFINING THE CONCERN 131

LIST OF FIGURES

LIST OF TABLES

LIST OF FORMS

LIST OF ACTIVITIES

Chapter 1

HUMAN RELATIONS TRAINING IN EDUCATION

This book, as the title suggests, is a comprehensive coverage of the topic of human relations development for educators. The training model advocated blends knowledge about different student populations and communication skills into an integral system. The communication skills component utilizes a problem-solving approach rather than therapeutic approaches of other texts. The problem-solving approach was chosen for the text because it is apropos to teaching and fits neatly in the teaching process.

The model advanced examines the nature of the communication pattern in a relationship. Suggestions are given to improve patterns of responding in a relationship which may be between spouses, parent and child, peers, nurse and patient, or teacher and student. In fact, human relations training programs tend to improve communication between any two people.

Most programs emphasize the equality of the individual in the relationship, eschew the use of power and authority to change behavior, and assume that most relations can be improved with systematic training. Changing communication patterns is seen as the key to improving relationships.

The following definition incorporates most of the features of many existing human relations training programs, however it is not as comprehensive as will be used in this book. *Human relations training is the development of skills which facilitates certain core conditions known to be essential in interpersonal relationships.* Core conditions (warmth, genuineness, empathy, respect, concreteness, self-disclosure, immediacy, and confrontation) mentioned in the definition are thought of as behaviors that can be integrated into a person's repertoire by systematic training.

Human relations training programs evolved from psychological and counseling concepts. Beginning in the early 1950s, a new direction in counseling was being forged. Greater emphasis was placed on the relationship between the counselor and the person seeking help. In some counseling approaches this relationship became the focal point of therapy.

This new approach quickly spread to other fields of human service professions. Social workers, nurses, and youth directors began to feel the influence of this new emphasis. Gradually, the approach solidified into what is termed human relations training. Several authors developed a number of systems that they called human relations training.

Despite the number of texts that present programs in human relations training, few attempt a definition of the term. However, authors have offered a variety of procedures for carrying out human relations training (Mahon & Altmann, 1977). For example, Carkhuff (1969), Gazda and associates (1977), and Egan (1975) each presented a three-phase helping model with remarkable similarities. Ivey (1971) developed procedures that he termed Microcounseling, and Kagen (1971) used video tapes of interactions as a process tool in a technique he labeled Interpersonal Process Recall. Still others such as Long (1978), Wittmer and Myrick (1974), and Gordon (1975) employed a basic communication model in their treatment of human relations.

DEFINITION OF
HUMAN RELATIONS TRAINING

The major problem with the previous definition of human relations training is its lack of comprehensiveness. Whether communication skills are sufficient for an effective human relations training program is questionable. The contention in this book is that human relations training is more than skills training. While skills training, especially in communication, is extremely important, it is not complete enough. Colangelo, Foxley, and Dustin (1979) made an astute conclusion when they wrote that other elements, such as ethnic, racial, and sexual awareness should be included in any definition of human relations. For true understanding to take place teachers need to have a working knowledge and awareness of the students they teach, and teachers need to be able to communicate this understanding and awareness accurately to their students.

What is needed is a *comprehensive approach* to human relations training, one that goes beyond skills training in communication, one that is more appropriate for current times, and one that includes all constituents of education—the handicapped, the gifted, the learning disabled, the Mexican-American, and others. A broad perspective is needed for diverse elements found in today's classroom.

To this end the following definition is offered as a foundation for this book. *Human relations training is a program which facilitates recognition and appreciation of differences in individuals and develops communication skills as the basis for effective interpersonal relationships.* This definition provides a comprehensive basis as it incorporates the concept of the diversity of individuals as a basic strength in interpersonal communication. Effective communication is enhanced by shared knowledge between the sender and receiver. Teachers need to have knowledge of effects of racism, sexism, ageism, and xenophobism on learning. This knowledge acquisition requires more than training in communications skills, and it requires more than awareness of certain stereotypes of students. Essential is a commitment to a philosophy that a teacher is more than a transmitter of information. A teacher is most effective when he/she exemplifies humanness, shares individual needs and values, and revels in the unique richness of individualities.

EXPECTED OUTCOMES

By studying the material in this chapter the reader will be able to

1. list at least four reasons for human relations being a part of teacher training,

2. describe components of a comprehensive model for human relations training, and

3. list major goals of a comprehensive human relations training program.

RATIONALE FOR HUMAN RELATIONS TRAINING IN TEACHER EDUCATION

Rationale for human relations training in teacher education rests on at least the following points. Special skills are needed when substantial differences exist between learners and teachers, when a common base of experiences and values between learner and teacher can no longer be taken for granted, and when differences seem to be increasing because of our changing society. Recent regulations and laws, pressures in living, and other features of contemporary times create further need for human relations training as an effective means of bridging the gap between these differences.

The United States is a nation of people of many different ethnic, racial, and religious origins. Characteristics of multicultural society have been portrayed as sources of both strength and weakness. Occasionally needs and wants of a pluralistic society have been divisive, sometimes resulting in catastrophic events. Examples of these are the Civil War and the riots of the 1960s. However, the promise of this country is in the character of its people. Despite problems of a pluralistic society, our cultural diversity could become our most basic strength. American society needs to reconcile its struggle for individuality on the one hand and its desire to foster a homogeneous society on the other. Education has a fundamental role in this process. It is probably the best agent to help facilitate individualism expressed in racial, ethnic, and sexual components, and at the same time forge a feeling of purposive unity in the American people.

Utilizing resources of our diverse society is perhaps the greatest contemporary concern of the United States. Other nations, such as Japan, have a more homogeneous culture expressed in religious, racial, and ethnic similarities. Thus, these countries do not have to expend the same amount of energy that the United States does in agreeing on values and customs governing societal behavior that contain contributions from all. On the other hand, diversity in America has provided a richness to society. Americans are a very dynamic and energetic people. Much of this dynamism can be attributed to cultural diversity.

Education, as a major social institution, has been used by society as the main agent for reconciling differences rather than facilitating their contributions. The American people have placed much of the responsibility for the integration of its diverse social elements in the hands of educators. So much so has this been the case that for most problems confronting Americans, formal schooling has been seen as the solution. This is typified by education assuming responsibility for problems such as sex education, racial integration, drug prevention, and moral education.

Reasons for this responsibility being placed on public schools can be far reaching. Schools provide a controllable environment; schools are places where children spend most of their waking hours; and in addition, the American public has recently accepted the judgment of education experts and thus believes that schools could be revolutionized to promote social change.

In general, school programs, however, have not kept pace with expanding concepts of the role of the school in society. The gap between what school personnel should do as defined by public expectations and what they actually do accomplish is probably of more serious consequence today than at any other period in history.

Many schools which stress achievement and command of the fundamental process of learning fail to accomplish other cardinal goals. While these objectives are indispensable, their emphasis does not preclude consideration of other objectives to which the public has long been committed, such as objectives concerned with health, economic adequacy, wise use of leisure time, and competence as a citizen. A major challenge of schools today is development of curriculum and teaching programs which express adequately the purposes schools are expected to serve.

FIVE FACTORS AFFECTING
HUMAN RELATIONS TRAINING PROGRAM

A realistic view of what education can and cannot do is being developed in contemporary education. A rationale for human relations training for educators must be tempered by this emerging view. Elements of this new ideology must be considered in a rationale.

Rationale for implementing human relations training in teacher preservice and in-service education focuses on five concerns affecting education today. These concerns include:

1. changing characteristics of school populations,
2. effects of recent legislation on teachers and students,
3. contemporary American stressful lifestyle,
4. ideological basis for human relations, and
5. research evidence indicating the efficacy of human relations training.

Overall effects of these concerns is that substantial differences exist between teachers and students. Shared commonalities, a basis for learning and understanding one another, may be severely strained or nonexistent in many classrooms. Generally, shared commonalities center around such characteristics as language, customs, and values. Today, more than at any other time in educational history, differences in characteristics between student and teacher are profound.

The fourth and fifth concerns provide a basis for human relations as the vehicle to bridge differences among teachers and students. An elaboration of each of these concerns follows.

Changing Characteristics of School Populations

Urbanization of the United States. Once a largely rural nation, today over 80% of Americans live in urban or suburban communities. This unprecedented shift in population came about through the process of industrialization which created changes in all facets of American life. Education has been affected by the ramifications of industrialization. Skills and demands of modern industry placed pressures on education to keep more students in school for longer periods of time. Consequently, the teacher of today is faced with a student population that likely differs from past students on a number of dimensions.

Differences among students are reflected in value systems, academic preparation, life expectancies, and goals. In many classrooms the teacher is confronted with children from diverse backgrounds. Commonalities and shared experiences by students and teachers are becoming less frequent, making mutual understanding and efficient learning more difficult. The student from an urban ghetto who has adapted admirably to his/her street culture may find interaction with middle and upper class teachers strained. The child with a concept of time different from most teachers may not be evaluated by teachers by the same criteria that the student is by his/her friends and family.

That is, values and customs which govern the behavior of the minority student may not be in concert with those of his/her teachers. Consequently, these differences may be looked upon as strange and in some instances, incomprehensible. When this situation exists, learning can be either enhanced by diversity or compromised by it. It takes skill and understanding for a teacher to be effective in these situations.

Multicultural and Minority Group Awareness. Added to urbanization and industrialization features of American society, there has been an awakening of cultural and minority group awareness in the last 50 years. Where once the melting pot phenomenon provided an ideological basis for an integrated society, currently many cultural groups are rejecting this concept. The melting pot theory had implications that were not taken into account by its supporters. Operating on the melting pot analogy unfortunately tends to devalue the individual's own ethnicity. To many members of racial and ethnic groups the message was clear, even if misunderstood. That is, the American ideal, usually equated with white middle-class values, was proper and others were improper. Specifically, white was preferred, Black was not; standard English was acceptable, Spanish was unacceptable; and Western European ancestry was valued, native American ancestry was devalued. While this seems to be an oversimplification, the effect undergirding the concept for minority groups is valid: their cultural or racial heritage is not as highly valued in society as a whole and specifically it is not valued in schools.

Thus, the minority student has the unenviable task of rejecting his/her heritage and accepting a new one. In effect this student suffers double jeopardy. Denied security, the minority student has to acquire values and behaviors of a new system. In many cases, these students are forced to accommodate new behaviors that have to be learned in a vacuum. They are not exposed to these behaviors in the home, thus they are deprived of appropriate models.

Related to this lack is the concept of compensatory education. During the 1950s and 1960s billions of dollars were spent on programs designed to upgrade (or compensate) certain students' experiences. Again, what stands out to many members of cultural groups is that their heritage and values are inferior and need to be brought up to "American standards" through compensatory education.

Currently, ethnic and racial groups are rejecting the notion of being treated as if they are inferior. They are saying that their value systems may be different but they are not inferior. Hispanics, Native Americans, and Blacks, for example, are beginning to act on the assumption that their way of life is as legitimate as anyone else's and they have contributions to make to society and the American lifestyle.

School personnel and involved parents must be responsive to this new thinking. Teachers, involved parents, and other school personnel must incorporate minority students value system into the contemporary curriculum so that students can feel that their heritage is worthwhile. *The concept that being different is not necessarily the same as being inferior will become a significant part of every teacher's and other school personnel's repertoire. More than any other one concept, this best signifies what human relations training is about.*

Most individuals have a difficult time coping with events, values, and behaviors that are different from their own. In many cases, differences are very unsettling and considered threatening. Others find differences dynamic and facilitating to learning rather than threatening. Because of differences, individual behavior is not always predictable and this uncertainty of how to react to differences often makes people angry. Knowledge and awareness of different cultures in the U.S. can help alleviate some of the anxiety that comes from interacting with different individuals.

The women's movement also has contributed to the changing characteristics of society. Full ramifications of this movement are not yet known. Certainly, however, family and male-female relationships are undergoing changes. Assumptions made about women in the past are no longer valid. Teachers and others involved in the educational setting especially need to be aware that women students are operating under different expectancies than those of a few decades ago. Teachers must be cognizant of the need to function without discrimination to women and others. Women in schools are full and equal participants in American society as are other individuals.

School personnel are powerful role modifiers for children as learners. Textbooks, films, and other instructional materials often present typical ways of behaving for males and females. School personnel can be instrumental by reinforcing nontraditional sex roles. Females can be presented in teaching materials that reflect an egalitarian approach. Textbooks can be very subtle in their approach to stereotyping behaviors of males and females. Reading series used in schools a few decades ago were notorious for depicting underdeveloped roles of women. Mothers were portrayed primarily as caretakers. Little girls were not very active whereas boys were shown to be adventuresome and spirited. Major decisions were delegated to the father and more stories were devoted to the activities of "Dick" than they were to "Jane."

What was valuable in these materials was not missed by students. Though subtle, the message was clear: Male behavior was more important and interesting than female behavior. Obviously, abuses such as these are no longer as blatant as they once were. However, schools must promulgate male and female roles as different but equal in value. Sex roles must not be bound up in occupational constraints. A fully functioning society asks each of its members to be all that *he/she* is capable of becoming.

Summarizing the foregoing content, conclusions can be drawn that the urbanization process, the multicultural awareness, and the women's movement contributed in part to fostering characteristics in student formulations different from that of the past. Further, this feature of society tends to make commonalities (values, customs, and so forth) between students and teachers more and more remote. When commonalities do not exist between individuals, the opportunities for misunderstandings, distrust, and suspicion increase. Clearly, this negation can create an impediment to learning

**Effects of Legislation and Court
Decisions on School Population**

Laws have been pased by state and federal legislators that have had significant impact on the composition of school populations. An early piece of legislation was the compulsory education law. The net effect of this kind of legislation was to change the composition of the student population. Mass education forced teachers to deal with students from a variety of backgrounds. Curricula have changed somewhat in response to different needs of diverse student populations. However, while changes occurred in *academic* curricula, little if any change occurred in *affective* curricula either in public schools or in teacher education programs. For example, a casual examination of curricula in teacher training programs for the past 50 years would reveal that little changes have been made. The emphasis has been and continues to be on teaching subject matter rather than teaching students.

In the past, American mass education has performed a tremendous mission by incorporating millions of students who immigrated from dozens of countries into its classrooms. Perhaps no other nation in history has performed such a task. However, the burden of change fell heavily on the student. To fit into the new American classroom was up to the student. New students had to abandon previous behaviors and had to acquire new ones appropriate to the classroom milieu. Other societal institutions at that time were capable of absorbing students who were unable or unwilling to change their behavior. Industry was in search of masses of semi-skilled and unskilled workers. Today these conditions no longer exist. Opportunities no longer exist for individuals who choose not to adapt to prevailing ethics of our industrial society.

A series of court decisions beginning in the 1950s has had pronounced effects on education. Court decisions of Brown (1954), Escobedo (1964), Rodriques (1971), and Lau (1974) are but a few of the important ones that reinforced the concepts of cultural pluralism in education (Valverde, 1978). The landmark Brown case established a legal basis for school desegregation. The court decision in the Lau case required a school district with non-English speaking students to include instruction in the students native language. General effects of these court decisions were to force educators to rethink policy from that of the "Americanization" of students to an appreciation of intergroup and intragroup cultural diversity.

Public Law 94-142 and Public Law 93-112 (sections 503 and 504) are recent pieces of legislation passed by Congress that may be as profound as the historic Brown case of 1954. In Public Law 94-142, the concept of placing the student in the least restrictive educational environment (mainstreaming) resulted in having students with a variety of handicaps placed in regular classrooms. Teachers are being faced with students with a variety of needs—academic, physical, social, and psychological. Communicating, understanding, and relating to these students will tax the resources of many teachers. Teachers are being confronted with students who may have handicaps that threaten their professional competency. Understanding why teachers feel frustrated with their new obligations is easy. Many teachers are placed in a position in which they have to sacrifice time with regular students in order to accommodate the previously labeled "special" student. A comprehensive human relations training program can provide help for these teachers, the kind of help not found in courses in pedagogy and methodology.

Some states are recognizing the need for human relations training for teachers. Several have required courses to be taken in human relations training by prospective teachers. Georgia, Iowa, Wisconsin, and Minnesota require all teacher education students to take such courses. Many higher education institutions which offer teacher training provide some kind of course in human relations training even though it may not be required by the state department. Minnesota Department of Education Curriculum Guide summarizes the position that some states are taking:

> A school may have an excellent over-all human relations program but individual teachers without a strong commitment to human rights may destroy such a program by prejudicial behavior. (Minnesota Department of Education, 1974, p. vii)

The Minnesota State Board of Education has demonstrated its sensitivity to this problem as well. New regulations require all elementary and secondary school teachers to complete training programs containing human relations components before receiving initial or continuing certification. At the very least, teachers must be able to act without expressing prejudicial or discriminatory behavior. Ideally they would internalize a set of values supportive of these guidelines (Minnesota Department of Education, 1974 p. viii). While legislating the spirit of human relations training is impossible, exposure to such programs affords the opportunity for teachers to examine the nature of prejudice, to clarify the nature of prejudice, to clarify values, and hopefully, to move this nation closer to its potential.

Contemporary American
Stressful Lifestyle

Public school classrooms reflect, to a large degree, the conflict and concerns of society. Drugs, violence, and racism are found in classrooms, and these concerns generally interfere with student learning. Teachers are faced with student problems unheard of just a short time ago. Many teachers feel that they are unprepared to handle these concerns. Much teacher time is spent on activities other than traditional activities. Dealing with stress in today's classroom environment consumes a large share of classroom time.

Students do not escape the stress found in and out of classrooms. Cases of teen drug and alcohol abuse are a national concern. Adolescent suicide has increased dramatically in the last 20 years. In the past, teen suicide was rarely acknowledged, today it is the second greatest killer of youth. Teen suicide has increased 203 percent over the past 20 years (Wendt, 1980). Three hundred thousand known suicide attempts by teens occurred in the U.S. during 1978. Reasons for teen suicide are many; however, the impact of today's stressful environment cannot be taken lightly. Apparently, many students today are choosing to deal with stress by consuming drugs and alcohol. The toll that these ineffective coping mechanisms take on youth is frightening. Clearly, many of America's teenagers need to be shown effective methods of living in the environment of a stressful society. Human relations training can provide skills to teachers to help with this alarming problem.

Teachers also personally feel the effects of today's stress in their classrooms. They are asked to handle students who do not want to be in school. The number of teacher assaults is frightening. In 1977, assaults on teachers were reported in 70,000 cases. Recently, a teacher in Chicago won an arbitration award for "battle fatigue" that came about when a student threatened to shoot him.

Instructor magazine reported that in a survey of teachers, the majority responding thought that teaching was hazardous to their health.

Further, as many as 33 % of teachers who took sick leave claimed that it was related to stress or tension experienced in classrooms. Not only are teachers deciding to be absent from school more often to escape the stress that is inherent in teaching, they are choosing not to remain in the profession. In a recent study of teachers in a large metropolitan county school system more than one-half (52%) of the teachers who responded stated that, if they had their lives to live over again, they would not become teachers (Moracco, D'Arienzo, & Danford, 1982). This represents a significant change from previous responses to this question. Over the past five decades, the percentage of individuals who would choose not to be teachers again has increased steadily from about 25% to about 50%. Results of this questionnaire can be a rough indicator of job satisfaction. Apparently, teachers in today's classrooms are not satisfied with their professional environment.

Clearly, today's school environment is taking a toll on teachers and other school personnel. Not quite so obvious is the conclusion that traditional teacher preparation in pedagogy and methodology is not sufficient. Human relations training added to a traditional program may provide skills necessary to facilitate the reduction of tension and stress that exist in today's classrooms for both students and teachers.

Many other features of our society act as indicators of a stressful environment. High divorce rate, single parent families, changing behavior, and value systems of American students are but a few features which call upon teachers to interact with students in a way for which they may have not been prepared adequately.

**Ideological Basis
for Human Relations**

The foregoing material was presented with the intent to support the claim that a diversity exists between student and teacher. This diversity takes on many forms. Some include differences in ethnic and racial values and customs. Diversity complicates the teaching-learning process. Learning takes place more easily and steadily when experiences and values of teacher and learner are common. When commonalities are lacking, learning becomes more difficult and impacts on both teacher and learner sometimes resulting in feelings of inadequacies and frustration on both the teacher and the student.

Compensatory education once provided the ideological basis to help bridge differences. However, compensatory education has not been very successful, and it is being increasingly rejected by minority and racial groups. Compensatory education has spawned a number of remedial programs costing huge sums of money. The fiscally conservative mood of the country beginning in 1980 makes funding quite unlikely for these programs to the extent that they once were. What is needed is a system of education that integrates rather than compensates. New approaches to this problem need to be investigated.

Human relations training can provide an ideological basis for education because one goal is to seek "an appreciation of diversity for pluralism, and the ability to take into account the dignity and worth of others as a requisite for mutual understanding" (Colangelo, Foxley, & Dustin, 1979, p. 81). *The accommodation of the American paradox; to encourage individualism and at the same time foster a unified culture, is the real task. Effective human relations training subscribes to the notion that everyone is a member of the human community. When the training fosters appreciation and awareness of the richness and uniqueness of different cultural, racial, and sexual groups, it can aid in the accommodation of the American paradox.*

**Research Basis for
Human Relations Training**

This section provides a research basis for human relations training in education. Flanders' (1970) research on seven major investigations which took place during a 20 year period found that teachers who attended to personal dimensions of learners produced in students higher achievement and more positive attitudes toward school.

> It appears that when classroom interaction patterns indicate that pupils have opportunities to express their ideas, and then these ideas are incorporated into the learning activities, students seem to learn more and to develop more positive attitudes toward the teacher and the learning activities. (Flanders, 1970, p. 401)

Teacher behaviors that were warm, understanding, responsible, caring, friendly, and stimulating were often part of the repertoire of effective teachers. These behaviors bear striking resemblance to behaviors thought to be important in human relations training.

Gazda et al., (1977) have identified three components of effective teaching that place interpersonal qualities of teacher behavior in proper perspective. First, the teacher must be knowledgeable about content to be taught. Second, the teacher must present this material in an appropriate sequence. Third, the teacher must be able to demonstrate interpersonal communication skills. Most institutions which have teacher education programs provide the first two requirements adequately. Teacher trainees who are preparing for the teaching profession complete several courses concerned with subject-content of the teaching specialty and with instructional methodology. All states also require a fifth year of study for permanent teacher certification.

However, few institutions offer courses and experiences which prepare individuals to interact effectively with others from a variety of backgrounds. When colleges and universities do offer courses, often these are in the form of a didactic experience. The prospective teacher is expected to transform the content from the didactic course into a meaningful system that can be incorporated into teaching behavior. A hazard of this approach is that it tends to be artificial and as such it never really becomes a part of the everyday repertoire of the teacher's behavior.

A MODEL FOR
HUMAN RELATIONS TRAINING

The foregoing definition of human relations training provides the foundation for a comprehensive model of human relations training. Basic components of the model include an awareness and knowledge of diversity in individuals and the personal affective growth of students. The model employs communications skills as a vehicle for facilitative interpersonal relationships. In Figure 1.1 is illustrated the relationship of the three components—skills and strategies, behaviors, and knowledge areas—in this model. The inner hub and spokes represent skills and strategies important in effective communication. This provides the foundation for relating to diverse elements in the school population. The spokes on the diagram represent some of the behaviors important in interpersonal communications. Those shown on the diagram are a few of many behaviors of effective communications. These behaviors are conceived as skills that can be accurately demonstrated, observed, and assessed. Also the vast majority of teachers are assumed to be capable of learning these skills.

Because communication skills are necessary but *not* sufficient conditions for a comprehensive treatment of human relations, five knowledge areas—multicultural education, nonracist education, nonsexist eduction, all children education, and psychological education—are essential and are shown in the outer circle. These components provide requisite knowledge and awareness of diversities in students so that an appreciation for the unique richness inherent in individuality can bring a heightened sense of humanness to personal relationships.

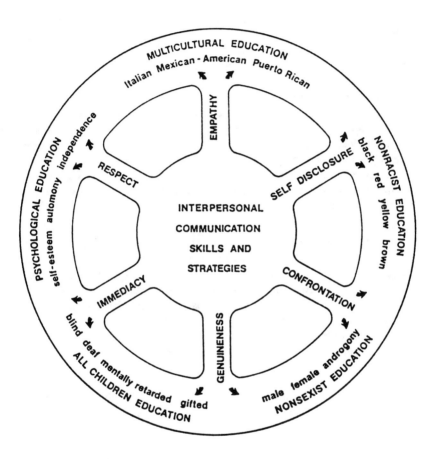

Figure 1.1. Model for comprehensive human relations training program: Skills and strategies, communication behaviors, and knowledge awareness areas.

The five knowledge areas are presented as though they are discrete. However, in reality these areas overlap to a degree. For example, multicultural education and nonracist education have a number of similarities. This should not be thought of as duplication. While minority and racial groups experience similar effects in schools because of their backgrounds, these effects always impact uniquely on the individual. What is really important is that teachers develop an appreciation of and respect for diversity in their students. Though this text groups student diversities into five knowledge areas, thousands of categories exist by which students differ. However, to try to isolate the many diverse characteristics of students is not practical. This text organizes student diversity by two criteria. One is the degree of positive impact the particular student diversity has on learning and the other is how frequently the diversity appears in students. Ideally each student represents a unique diversity and should be viewed as such; however, to attempt to cover all the possible diverse elements that students possess presents an overwhelming task. Diversity needs to be organized into collections of individuals for parsimony and enhancement of learning.

As indicated in Figure 1.1, interpersonal communications skills and strategies are the heart of the comprehensive human relations training model. Behaviors are placed in the spokes of the model. They represent links to the knowledge areas which include important concepts in contemporary education. This model intends to use communication skills as the integrating and cohesive agent to the five important knowledge areas listed in the outside rim — Nonracist Education, Multicultural Education, Psychological Education, Nonsexist Education, and All Children Education.

Concepts in the outer rim represent major elements of diversity among school populations. If appropriate appreciation for and awareness of these concepts (knowledge areas) are mastered, and if the concepts are combined with a delivery system (communication skills), then major components of an effective human relations training program have been implemented.

In later chapters each area will be considered as a separate section of the text. The main purpose of this section is to give an overview of some of the main features of the major cultural and ethnic groups in our society. For example, in the Mexican-American population the concept of honor maintains a major role in behavior. This must be understood fully if teachers are to understand some of the behaviors of Mexican-American students.

The English language as developed in U.S. society has potential for racial overtones. The English language sometimes encourages racist attitudes. The competent teacher must be aware of this feature.

Females have not always been treated equally in school. We have come a long way from, "You don't want to be a doctor, Mary. You want to be a nurse," attitude. However, in numerous other subtle ways females are told that they have certain stations in life. The contemporary teacher is aware of this ubiquitous phenomenon. The chapter regarding Nonsexist Education aims at bringing to light some of the ways females are treated unfairly.

Since the enactment of Public Law 94-142 and similar state laws, great changes are taking place in the regular classroom. "Mainstreaming," a feature of this law, has transferred many students who were in special education classes into regular classrooms. The classroom teacher is now faced with children with a myriad of handicaps and disabilities. How to deal with these concerns is the focus of the chapter called All Children Education. Attitudes toward the handicapped will be explored as well as explication of strategies that can be used when interacting with handicapped children.

Most teachers are aware of the importance of children's self-esteem in the learning process. Practicing teachers are witnessing the penalty that poor self-esteem exacts from students' growth in the affective domain. Teachers realize that schooling goes beyond teaching the 3 R's. While the 1980s are experiencing a conservative back-to-basic movement in education, a forceable argument can be made that positive self-image is just as basic in a student as is knowledge of the state capitals. In fact interplay exists between learning and one's image. The effective teacher knows how to encourage and develop both of these aspects. Positive self-esteem is just one of the topics in the chapter entitled Psychological Education. Other topics are autonomy and independence.

GOALS OF A COMPREHENSIVE HUMAN RELATIONS TRAINING PROGRAM

A human relations program cannot actualize its potential without definitely stated goals. Too often good intent suffices for lack of explicit goals for human relations training. "Goals unexpressed are goals that will not be reached. Implicit goals can be overlooked as well as misunderstood; a program without clear and worthy objectives flounders into irrelevance" (Minnesota Department of Education, 1974).

Hundreds of goals are suitable for a human relations training program. Goals chosen for a particular model reflects a certain philosophy. The ten goals listed in Table 1.1 represent what can be expected from individuals properly trained in human relations. The table also includes a limited elaboration of the goal (second column), objectives for the goal (third column), and at least one activity that can be performed to indicate understanding of the goal (last column). The intent is not to list all objectives and activities because they may vary from situation to situation. Rather, the intent is to give illustrative materials so that individuals can devise others in keeping with their own needs. For example, human relations training geared for teachers who intend to work with Mexican-Americans may incorporate different activities from training programs for teachers who intend to work with Native Americans.

These goals attempt to reflect the global philosophy of this human relations training model. Specifically, the concept that underlines all the goals is that while individuals are "all of a piece," it is the individual's uniqueness when shared with others that enhances all.

Without an internalized philosophy human relations training will remain only a set of unapplied skills. More important than skills or any particular model of training is an attitude that includes a commitment to implement human relations skills (Mahon & Altmann, 1977). Learning human relations skills does not guarantee their application in a school setting. The example of the teacher who completed a human relations class and still "counted Indians" when dividing the class into groups bears witness to the fact that human relations training cannot be compartmentalized if it is to be successful.

Figure 1.2 represents the relationship among the components of this human relations program. The definition, goals, and delivery model of the program are shown in their respective relationships. In Figure 1.2 is indicated that the definition of human relations training serves as the fountainhead for the remainder of the model. The ten goals of the program are developed from the definition and are consistent with the philosophy underlying the definition. The third component, the delivery model, is represented as a wheel. Its main purpose is to provide means to accomplish goals of the human relations training program.

In this chapter is presented a rationale for human relations training that is both comprehensive and conceptually sound. The approach advocated in this text integrates human relations training into the teaching act. We believe that attempts to "teach" human relations at 10:00 each morning can not be successful. A piecemeal approach leaves much to be desired.

Students learn much in school in addition to cognitive information. Teachers model certain behaviors and attitudes whether they acknowledge it or not. This modeling is a powerful influence, especially to the very young student. Effective human relations training begins with teachers modeling appropriate behaviors. Effective human relations programs have committed, dedicated teachers who believe in each student's uniqueness.

SELF-TEST, CHAPTER 1

1. Which of the following is *not* a rationale for human relations training in education?

    a. Our school population is more diverse now than it ever was.
    b. Our society will never become integrated until we become a fully homogeneous society.
    c. There is increasing stress in today's environment.
    d. Recent legislation makes human relations training needed more.

2. Most models of human relations training emphasize

    a. how to interact with different races.
    b. how to be friendly with students.
    c. how to teach children with handicaps.
    d. how to use communication skills.

3. Teachers report the following about stress in teaching:

    a. Stress only happens to poor teachers.
    b. Stress accounts for one-third of sick days taken by teachers.
    c. Stress is felt mostly by older teachers.
    d. Stress is not a significant factor for teachers leaving their jobs.

Table 1.1

Major Goals of a Comprehensive Human Relations Training Program

GOALS	ELABORATION	OBJECTIVES	ACTIVITIES
1. To understand and respect the basic similarities among peoples.	The kinship among peoples is tied up by their common needs: physical, emotional and social. Human relations education is possible only when basic similarities among people is recognized as the link between all of us.	1. To identify the basic needs of all people. 2. To identify identical rituals in various cultures (e.g., marriage).	1. Research the common rituals associated with death in at least 3 cultures. 2. Examine art of different cultures for common themes.
2. To acquire knowledge of human and cultural diversity.	There is notable neglect in teaching about non Western cultures in schools. It is no longer possible to judge civilizations by strictly Western judgments and values.	1. To demonstrate knowledge that our cultural heritage comes from a variety of sources. 2. To be able to compose an individual definition of civilization.	1. Write a definition of civilization which is capable of including nontechnical cultures and societies. 2. Identify words from Mexican-American culture that have been integrated into the English language.

3. To identify empathically with people from other groups and cultures.	To have an impact on training, an emotional involvement and commitment is necessary. Empathy can be used as a means to appreciate fully other people's culture.	1. To grow in the capacity to share and value the feelings and attitudes of others.	1. Respond empathically to persons from different backgrounds and cultures. 2. Role play authentically a value position substantially different from one's own.
4. To understand the dehumanizing effects of superior/inferior relationships.	Superior/inferior relationships have negative impact for both positions. Exclusivity in group identification is a major promoter of superior/inferior relationships.	1. To become aware of the impact superior/inferior relations has on the people involved. 2. To be able to identify techniques used to keep "people in their own place."	1. Recognize words in our language that support superior/inferior relationships. 2. Review old textbooks for derogatory references to American Indians.
5. To recognize the pervasiveness and consequences of stereotyping.	Stereotyping plays a major role in fostering prejudice. To be free of most kinds of stereotyping is to view the world in its fullest sense.	1. To be able to identify personal stereotypes. 2. To examine myths about cultures and peoples.	1. Devise a list of derogatory phrases that describe blacks. 2. Devise a list of adjectives that best describes males.

Table 1.1 Continued

GOALS	ELABORATION	OBJECTIVES	ACTIVITIES
6. To make unbiased rational judgments about evidence and individuals without either prejudice or overcompensation.	Prejudice results in tunnel vision and diminishes a person's ability to experience fully the impact of events. Making unbiased judgments requires suspending previously held ideas.	1. To understand how prejudice limits the range and richness of the experiences of the prejudiced person. 2. To recognize examples of prejudice found in books and media.	1. List ways prejudged behavior limits a person's experience. 2. Examine TV commercials for evidence of prejudice.
7. To accept and value democratic rather than paternalistic practices.	Paternalistic practices run counter to a democratic society. Paternalism always includes the concept that there are other people who are not acceptable and thus must be assisted.	1. To be able to identify paternalistic statements reflecting white or male superiority. 2. To be able to uncover paternalistic activities in specific social institutions.	1. Identify paternalistic statements in today's society (e.g., "For a woman driver, she is doing O.K."). 2. Review a week's television programming and list paternalistic statements made during the programs.
8. To assist all children in developing strong positive self-images.	Social maturity in people is marked by individuals who have a sense of indentity. Strong self-images in peo-	1. To have students take pride in their particular heritage. 2. To have students	1. Write a critical analysis of themselves in terms of goals and realities. 2. Construct personality

	ple facilitate open and honest relationships between individuals.	demonstrate growth in realistic and positive understanding of self.	profiles of themselves as they are perceived by others.
9. To realize that improving the quality of human interaction is a never-ending process.	Skills in human relations training must include the realization that human relations is a process rather than a product. As such the process is continually unfolding, enriching the individual's life.	1. Students are able to predict future directions and concerns and legislation in human relations and civil rights. 2. Students can apply previously learned goals to new and unique situations.	1. Identify people in the past who through progressive thinking were able to predict quality human relations and civil rights events. 2. Identify issues and concerns in human relations not yet recognized by the general public.
10. To recognize the debilitating effects of sex role stereotyping and prejudice.	Many individuals are unaware of sex prejudice in themselves and others. Social, economic and political benefits are increased when people act in sex-free ways.	1. Students are able to analyze the errors of sex stereotyping. 2. Students are able to identify sex stereotyping in themselves.	1. List sex role stereotyping after viewing 10 T.V. commercials. 2. Construct 5 misconceptions about women commonly held by people in our society (e.g. women are unpredictable).

Note. Table is original. Some material adapted from *Human relations guide I: Inter and intracultural education* (1974).

Definition

Human relations training is a program which facilitates the recognition
and appreciation of differences in individuals and develops communication
skills as the basis for effective interpersonal relationships.

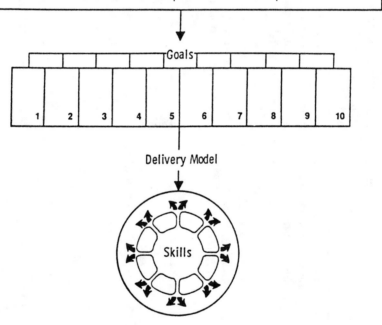

Figure 1.2. Components of human relations training.

4. Which of the following is *not* true about teen suicide?

    a. It happens most frequently in Blacks.
    b. The rate of teen suicide has been increasing dramatically.
    c. Girls commit more suicide than boys.
    d. Suicide may be an expression of stress in today's environment.

5. Which of the following is *not* a cause of the changing nature of the school population?

    a. American's transition to an urban society.
    b. Rising incomes of Americans have led to rising expectation of parents.
    c. Recent legislation such as PL 94-142.
    d. Awareness of certain minority groups.

6. The court case that abolished segregated schools was

    a. Lau
    b. Brown
    c. Smith
    d. Parks

7. The position taken in this text regarding the teacher-learner is that

    a. learning is most effective when it is made practical.
    b. learning is more difficult when commonalities between teacher and learner are large.
    c. good teachers are firm but fair.
    d. teachers are responsible for most learning situations.

8. The main vehicle for delivering human relations is

    a. communication skills in interpersonal relationships.
    b. understanding racism in schools.
    c. appreciation of all children including the handicapped.
    d. students' own positive self-image.

9. The model of human relations training presented in this book differs from most others by

    a. using different communication skills.
    b. concentrating on confrontation skills.

c. combining awareness and knowledge of cultural diversity with communication skills.

d. emphasizing the psychological nature of the learner.

10. Which of the following is *not* a goal of the comprehensive human relations training present in this book?

a. To foster the ideal of awards based on merit rather than prejudice.

b. To understand how stereotyping demeans everyone.

c. To provide sound choices for vocational choice.

d. To appreciate diversity in people.

ANSWERS: 1. (b), 2. (d), 3. (b), 4. (a), 5. (b), 6. (b), 7. (b), 8. (a), 9. (c), 10. (c)

11. Discuss why knowledge of subject matter and theory are not always sufficient for effective teaching.

12. Describe why human relations training is valueless unless a commitment is made to use it in all of our activities.

13. Define human relations training for educators. Explain how you arrived at this definition.

14. Discuss four reasons for teachers having training in human relations.

15. Discuss how communication skills are at the heart of the human relations training model presented in this book.

ACTIVITIES

Activity 1.1 Teacher Survey Concerning Stressful Activities

1. Survey five teachers as to their opinions about the most stressful activities in their teaching.

2. Review the information collected and determine whether or not commonalities exist among the responses obtained.

Activity 1.2 Life Enrichment Through Another Person

1. Choose someone in your life to observe who is substantially different from you.

2. List and explain three ways this difference has enriched your life.

Activity 1.3 Description of a Typical American

1. Describe the typical American.

2. How does he/she differ from you?

Activity 1.4 Experiences with Racial or Ethnic Minorities

1. List previous experiences you have had with racial or ethnic minorities.

2. What have you learned from these experiences?

Activity 1.5 "Melting Pot" Theory No Longer Applies

1. Describe why the "melting pot" theory no longer applies to many racial and ethnic groups.

ADDITIONAL RESOURCES

Books and Publications

Avila, D. L., Combs, A. W., & Purkey, W. W. (1977). *The helping relations sourcebook* (2nd ed.). Boston: Allyn and Bacon.

Carkhuff, R. R. (1969). *Helping and human relations: A primer for lay and professional helpers.* Vol. 2 *Practice and research.* New York: Holt, Rinehart and Winston.

Colangelo, N., Foxley, C. H., & Dustin, D. (1979). *Multicultural nonsexist education.* Dubuque: IA: Kendall/Hunt.

Egan, G. (1975). *The skilled helper: A model for systematic helping and interpersonal relating.* Monterey, CA: Brooks/Cole Publishing.

Gazda, G. M. (1971). Systematic human relations training in teacher preparation and inservice education. *Journal of Research and Development, 4,* 47-51.

Gordon, T. (1970). *Teacher effectiveness training.* New York: Peter H. Wyden.

Human relations guide I: Inter and Intracultural education. (1974). St. Paul, MN: Department of Education.

Long, L. (1978). *Listening/responding: Human relations training for teachers.* Monterey, CA: Brooks/Cole Publishing.

Redman, G. L. (1971). A model for human relations inservice training. *Journal of Teacher Education, 28,* 34-8.

Films (F) and Filmstrips (FS)

Cipher in the Snow (F). University of South Carolina, Film Library, Instruction Services, Columbia, SC 29208.

The Art of Human Interaction (FS). Human Relations Media, 175 Tompkins Avenue, Pleasantville, NY 10570.

What's The Difference Being Different? (F). University of South Carolina, Film Library, Instruction Services, Columbia, SC 29208.

Organizations

Anti-Defamation League. 303 Gorham Building, 127 North 7th Street, Minneapolis, MN 55403.

Racism/Sexism Resource Center for Educators. 1841 Broadway, New York, NY 10023.

State of Minnesota. Department of Education, Division of Instruction, Capitol Square Building, 550 Cedar Street St., Paul, MN 55101.

Women's Educational Equity Communications Network. Far West Laboratory for Educational Research & Development, 1855 Folsom Street, San Francisco, CA 94103.

REFERENCES

Brown v. Board of Education, 347 U.S. 483 (1954).

Carkuff, R. R. (1969). *Helping and human relations: A Primer for lay and professional helpers. Vol. 2 Practice and research.* New York: Holt, Rinehart and Winston.

Colangelo, N., Foxley, C. H., & Dustin, D. (Eds.) (1979). *Multicultural nonsexist education: A human relations approach.* Dubuque, IA: Kendall/Hunt.

Egan, G. (1975). *The skilled helper: A model for systematic helping and interpersonal relating.* Monterey, CA: Brooks/Cole.

Flanders, N. A. (1970). *Analyzing teacher behavior.* Reading, MA: Addison-Wesley.

Gazda, G. M., Asbury, F. R., Blazer, F. S., Childress, W. C., & Walter, R. P. (1977). *Human relations development: A manual for educators* (2nd ed.). Boston: Allyn and Bacon.

Gordon, T. (1975). *Teacher effectiveness training, T. E. T.* New York: Peter Wyden.

Instructor survey reveals stress, weight top concerns of teachers nation-wide. (1977, February). *Instructor, 86,* 12.

Ivey, A. (1971). *Microcounseling: Innovations in interviewing training.* Springfield, IL: Thomas.

Kagen, N. (1971). *Influencing human interaction.* East Lansing, MI: Michigan State University CCTV.

Lau v. Nichols, 414 U.S. 563 (1974).

Long, L. (1978). *Listening/Responding: Human relations training for teachers.* Monterey, CA: Brooks/Cole.

Mahon, B. R., & Altmann, H. A. (1977). Skill training: Cautions and recommendations. *Counselor Education and Supervision, 17,* 42-50.

Minnesota Department of Education. (1974). *Human relations guide I: Inter and intracultural education.* (Curriculum Guide No 39). St. Paul, MN.

Moracco, J. C., D'Arienzo, R. V., & Danford, B. (1982). The measurement of stress among regular and special education teachers. *Diagnostique. 7,* 229-241.

San Antonio Independent School District v. Rodriques, 411 U.S. 1(1973).

Wendt, J. A. (1980). Adolescent suicide on the rise. *Guidepost, 22,* 1, 10.

Wittmer, J., & Myrick, R. (1974). *Facilitative teaching: Theory and practice.* Pacific Palisades, CA: Goodyear.

Chapter 2

COMPREHENSIVE HUMAN RELATIONS TRAINING MODEL

The purpose of this chapter is to elaborate on the human relations training model presented in Chapter 1, Figure 1.1. Communication skills and strategies, the core of the model, are described first followed by an explication of the five· major knowledge areas. Training procedures thought to be most effective are highlighted with special attention given to the use of constructive feedback.

EXPECTED OUTCOMES

By studying the material in this chapter, the reader should be able to

1. list and explain three out of the four major assumptions underlying the model,

2. replicate the stages of the communication paradigm used for the relationship skills,

3. explain the relationship between awareness of the five large knowledge areas of school populations and the use of effective interpersonal communication skills, and

4. discuss feedback as a process and major considerations about using feedback effectively.

REVIEW OF CURRENT MODELS

A number of human relations programs for educators are available. Most reflect the personal philosophies and biases of their authors. However, a common thread among these programs is an humanistic approach to education. Rogers' (1957, 1961) writings on the core conditions of therapy—empathy, genuineness, and respect—provide the basis for most of these models. Carkhuff (1969) working with Rogers' ideas, translated the core conditions into what he stated are discrete, observable, and trainable behaviors. Moreover, Carkhuff introduced quantification in the training process by constructing rating scales for each of the skills. These scales have received criticism on both methodological and ideological grounds (Long, 1978).

Because scales are capable of being quantified, individuals may become too concerned with scores rather than evaluating the affective impact of a certain segment of communication. Another criticism of this approach is that classifying behaviors into minute skills may have the effect of destroying the actual intent of the skill. That is, dissecting the communication process may cause the learner to lose track of the overall goal.

Whether a skills approach to communication training that utilizes a scaling process is more effective than a traditional approach is debatable. The rating scale procedure is an attempt to provide helpers with objective measures of their communication behaviors. Figure 2.1 is an abbreviated scale for the skill labeled empathy. The procedure for rating is that an observer rates each communication segment on a scale from one through five.

1	2	3	4	5
Not Helpful	Somewhat Helpful	Minimally Helpful	Helpful	Very Helpful

Figure 2.1. Rating scale for empathy.

Carkhuff also presented a three-phase model of the helping process, going beyond Rogers' conditions by introducing an action base. The stages are exploration, understanding, and action. This model allows the helper (counselor, teacher, parent, and so forth) an active intervention role in the helping process, and it acknowledges that listening may not be enough for effective behavior change.

Gazda (1971) and Egan (1975) have developed helping models for educators, helpers, and health professionals that reflect remarkable similarities to the Carkhuff three-stage model. Slight changes in wording and more direct application to teachers and health professionals seem to be the only differences between the Carkhuff and Gazda training programs.

These three major models of human relations training take the common approach that one relates to an individual best when one understands the perceptual field of the other. By understanding the individual's internal frame of reference and by acknowledging that individuals are proactive as well as reactive in their environment, the helper establishes the foundation for a relationship that can be instrumental in behavior change. This position is similar to Rogers (1957), Combs and Snygg (1955), and other leaders in humanistic psychology. Additionally, these models add an action phase including strategies derived from learning theory. This can be interpreted by some as moving away from a strictly nondirective point of view to a blend of humanistic and learning theories.

In summary, most models of human relations training programs have roots in counseling and psychology. Interpersonal relations skills are featured in all the models. Viewing behavior from the individual's "internal frame of reference" is central to human relations training.

However, interpersonal relations skills, while important, are not the only characteristics of effective communication. This position can be summarized by stating that interpersonal relations skills are necessary but not sufficient for effective communication involving a variety of people. This text acknowledges the previous statement and makes it a focal point of the training program by integrating interpersonal relation skills and knowledge about diverse student populations (for example, handicapped, race, sex). The central concept of the model is that communication is best practiced by having the skills of interpersonal relations and by knowing something about individuals with whom one communicates.

Application of Counseling
Techniques to Teaching

The model presented in this text recognizes and utilizes the premise that counseling and teaching differ on a number of dimensions. While concepts derived from counseling are appropriate for classroom use, actual counseling models are difficult to apply directly to teaching because of a number of unique differences between counseling and teaching. For example, the milieu under which each occurs is so diverse that teaching and counseling, though related, employ different processes. Counseling is usually associated with one-to-one interactions at several limited points in time. Counseling is generally an intense interaction conducted in an intimate atmosphere. Teaching, on the other hand, occurs in a many-to-one interaction during one-to-six-or-more-hours-a day stretching over the academic year. Teachers may work with students individually, but other students are in close proximity. The teaching atmosphere is less intimate because it is diffused by many students and its main focus is on learning.

The teacher's role in the classroom is not the same as the counselor's role because teachers have different responsibilities. In comparison with counselors, teachers may have to take more direct action and make more decisions that are based on professional role definitions and responsibilities.

The teacher's role influences and in some cases restricts behavior. A teacher is responsible for most student behavior and in many cases teachers are called upon to evaluate student conduct. Teachers assign grades to students, and because of this evaluative role the relationship between teacher and student takes on aspects different from those that would exist if teachers did not have to assign grades. The different roles of teachers and counselors restrict the counseling approach to human relations training.

Problem-solving Approach

Communication skills in this text are based on a problem-solving approach. Traditionally, communication skills are based on a three-stage therapy model of exploring the problem, understanding the problem, and acting to resolve the problem. In this process the helper (teacher) facilitates the progress by exhibiting certain communication skills. This approach is borrowed from counseling and psychological theory with very little modification.

The rationale behind the approach used in this book is that problem solving, rather than counseling approach, more accurately approximates the teaching-learning act. The classroom problem-solving model that is posited herein is not presented because other models are invalid, rather it is presented because this model is more appropriate for classroom use. The model can be applied to any classroom regardless of level and subject matter. In addition an effective communication model should not be restricted to the classroom; this model is appropriate for living and interacting outside the classroom as well as inside it. In all probability the teacher who uses the model in both personal and professional roles will profit more from his/her improved communication skills. These persons also will experience more satisfying relationships with significant others in their lives.

The problem-solving model is less therapeutically oriented than the traditional approach to human relations training. However, many skills and techniques found in traditional models are incorporated in this problem-solving approach. The blend of counseling approach with the problem-solving approach provides a model that incorporates the best from both.

ASSUMPTIONS UNDERLYING THE HELPING PROCESS MODEL

A number of assumptions underlie the helping process model. The most important ones follow. While no assumption can be proven, the ones listed appear to be universal in their acceptability.

1. Most individuals are interested in fair and equitable interactions. People usually do not take advantage of others if they perceive genuine concern. When genuineness is lacking in relationships interest turns from thinking what is the best solution to mutual problems, to what is the best solution to individual problems. In this regard, individuals become very sensitive in gauging others' genuineness.

2. Individuals work best when they trust others. Similar to the first assumption, trust in others allows an individual to devote more energy to solving concerns in a mutually benefiting way. When trust in others is lacking, a great deal of time is spent pairing, fencing, sparing, and using other tactics to heighten individual's self-esteem. These acts, in addition to consuming time and energy, take the focus away from finding the best solution for the group and place the focus on finding the best solution for the individual.

3. The use of power and authority is seldom employed in fair and equitable interactions. Recipients of solutions arrived at through the use of power often feel anger and hostility toward others. Revenge, or the attitude that "I will get back at you," is sometimes a by-product of the use of power. While a feeling of winning is apparent when power is used, no one really wins. For this reason, teachers should avoid its use.

4. Solutions arrived at by mutual agreement are usually most lasting. Unlike imposed solutions which often solve concerns temporarily, mutually agreed upon solutions are lasting because trust and genuineness have gone into the process. A vested interest in the relationship helps to insure that solutions are long term. Each person sees how the solution benefits not only him/her but everyone involved.

Before any real understanding and appreciation for the problem-solving communication model can be developed, the foregoing assumptions must be internalized by the reader to some degree. The spirit and attitude behind these four assumptions need to become part of the reader's repertoire of behavior. The main attitude being advanced is that use of force and authority by teachers does little to encourage real learning. Obviously the potential teacher who insists on using authority as a means of control may find it difficult to understand, appreciate, and apply the material in this text.

STAGES OF THE PROBLEM-SOLVING COMMUNICATION MODEL

The problem-solving model used for communication in this text has six stages: *expressing feelings, defining the concern or problem, generating alternatives, selecting an alternative, implementing a strategy,* and *evaluating the strategy* (Table 2.1). This is a developmental, sequential process in which each stage is to be completed adequately before moving to the next stage. While it is entirely possible to skip a stage and still arrive at a solution, solutions are usually more satisfying and effective if all stages are completed consecutively. This model is valid for use inside or outside the classroom and can be taught to students as a strategy that they can use in their everyday interactions.

The teacher enacts one of two roles in the model depending on the particular concern. Concerns may lie between student(s) and teacher, or they may lie between two or more students. If the concern is between students, the teacher may act as a mediator in the process. The mediator's basic function is that of a facilitator. If the concern lies between student and teacher, then the teacher must assume two roles: one is as a party to the concern and the other as a facilitator. In this type of situation, the teacher has to be very careful that both roles function effectively. Obviously, dual roles are more demanding than being a facilitator only.

Each stage of the model has goals for participants. If concerns or problems are student ones, the student is called the *helpee* and the teacher as a facilitator is called the *helper.* In each of the stages the helpee must arrive at some distinct behavior before moving to the next stage.

Table 2.1

Explication of the Six-stage Helping Process

STAGE	HELPEE GOALS	HELPER GOALS	HELPER SKILLS
EXPRESSING	Helpee is able to explore and to identify underlying feelings and emotions of his/her concerns.	Helper is able to facilitate helpee by establishing a growth relationship.	1. Primary accurate empathy 2. Concreteness 3. Respect 4. Genuineness
DEFINING	Helpee is able to identify his/her concern and is able to place it in a proper perspective and make a commitment to change.	Helper is able to facilitate helpee by providing and clarifying parameters of concern and facilitating to "own the concern."	1. Immediacy 2. Advanced accurate empathy 3. Self-disclosure 4. Primary confrontation 5. Clarifying
GENERATING ALTERNATIVES	Helpee is able to list several alternatives as possible solutions to concern.	Helper is able to facilitate helpee by assisting and promoting the generation of alternatives.	1. Brainstorming 2. Summarizing 3. Prompting 4. Open-ended questions
SELECTING AN ALTERNATIVE	Helpee is able to select one alternative from several possibilities.	Helper is able to facilitate helpee by assisting in the decision-making process.	1. Open-ended questions 2. Reinforcing 3. Suggestions and strategies

Table 2.1 Continued

STAGE	HELPEE GOALS	HELPER GOALS	HELPER SKILLS
IMPLEMENTING A STRATEGY	Helpee is able to list and sequence all the steps necessary in order for the strategy to be carried out effectively.	Helper is able to assist the helpee in arranging for contingency of the strategy.	1. Open-ended questions 2. Confrontation 3. Clarification 4. Prompting
EVALUATING THE STRATEGY	Helper is able to assess whether the proposed alternative is effective.	Helper is able to facilitate helpee by assisting in the evaluation process.	1. Summarizing 2. Open-ended questions

Note. Helpee refers, in most cases, to students and helper to a teacher. However, there are situations when teachers interact with other teachers, principals, and other school personnel in the helper role. In these situations, teachers, principals, and other school personnel are considered the helpee.

The teacher (helper) facilitates this process by displaying certain kinds of skills that are known to be helpful at the particular stage.

In Table 2.1 is outlined the helping-process model. The six stages are listed along with expected helpee and helper goals. Helper skills that facilitate communication with the helpee at each stage are listed in the last column.

Movement through these stages is contingent on a number of variables. Characteristics of helpee, ability of helper as facilitator, and nature of concern influence how quickly each stage is completed. Quality help is not a matter of time; the amount of time spent in the helping process is not nearly as important as the quality of time consumed.

Some concerns are solved in a matter of a few seconds, while others take days and sometimes months. A teacher should not be too anxious to resolve concerns immediately for this may actually impede progress. Some teachers need closure on a problem more than they need a fair solution to it. These teachers have a difficult time relating to students

38   *Comprehensive Approach To Human Relations*

unless all the loose ends are tied up. In their efforts to arrive at closure they may rush to a solution that is not very effective.

Sometimes teachers need to realize that they are not responsible for solving all their students' concerns. If teachers believe that students are ultimately responsible for their own concerns, this belief may relieve the teacher of the burden of having to solve all problems.

Expressing Feelings—Stage I

In this stage the important goal is for the student to express his/her feelings about the problem. For example, if student A comes in from the playground and tells the teacher that he/she should punish student B for some misbehavior exhibited on the playground, student A needs to be able to identify the feelings involved in this concern. In this example, student A may have tattled on student B because student A was feeling anger toward student B and would like to see student B punished.

Teachers characteristically interact with students at Stage I that actually inhibit students' expressing their feelings. For instance, in the previous example, the teacher may tell student A not to be a tattletale. Another example is when a teacher suggests to a student that he/she should not interrupt the lesson and that the class has more important business than to be bothered by the student.

Though a caring attitude such as, "Are you hurt?" appears to be a good response, it does not facilitate the student expressing his/her feelings about the problem. Until these feelings are fully identified and expressed, the student most likely cannot devote him/herself to the other stages of the helping process. In the problem-solving model the helpee needs the opportunity to explore and identify the underlying feelings behind his/her concerns.

The helpee may not be aware of the true underlying feelings behind the concern. Or as happens in many cases, the initial concern is not the most important one. A teacher who rushes to provide solutions at this point may be acting prematurely. The helper in Stage 1 works with the helpee to uncover hidden feelings. Jumping in with solutions may interfere with this important process and may prevent real concerns from surfacing.

Barriers to Communication in Stage I. Often traditional ways of responding to students do not facilitate the goal of Stage 1. In the following example is illustrated use of some typical ineffective ways that teachers interact with students.

Example:

Tommy, 14 years old, in math class (slamming his book on his desk). *Why do I have to do this dumb stuff! It doesn't make any sense and it's no use to me anyway. I'm not going to do this homework!*

Teacher A. "You open that book immediately and begin your work right now!" (This response resorts to authority. In no way does it facilitate the student expressing his feelings about the concern.)

Teacher B. "Now, Tommy, you can do the work if you really put your mind to it." (This response appears to be helpful. However, it does not facilitate Tommy expressing his real feelings. In fact, it denies that Tommy should have any feelings about doing homework.)

Teacher C. "Tommy, if you were paying attention you would know how to do your homework. Now, buckle down and get started." (Again, this response does not attend to Tommy's feelings.)

Teacher D. "Tommy, what's bothering you? You know better than to act like that." (Similar to the other responses, this one does not get Tommy to express his feelings.)

These examples of teacher responses illustrate some ineffective ways that teachers strive to cope with classroom concerns. These roadblocks to communication usually take the form of advising, reprimanding, ridiculing, reassuring, dismissing, or commanding the student. Interactions such as these do not facilitate students' expressing their feelings about the problem. Expressing feelings is necessary as a catharsis, helps students explore their concerns, and is extremely important in the process of finding long-term solutions to problems.

Facilitating Skills in Stage I. A number of skills can help students identify underlying feelings about their concerns. These skills involve a set of behaviors that Rogers (1957) identified as the core conditions of helping. These are very powerful behaviors that indicate to the student that the teacher cares for the student and is concerned about the problem.

Facilitating skills involved in Stage I behaviors include *empathy, genuineness, concreteness,* and *respect.* Each of these skills will be defined and discussed in detail in Chapter 4. At this point, note that these skills convey the notion of involvement, promote awareness of feelings, and focus attention on the student. These skills are exhibited by the teacher for the benefit of the student and do not directly intervene in the solution of the problem.

Defining Concerns or Problems—Stage II

The main purpose of the *defining stage* is for the student to define the problem objectively and to identify "ownership" of the problem. This stage requires the student to view all aspects of the problem, to weigh various points of view fairly, and to come to a conclusion about who owns the problem. The teacher in this stage promotes defining behavior in students by engaging in Stage I skills and by exhibiting Stage II skills which are *advanced empathy, immediacy, clarification, self-disclosure,* and *primary confrontation.*

The teacher takes a more active role in Stage II. While the focus is still on the student more direct interplay takes place between the teacher and the student. This style also involves more personal risk on the part of the teacher. A solid relationship based on trust between the student and teacher needs to have been established if these skills are to be effective.

Ownership of Problem. Identifying who "owns" the problem is very critical in this stage. The person who owns the problem takes the responsibility for solving it. Students should not be encouraged to place the problem of ownership where it does not belong, and students should not be encouraged to take responsibility for owning another's problem. A major philosophy of this text is that most individuals are capable of solving their own problems if appropriate conditions exist and if the opportunity to engage in problem-solving strategies is encouraged.

Commitment to Change. Expressing feelings and identifying the problem are necessary but not sufficient conditions for problem solving. One other component must be present before problem-solving strategies can be implemented. Individuals need to make a commitment to change before any lasting solutions to concerns can be found. This personal commitment to take action and responsibility is a very important part of Stage II. Teachers can help students make this commitment by using skills appropriate in the previous stage and by exhibiting advanced confrontation and clarification.

Teachers mistakenly believe that for every problem students have a quick solution can be found. This helps to explain why teachers engage in much advice giving. However, this approach denies individuals their right to wrestle with their concerns and to grow in the process. Growth is possible when the person knows how to apply facilitative problem-solving strategies. *Problem solving is a process strategy; advice giving is a product strategy.*

The main focus at Stage II is to have the student look at the concern realistically and objectively, place ownership where it rightfully belongs and if warranted, take responsibility for solving the problem. This may mean that the teacher challenges the student on a number of occasions, clarifies any misunderstandings, and encourages the student to act on unresolved issues.

Many people give lip service to their commitment to change their behavior. How many times have you heard a friend claim that he/she is going to lose weight or give up smoking? To some people making a declaration to change is sufficient in and of itself. These people often deceive themselves. The teacher's main task in this situation is to extricate a valid commitment from the student to change.

Generating Alternatives—Stage III

The previous two stages laid the proper foundation for Stage III. In this stage, the student(s) generates a set of alternatives which may serve as possible solutions to the problem. The teacher in this stage facilitates such action by using *brainstorming, summarizing, encouraging, open-ended questioning,* and *prompting* skills. These skills create an environment that is conducive to imaginative problem solving. The teacher acts as a disinterested mediator because he/she does not have an investment in any one solution. In this stage the teacher must make certain that all students who are involved in the concern receive an opportunity to posit alternatives.

Teachers transmit a number of subtle nonverbal clues to indicate approval or disapproval of behavior. The teacher must not unfairly influence the process of generating alternatives by his/her nonverbal behavior. Also, the teacher's preconceived ideas about what the solution should be may interfere with generating alternatives. If this is true, the teacher may reinforce students who volunteer alternatives similar to the ones held by the teacher.

Selecting an Alternative—Stage IV

After all possible alternatives are brought forth, alternatives are evaluated to determine the best strategy for each person involved in the concern. The teacher facilitates this process by using skills of *open-ended questioning, reinforcing, suggesting,* and *summarizing* points of view. The teacher has to be very carefully trained that power and authority are not used in selecting an alternative. This is especially important when the teacher also happens to be involved in the problem. Each person must be contented with the solution. Also, each person needs to understand his/her role in the solution and needs to be able to implement fully his/her role.

As with the generating alternatives stage (Stage III), the teacher's nonverbal behavior must be closely monitored. In selecting one alternative from the several possible, the teacher should not influence the selection process. This action can be done very subtly by a frown indicating a lack of approval or a slight smile indicating favored approach. Students become very adept at fathoming the nuances of teachers' nonverbal behavior.

Implementing the Strategy—Stage V

In order for strategies to be successful they must be well planned. In this stage is described some techniques that are useful for arranging and planning steps that are necessary for implementing strategies. In addition, the roles and responsibilities of all the individuals involved are identified and explained to participants. Sometimes strategies fail because people do not know what is expected from them. The problem may have been so vaguely defined or the responsibilities so poorly appointed that the strategy is doomed from the start. Contracts, as responsibility checklists, may be drawn up to publicly identify each person's role in implementing the strategy. The purpose of this stage is to ensure that the strategy has the best opportunity to succeed through efficient planning. The helper skills include *open-ended questioning, confrontation, clarification,* and *prompting.*

Evaluating the Chosen Strategy—Stage VI

Hopefully, an alternative will be attractive to all persons involved in the concern. Providing an evaluation process for the solution is crucial. The teacher provides for evaluation by structuring a time when persons involved can evaluate the progress of the solution. At the evaluating session, the teacher facilitates an honest and forthright evaluation to the solution. Each person involved should have equal input as to whether or not the solution is working, if adjustments need to be made, and how each feels about the process. The helper skills include *encouraging, summarizing,* and *open-ended questioning.*

Summary of the Problem-solving
Communication Process

An overview of the six-stage problem-solving model has been presented. It provides the core of the human relations program for this text. Each stage, with all its components, will be explored in detail in later chapters. This model can be utilized in the classroom with very little adjustment. In fact, the problem-solving aspects of this model have been used traditionally as a vehicle for effective teaching in the classroom. As such it should not take on an artificial flavor, rather it should be seen as an integral part of the teaching process. This is true whether the problem centers around academic concerns or whether it involves interpersonal problems.

AWARENESS COMPONENTS

Training in communication skills is not necessarily the same as human relations training. Human relations training is a more global concept embracing cognitive aspects of human diversity as well as training specific to communication skills. Individuals can develop growth enhancing interpersonal relationships if they have knowledge of and an appreciation for the background and heritage of others and if they have skills in effective communication.

In this section is discussed the knowledge awareness components of the human relations model presented in Chapter 1. These components were represented in the outer rim of Figure 1.1 and constitute five major areas of student diversity. A brief description of the content of each of these areas is given to orient the reader.

Multicultural Education

Knowledge of concepts of multicultural education gives teachers an appreciation of diversity in the student population. In turn this facilitates the process of viewing behavior from the individual's "internal frame" of reference. This special viewing is essential for true understanding to take place between individuals or groups of individuals.

Multicultural education seeks to examine without evaluation various cultures in the U.S. "The vibrancy of multicultural education is that it is not based on assumptions that there are advantages or disadvantages according to cultural groups, but on *differences* that need to be recognized and respected" (Colangelo, Foxley, & Dustin, 1979, p. 83). However, differences are not always easy to accommodate in individuals.

Awareness of multicultural difference may make this accommodation less difficult.

Nonsexist Education

Nonsexist education is a system for delivering knowledge without regard to gender of students. Schools as major institutions for socialization have portrayed female roles in society in a number of disparaging ways. Sexism in education is both subtle and pervasive. Institutional sexism still exists today; this section aims at analyzing sexism in our school and its effect on boys and girls.

Nonsexist education is not another term for women's liberation movement. While nonsexist education has many features of the women's movement, it encompasses being free of misleading or implied evaluation of a person or a group of people on account of gender.

What is advocated is an approach to education that enhances students' total well-being. Students should be able to confront the many vicissitudes of life without being penalized by their gender.

Nonracist Education

Despite the strides made in the last 20 years, racism still exists. It takes a psychological toll on all members of our society.

Effects of racism will be examined to gain an appreciation for some concerns with which students from different races have to contend. This section also will examine language and heritage in the U.S. to understand the subtle process of maintaining racism in society.

Teachers need to recognize certain characteristics of students from certain groups that may impact teaching. Learning styles and psychological variables are special areas about which teachers must have some understanding.

The strength of American society is directly proportional to the cohesiveness existing in its many diverse elements. School, perhaps more than any other societal institution, incorporates diversities of cultures. If its classrooms are as isolated from interaction among these elements as is our society at large, little reason exists to believe that society will become truly cohesive.

This cohesiveness cannot be effectively fostered by force. It must be a national commitment that is reflected in the classroom by all involved, both teacher and learner. Furthermore, it is not a topic that can be taught as is algebra; nor can a truly integrated society be accomplished by merely exposing students to a class in human relations each morning.

All Children Education

Because of recent legislation, educators will be asked to teach students with handicaps who were placed previously in special classes. Public Law 94-142 mandated a number of conditions that may present teachers with problems. Most teachers have not been trained to work with the handicapped or exceptional child. Some teachers have fears and biases that may prevent them from teaching these students effectively.

A rethinking is necessary before mainstreaming can become effective. This section provides the basis of that rethinking; that is, competition and uniformity, the foundation of contemporary education, is an antithesis to mainstreaming. Mainstreaming appreciates diversity in students even if that diversity happens to be blindness, hearing impairment, or some other handicap.

Psychological Education

Psychological education has a number of components. The heart of psychological education is to facilitate the affective growth of students. The interaction between affective and cognitive learning is complex. Without attending to both, teachers may risk ignoring the influence one has on the other.

Some components of psychological education are self-concept, moral development, sexual identification, independence, and autonomy. This section provides a basis for understanding these concepts.

This completes the overview of the five areas of student populations targeted for examination in human relations training. Chapters 10-14 elaborate on each of the five areas in detail. These five areas plus the communication skills incorporated in the problem-solving model constitute the major components of the human relations training approach employed in this text.

TRAINING PROCEDURES
FOR HUMAN RELATIONS

This text agrees with the position taken by Egan (1975) and Carkhuff (1969) about the mode of training for helpers in human relations. A group approach which combines skills training with an experiential format has some advantages. The group affords opportunities for interactions and learning among members. In this sense the group approach is both a method of training and a method of treatment (Egan, 1975).

The treatment aspect of the group approach is evidenced when individuals use the training sessions as an opportunity to explore and understand their behaviors as they move through the human relations program. The person who utilizes the training sessions as a vehicle for exploring his/her positions on controversial subjects treated in this text is effectively making use of the group process. In this manner, personal growth may be enhanced as a result of applying skills in training sessions. Training-as-treatment outcomes very often revolve around such parameters as feelings, attitudes, and behaviors necessary to learn human relations skills. Clearly, these refer to interpersonal and intrapersonal dynamics (Byer & Egan, 1979).

Whether or not a teacher can implement human relations in the classroom if he/she has not internalized the element of the program is doubtful. More harm than good can come from a person who is teaching the concepts without really adhering to the attitude and spirit behind them.

The powerful influence a teacher has as a model cannot be overrated. Students continually monitor a teacher's behavior for attitudes and behaviors that are portrayed "between the lines." Students quickly assess which teachers are fair and which ones harbor prejudicious attitudes. Rarely is the teacher's behavior overt. By observing subtle messages transmitted by nonverbal cues or couched in semantics students assess their teachers' attitudes.

Training Sequence

Skills in this text can be implemented in a number of ways. The procedures outlined in this section are suggestive only. In the authors' experiences these procedures have been effective in skills training. The sequence for instruction is *input, demonstrate, practice,* and *feedback.*

Input. Input refers to instructor's lectures, handouts, readings, and so forth, about the skills that provide the necessary conceptual framework for the particular human relations skill. The input material facilitates understanding of the skill in terms of its purpose. Without such understanding it is doubtful whether the skill can be applied effectively.

Demonstrate. Demonstration, the next step in the sequence, can be accomplished in several ways. Videotape, live, or film demonstrations are some ways to illustrate the behavioral aspects of the particular skill to be learned. Demonstration serves several purposes. First, it models behavior for the student. In modeling the student places him/herself in the role of the actor doing the demonstrations. In effect this serves as a rehearsal for the student. Second, demonstrations can be used to clear up misunderstandings that students may have about the skill. Because students themselves are not in the demonstration, questioning the behavior they have seen may be easier. Later live demonstrations utilizing classroom students can be used. If students participate in demonstration, they need to feel that they do not have to be perfect. Life has plenty of opportunities for errors. If the intention is sound, making occasional mistakes is not harmful. In fact errors can demonstrate that we all are capable of mistakes and that mistakes do not diminish our worth.

Practice. A practice session follows input and demonstration. Members of the group divide into dyads or triads and practice the skill with one another. This method of practice includes role playing. Other kinds of practice include activities, homework assignments, and videotaping. The importance of allowing adequate time for practice cannot be undervalued. Similar to any skill, the behavior must be practiced until it becomes a natural part of an individual's repertoire. For example, as in tennis learning the backhand stroke at first is difficult and somewhat clumsy. However, the skill is broken into subskills and each is practiced until every motion flows as a unit. The same procedure holds true for the communication skills presented in this text. Unless they are practiced diligently, they will remain bits of isolated behaviors.

Feedback. In order to make full use of practice, feedback to members is necessary. Honest and objective feedback can provide information for behavior change. Because feedback is potentially very effective in skills training, the next section explains and elaborates on feedback procedures for training sessions and for developing strategies to facilitate human relations training in a developmental framework.

Use of Feedback
in the Training Process

Individuals learn more effectively when they are presented information about their behavior. This are information provides people the opportunity to choose to continue behavior or to change it. Continuous information about behavior affords opportunities to change behavior. *Information given to people for behavior change is called feedback.*

Throughout the training procedures feedback should be provided to peers. This is an important feature of the training process. The skills that are discussed in this text need to be practiced thoroughly. Feedback helps to insure that the skills are learned effectively.

Feedback is a powerful technique for behavior change. In the absence of feedback a person may not be aware of the reaction that his/her behavior has on people. Because most people are sensitive to how others view their behavior, tact is an important ingredient in any feedback process. Very often feedback given to people is not heeded. These cases may be due to the method of how the feedback was given or due to the fact that interpersonal climate between the communicants was not appropriate. Feedback is sometimes confused with advice.

Guidelines for Providing Feedback

Some characteristics when applied to feedback lessen its threatening nature and increase the possibility that the feedback will be used effectively. Johnson and Johnson (1975, pp. 16-18) has identified characteristics which provide a helpful framework for giving feedback. When individuals become defensive, the possibility that they will listen accurately to feedback is greatly reduced. When persons employ defensive postures, they devote more energy to responding than to listening. They adopt a restricted thought process that mitigates any creative or constructive feedback from being internalized. For this reason feedback must always be given with as much tact as possible. No one likes to hear comments about his/her inadequacies. However, if these comments are given in a context of trust and genuine desire to help, feedback can be a powerful tool for changing behavior.

1. *The focus of feedback is a person's behavior rather than the person.* Commenting on behavior rather than personality tends to make the receiver of feedback less defensive. *Focusing on behavior involves using adverbs; focusing on personalities involves using adjectives.* "Your questions were inadequate" is different from "You're stupid." In giving feedback individuals should be separated from their behaviors. Doing a foolish act is very much different from being a foolish person. We are all capable of doing foolish things, but we are not all foolish people.

2. *Feedback should concentrate on observations rather than inferences.* Only what is seen or heard in the other's behavior should be reported. Attempts to interpret behaviors should not

be made. Inferences are subject to being incorrect and this may hinder constructive feedback. Inferences may also ascribe incorrect motives to an individual's behavior which may cause the individual to become defensive.

3. *Descriptions rather than judgments should be the focus of concern.* Similar to number 2, judgments involve personal subjectivity. Accurate descriptions do not involve evaluation of behavior. Describing a teacher's behavior as responding positively to a certain student twice during a class period is different from describing a teacher as being cold or indifferent to students.

4. *Descriptions of behavior need to be made in terms of quantity rather than quality.* Statements that reflect quantity are measurable and capable of determining change. "You made less than six open-ended responses," is more helpful than "Your open-ended responses were poor." Value judgments ultimately come to rest on a good-bad continuum. Labeling one's behavior as bad has a disastrous effect on one's self-esteem. This cannot help but interfere with behavior change.

5. *Feedback should concentrate on behavior in the present rather than behavior that has occurred in the past.* Descriptions should address behaviors that occurred in a given time context. Dredging up past behavior is largely irrelevant for effective feedback on present behavior. Having past experiences recounted is discouraging and detrimental in motivating behavior change.

6. *Feedback needs to be information sharing rather than advice giving.* One important feature of feedback is that it provides information so that people can make better decisions for themselves. Advice giving reduces the possibility of persons taking the responsibility of assessing and acting on information. People who act on information and take the responsibility of decision making are apt to have a greater commitment to the action. When one is vested in the decision-making process, one generally tries hard to make it work.

7. *Feedback should seek alternatives instead of solutions.* Problem-solving techniques help individuals make effective decisions. Exploring alternatives is a valuable procedure in this process. For this reason, the process may be more important than the product. Knowing how to explore alternatives is a very valuable strategy.

8. *The receiver is to be the potential beneficiary of feedback not the individual who gives the feedback.* Feedback is for the receiver's benefit, as such it cannot be foisted on others. The purpose of giving feedback is *not* to enhance the position of the sender. The focus of feedback shold always be on the receiver and is not to demonstrate the adequacies of the sender.

9. *Feedback can be gauged to avoid information overload.* Too much information may serve the reverse purpose by overwhelming the person. Pacing is an important component of effective feedback. Information overload can "shut" down the receiver.

10. *Feedback needs to be given in the appropriate content.* Knowing when to give feedback and using an appropriate approach help to insure that feedback will be utilized. Feedback given in the incorrect context (time and place), regardless of its value, will probably go unheeded. Here again, the question of tact takes precedent. To give feedback, especially if it is not pleasant, in front of peers can be dangerous.

A Final Word About Using Human Interaction Skills

The skills discussed in this text apply to a wide range of human interactions. Teaching is just one of many interactions in life. Skills will not be used as effectively as possible if they are restricted to classroom interactions. Applying these skills in a variety of situations with a variety of people ensures maximum usefulness.

At first the skills will seem somewhat artificial; that is, until these behaviors are fully integrated, they will seem contrived. One of the best ways of integrating skills is to deliberately apply them to all aspects of life. In the beginning your responses may be inappropriate; gradually adjustments will result in more accurate responses. In time this process will become automatic.

At first new communication skills will not result in much success. This may be because people have come to expect a certain manner of response. A new pattern of communication may upset their expectancies. Because people can no longer predict accurately what your behavior will be, they become very anxious when their expectancies about your behavior are changed.

Persistence and consistency with use of these new communication skills will result in the establishment of new patterns of communication. Eventually new behaviors will be accepted as genuine.

The rewards that come with being an effective helper make the effort worthwhile. Knowledge of having been a helpful agent in another person's life is a great feeling—this feeling is what human relations training is all about.

SELF-TEST, CHAPTER 2

1. Which of the following is the stated assumption behind the helping relations model?

   a. All people need help at some time.
   b. Most people are capable of solving their problems.
   c. Blacks have particular problems that teachers must address.
   d. Some problems should not be solved by school personnel.

2. The danger of offering advice too soon is

   a. some subgroups reject the notion of advice giving.
   b. that the first concern voiced is not always the real concern.
   c. good teachers do not offer advice.
   d. advice giving implies authority and status.

3. Which of the following is a roadblock to communication?

   a. Reprimanding.
   b. Criticizing.
   c. Advising.
   d. All of the above.

4. Which of the following is true about the stages in the helping model?

   a. Each of these stages take approximately the same time.
   b. Evaluating alternatives is the most difficult stage.
   c. The first three stages are more important than the second three.
   d. It is best to complete all stages in the model.

5. The stage at which the student can take a balanced view of his/her concern is

    a. expressing.
    b. defining.
    c. committing.
    d. generating alternatives.

6. The stage in which the helper establishes a relationship is

    a. expressing.
    b. committing.
    c. generating alternatives.
    d. evaluating.

7. What is often a by-product of solutions achieved through the use of power?

    a. Anger.
    b. Hostility.
    c. Revenge.
    d. All of the above.

8. Which of the following is most important in behavior change?

    a. Feedback.
    b. The student liking the teacher.
    c. Age of the student.
    d. Sex of the student.

9. Which describes the relationship between counseling and teaching?

    a. Counseling and teaching processes are much the same.
    b. A good counselor is a good teacher.
    c. Counseling concepts can be applied to teaching with modifications.
    d. A good teacher is a good counselor.

10. Human relations training is accomplished most effectively through

    a. individual instruction with a teacher.
    b. small groups.
    c. life experience.
    d. none of the above.

ANSWERS :   1. (b), 2. (b), 3. (d), 4. (d), 5. (b), 6. (a), 7. (d), 8. (a),
9. (c),   10. (b)

11. Discuss four assumptions underlying the human relations model presented in this chapter.

12. Give reasons why the use of power and authority should be limited in the classroom.

13. Discuss the relationship between knowledge of student diversity and communication skills, and global human relations training.

14. Describe feedback procedures outlined in the chapter.

15. What advantages occur by using a group approach in human relations training.

Activity 2.1 Classroom Observation

Objective: To become aware of teaching styles.

Group Size: This is an individual exercise.

Time: Approximately one hour.

Procedures:

1. Choose a classroom, preferably a public school, but a college classroom will do.

2. Observe how classroom conflicts are resolved.

3. Points to consider when observing.

     a. What were issues in the conflict?
     b. Describe the issues without evaluation.

     c. How was the conflict resolved?
     d. Describe the teacher's behavior during the conflict.

Activity 2.2 Practice in Giving Feedback

Objective: To practice feedback procedures before actually using them in class.

Group Size: This is an individual exercise.

Time: This exercise can be done outside of class.

Procedures: Hand out paper with the following instruction:

Use the following situations for practicing giving feedback. Pretend you are an observer in a practice situation where you are to provide feedback to your peers. Write the feedback you would give to the descriptions below. Supplement the material to make the feedback most effective.

1. The helper is voicing a concern for the helpee but he/she displays other nonverbal behavior such as lack of eye contact and a lot of fidgeting.

2. The helper makes the following empathic statement, "Mary, you're angry at your mother because she treats you as though you're a child." The helpee lights up and says, "Yeah, she really does!"

3. The helper has changed the focus on the helpee several times. Each time that this happens, the helpee makes a puzzled face.

Activity 2.3 Giving and Receiving Feedback

Objective: To become familiar with feedback procedures.

Group Size: Class divided into triads.

Time: Approximately 20 minutes.

Procedures:

1. Divide groups into triads. Appoint one as the helper, one as helpee, and the third as the observer.

2. The observer is to take notes on the interaction between helper and helpee.

3. The observer gives feedback to helper and helpee.

ADDITIONAL RESOURCES

Books and Publications

Colangelo, N., Foxley, C. H., & Dustin, D. (Eds.). (1979). *Multicultural nonsexist education: A human relations approach*. Dubuque, IA: Kendall/Hunt.

Phi Delta Kappan. This journal publishes many fine articles on educational issues. The issues from 1976-78 have articles dealing with human relations in teaching.

Films

What is Prejudice? Visual Aids Service, University of Illinois, Champaign, IL 61820.

The Teacher's View. Visual Aids Service, University of Illinois, Champaign, IL 61820.

Communication: The Nonverbal Agenda. University of South Carolina, Rental Library, Instruction Services Center, Columbia, SC 29208.

Prejudice: Causes, Consequences, Cures. University of South Carolina, Rental Library Instruction, Services Center Columbia, SC 29208.

Organizations

Council on Interracial Books for Children. 1841 Broadway, New York, NY 10023.

Racism/Sexism Resource Center for Educators. 1841 Broadway New York, NY 10023.

Women's Educational Equity Act Program. U.S. Department of Education, Washington, DC 20202.

REFERENCES

Byer, W. B. Jr., & Egan, G. (1979). *Training the skilled helper.* Monterey, CA: Brooks/Cole.

Carkhuff, R. R. (1969). *Helping and human relations: A primer for lay and professional helpers. Vol. 2 Practice and Research.* New York: Holt, Rinehart and Winston.

Colangelo, N., Foxley, C., & Dustin, D. (Eds.). (1979). *Multicultural non-sexist education: A human relations approach.* Dubuque, IA: Kendall/Hunt.

Combs, A., & Snygg, D. (1959). *Individual behavior: A perceptual approach to behavior.* New York: Harper & Row.

Egan, G. (1975). *The skilled helper: A model for systematic helping and interpersonal relating.* Monterey, CA: Brooks/Cole.

Johnson, D. W., & Johnson, F. (1975). *Learning together and alone: Cooperation, competition, and individualization.* Englewood Cliffs, NJ: Prentice Hall.

Gazda, G. M. (1971). Systematic human relations training in teacher preparation and inservice education. *Journal of Research and Development, 4,* 47-51.

Long, L. (1978). *Listening/responding: Human relations training for teachers.* Monterey, CA: Brooks/Cole.

Rogers, C. R. (1957). The necessary and sufficient conditions of therapeutic personality change. *Journal of Consulting Psychology, 21,* 95-103.

Rogers, C. R. (1961). *On becoming a person: A therapist's view of psychotherapy.* Boston: Houghton Mifflin.

Chapter 3

NONVERBAL COMMUNICATION

Observation and interpretation of nonverbal behavior will be highlighted as applied to a human relations training program. Strategies will be offered that teachers can utilize for effective nonverbal behavior in teaching. Subcultural differences in nonverbal behavior will be explored followed by two objective methods of assessing classroom nonverbal communication patterns.

EXPECTED OUTCOMES

After reading the material in this chapter the reader will be able to

1. list four body parts that are used to express nonverbal behavior,

2. demonstrate open and closed body positions,

3. demonstrate effective attending behavior,

4. explain some potential hazards of sending inconsistent messages,

5. explain the relationship between culture and nonverbal behavior, and

6. discuss subcultural differences in expressions of nonverbal behavior and implications to teachers.

ATTENDING SKILLS AS
NONVERBAL BEHAVIOR

Content and experiences in this book are designed to improve communication skills. Some skills will be new to the reader while others will build on previously learned ones. All communication skills have a common set of behaviors regardless of nature and intent of the communication. These are called the *attending skills* of communication. Most attending skills are expressed nonverbally. Developing attending skills is necessary before learning other skills presented in this model.

Attending skills are presented separately; however, they are an important and integral part of each of the other communication skills. That is, all skills presented in this model have attending behavior as a part of them. Good attending behavior is assumed to be a fundamental aspect of skills such as empathy, genuineness, self-disclosure, and others.

Incorporating good attending behaviors in classroom communication conveys to students that the teacher is interested and ready to devote full attention to what they are saying. Effective teachers devote full attention to their students. By exhibiting good attending behavior, teachers demonstrate to students that they are the focus of their communication. The full impact of this skill cannot be underestimated: students prize empathic components of teachers and believe them to be one of the major features of effective teachers.

Majority of attending behaviors are demonstrated through *nonverbal* messages. Nonverbal messages are transmitted by behaviors such as posture, body position, facial expressions, clothing, gestures, eye contact, distance between people, and vocal cues. Before examining specific attending skills demonstrated by nonverbal behavior, five important areas of nonverbal communication in the classroom will be explored.

NONVERBAL MESSAGES

Messages we send to others contain verbal and nonverbal components. In Figure 3.1 is illustrated the relationship between two components of communication—verbal and nonverbal.

The verbal component refers to semantics of the language. The verbal component is easier to understand for some individuals when the level of the language used is appropriate for the receiver. Language that is too abstract or too concrete for the receiver handicaps clear communication. Slang or unconventional language that is not common to sender and receiver presents problems in communication.

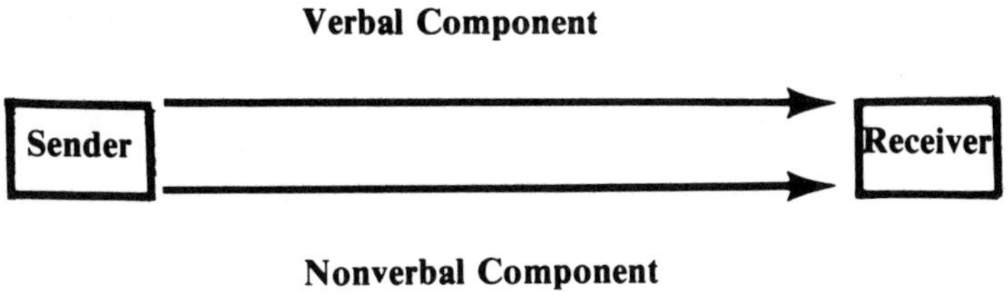

Verbal Component

```
┌─────────┐ ─────────────────────────────▶ ┌──────────┐
│ Sender  │                                 │ Receiver │
└─────────┘ ─────────────────────────────▶ └──────────┘
```

Nonverbal Component

Figure 3.1. Relationship between two components (verbal and nonverbal) of communication.

The nonverbal component of communication refers to behavioral cues employed by the sender to enhance the understanding of the message. Unfortunately, the nonverbal component also can add confusion to understanding when it is at variance with the meaning of the verbal component of a message.

Mehrabian (1971) estimated that as much as two-thirds of the affective or feeling meaning of a message is conveyed nonverbally. This means that behaviors which indicate feelings and preferences are communicated more nonverbally than verbally. Expressing happiness nonverbally is easier than expressing it verbally.

Consistent interpretation of nonverbal behavior is sometimes difficult. This is because people attach different interpretations to the same nonverbal behavior. One reason nonverbal behavior is ambiguous is that it is not codified to the extent of verbal language. For instance, verbal language has a syntax that is known and standard, whereas nonverbal language is expressed differently in different subcultures.

To complicate matters, a particular emotion can be expressed nonverbally in several ways. For example, anxiety may be expressed behaviorally by rapidly tapping fingers, assuming a rigid, statue-like stance, or by pacing back and forth. In each case, the same emotion is expressed in different ways.

In addition to the difficulty in interpreting nonverbal behavior, some individuals send nonverbal and verbal messages that are inconsistent with each other. Inconsistent nonverbal and verbal messages may cause anxiety and feelings of distrust on the part of the receiver.

An illustration of this double message is when two people are talking and one of the persons indicates verbal interest by vocalizing "Yes" and "Is that right," but constantly looks at his/her watch or slowly backs away from the speaker. The sender probably will conclude that the other person is not really interested based on the nonverbal behavior displayed. Contradictory messages are called "double messages" because they place the receiver in conflicting positions. They often have a part in interfering with effective communication in teaching.

Recipients of conflicting messages usually rely on the nonverbal aspect of the message to convey true feelings. Because nonverbal messages are more difficult to disguise, individuals tend to rely on their perception of the nonverbal aspect when confronted with an inconsistent message. An illustration of the results of inconsistent verbal and nonverbal behavior is when a 12-year-old boy, after much deliberation and debate, went to see his teacher after school about a problem. While he was explaining his problem, the teacher seldom looked up from correcting papers though she expressed interest verbally to the student. He got the impression that the teacher was not really very interested in his problem and never went to see her again.

ASPECTS OF NONVERBAL BEHAVIOR IN THE CLASSROOM

The preceding discussion defined and examined inconsistencies in communication based on nonverbal behavior. Nonverbal communication also affects classroom interaction and learning effectiveness. Nonverbal messages are transmitted by such things as clothing, body position, and physical arrangements of the classroom. Teachers need to be sensitized to what they are communicating nonverbally. Only through awareness can teachers improve the quality of their nonverbal behavior. In this section are discussed nonverbal aspects of environment, physical delivery style, eye contact, facial expression, and vocal cues, as they affect classroom behaviors.

Environment

The physical classroom environment affects communication. Teachers influence learning behavior by the colors they use, seating arrangements, architectural design features, and control of noise (visual and vocal). Teachers communicate much about themselves by the way they use and decorate space in a classroom.

If possible, the learning environment should be a pleasant place. In early grades, teachers have few restrictions and are free to increase the room's attractiveness by hanging examples of children's artwork, creating attractive bulletin boards, and using visual aids to reinforce verbal messages. Visual stimulation can be effective. However, at times teachers present too much visual stimulation which creates *visual noise.* Visual noise makes learning difficult because too many "eye catchers" exist which distract attention.

Throughout elementary and high school, innovative teachers can present visual examples to increase interest and attention. Appropriate posters, class projects, and quotations can reinforce what teachers are trying to communicate in their classrooms.

Teachers also can facilitate learning by their seating arrangements. Seating arrangements that are semi-circular or circular have certain advantages. They enable teachers to establish eye contact with students. A variety of seating arrangements is possible in any classroom; subject matter and personal preference are considerations in determining a seating arrangement.

For teachers to establish eye contact with students is extremely important. By making eye contact with each student in the room, the teacher invites involvement. The teacher should make it a point to "touch base" every few minutes by engaging in eye contact with each person in the classroom.

Sometimes teachers use moveable objects as barriers to communication. Moving behind a lectern or sitting behind a desk are typical examples. Teaching is an exhausting act and at times legs will ache from standing for long hours. Rather than sitting behind the desk the teacher can pull up a chair and sit among the students. Standing behind a lectern or sitting behind a desk is often seen as a symbol of power. It gives the impression that the teacher is operating from authority, while sitting among students gives the impression that the teacher is more open to the students as individuals. All this assumes that the teacher can engage in these nonverbal behaviors as natural expressions.

Teachers usually arrange their classroom to meet individual preferences and students usually choose their seats based on the same preferences and needs. In rooms with straight rows, Sommer (1967; 1974) found that the tendency exists for participation to occur in the middle section of each row, for participation to decrease from the front to the back of the room, for students within eye contact of each other to participate more often, and for participation to decrease as the class size increases. These studies have shown that most student participation comes from students sitting in the center of the room. Teachers who are aware of this tendency, then, have an advantage in encouraging those students who are less likely to participate.

Physical Delivery Style

One of the first concerns that teachers have is how they will look in front of the class. Teachers should be concerned with their personal appearance, use of body movement, posture, and positioning in the classroom.

Teachers are not always aware of how much they communicate by their physical appearance and they sometimes fail to appreciate that they present an image to students by how they dress. The dress of teachers needs to be consistent with their other behavior. For example, informal clothing, if appropriate for teaching, should be consistent with an informal classroom.

The composure-control use of gestures and body movements helps maintain attention and interest. Teachers who exhibit physical enthusiasm can elicit interest even in boring material. Teachers need not think of themselves as entertainers in front of class, but they should demonstrate physical involvement.

One way to show involvement is physical closeness. Students can lose interest simply by being too far from the teacher. A skillful teacher can "pull" students into the lesson by moving among the students in a deliberate way. As the teacher stops by a student's desk he/she can give a nonverbal sign of recognition to that student. The sign can be an ever-so-slight smile, a wink, or any of the countless ways recognition can be demonstrated nonverbally. This action helps maintain student interest and attention.

Too often teachers teach to only a select few students in their classes. If teachers are not alert to this phenomenon, they may find themselves attending to a minority of students. Other students' interest may be extinguished by this action. It is important that the teacher "spread" him/herself around the classroom.

Physical delivery also includes posture and the position of the teacher in the classroom. The best teachers maintain a posture of relaxed alertness. This is neither erect attention nor slouched stooping, but rather a high energy level posture that shows interest in what they are communicating.

Eye Contact

One of the most powerful forms of nonverbal communication is eye contact. Eye contact communicates interest in what students have to say. By maintaining eye contact teachers communicate to their students that they are concerned and that students have the teacher's full attention. Teachers can be taught the importance of eye contact to the teaching and the learning situation.

Engaging in eye contact does not mean staring or exhibiting a cold fixed gaze. It does mean looking at each student individually. Some students find direct eye contact uncomfortable and teachers need to be careful not to maintain eye contact with them for too long. However, teachers should not avoid eye contact entirely with these children. Teachers are models for students and by engaging in attentive nonverbal behaviors they have a potential to demonstrate quality nonverbal interpersonal communication.

Eye contact can be useful to teachers. By looking at students individually, teachers can tell whether or not they are being understood, are keeping students' attention, or need to clarify a concept. Eye contact is useful in keeping students actively involved. For example, when students are doodling in notebooks, a teacher may concentrate eye contact until obtaining attention. When teachers make direct eye contact with students who are not paying attention, students are more likely to continue paying attention later; however, this use of eye contact should not demonstrate disapproval.

Facial Expressions

Feelings and reactions are communicated by facial expressions. Disguising a blush or flash of anger can be difficult. Facial expressions indicate to students whether or not teachers are interested, bored, or indifferent to what is happening in the classroom.

Students "read" teachers' facial expressions to assess how they are being received. Teachers find that being especially sensitive to two considerations of facial expressions is helpful in teaching. First, facial expressions should reflect accurately content and feeling dimensions of teacher verbal statements. If a teacher makes a statement about how he/she understands the anguish or disappointment that a student is feeling, then his/her face should reflect that anguish or disappointment, too. Second, students assess teachers' facial expression to determine the teacher's reaction to what has been said. Sometimes facial expressions *cannot* be controlled because the content is upsetting or the language is disturbing to teachers. In these cases, teachers need to relate their feelings to students rather than presenting contradictory messages.

Just as important as teachers displaying accurate facial expressions is the factor of teachers being sensitive to the facial expressions of their students. Awareness can help teachers know how well they are communicating their ideas. Sometimes teachers and students try to cover a felt emotion by displaying a different facial expression than would be expected. This behavior is known as *masking*. For example, John was told that he was elected class president. A few minutes later, after a recount, he found out that he had lost by two votes. John probably would try to cover his felt disappointment with a smile and verbal statement, "It's OK." Some indications of masking behaviors include wringing the hands, tapping fingers, quivering voices, or kicking feet.

Paralinguistic Behavior

Characteristics of the voice (tonal quality, pauses, inflection, pitch, and so forth) give cues to the true feelings of the communicator. For example, "no" can really mean "yes" if the correct tone of voice and emphasis is placed on the words, and rapid speech may indicate speaker anxiety. These clues are *paralinguistic behaviors.* In paralinguistics more attention is given to how something is said, rather than to what is said. As with other nonverbal behaviors, consistency with verbal behavior is very important.

Paralinguistic behavior helps teachers to interpret true meanings from students' verbal messages. Teachers that learn to observe and interpret paralinguistic behavior can gain valuable information about student feelings and reactions. For example, if students have their arms tightly wrapped around their books, legs crossed, and if their speech pattern is rapid, they may be experiencing some anxiety. Teachers need to find a way to help students relax so that problems can be discussed. One way teachers can help is to serve as models by demonstrating a relaxed manner in interactions.

GUIDELINES FOR NONVERBAL
BEHAVIOR WHEN INTERACTING
IN THE CLASSROOM

One-to-one or small group interactions are potentially more intimate than large classroom interactions. Nonverbal behavior in a small group is especially important. The following suggestions will help structure nonverbal behavior so that it can be consistent with verbal behavior and increase the possibility of facilitative communication.

Teachers choosing to interact with students on a personal dimension should make sure they have the time to do so. This is especially important for personal interactions. Teachers run the risk of sending inconsistent messages when they engage in conversation in which they are not prepared to devote their full attention and time. Nonverbal behavior conveys levels of involvement. Teachers can demonstrate that their full attention is directed toward the student by their nonverbal behavior. Any activity which may indicate impatience or a lack of time should be avoided. Scheduling another time for interacting is preferable rather than anxiously checking a clock while the student is talking.

Teachers assuming an *open body posture* demonstrate that they are interested in what students have to say and that they are receptive and accepting of students' ideas. An open body posture is one that has the individual sitting at ease in a relatively relaxed position with arms and legs uncrossed and the head tilted toward the speaker.

A *closed body posture* conveys an entirely different meaning. It sends messages that may mean defensiveness, hesitation, confrontation, anxiety, and so forth. Researchers who have studied nonverbal communication have determined that movements and positions which tend to compress the body indicate defensiveness and closedmindedness. A closed body position is indicated by crossed limbs and an attempt to make the body rigid. When communication patterns are threatening, the individual may attempt to compress the body by wrapping the arms around the chest. An extreme example of this is the frightened child who curls into a ball in a corner of the room.

The teacher who is aware of these dynamics of behavior enhances his/her communication by observing nonverbal behavior in students and acting on these observations. For example, if in talking with a student a teacher notices that the student has arms wrapped tightly, clutching a book to the chest, that the student is undergoing some anxiety would be a fair assumption. The teacher can increase his/her effectiveness by first addressing the anxiety the student is experiencing. This can be done by trying to understand what is generating the anxiety. If in this example the teacher is having a conference with the girl about her poor performance in class, the assumption that the conference is anxiety provoking for the student is not unreasonable.

The teacher can ease anxiety in the student by acknowledging stress in the situation. A simple statement like, "Mary, I sense that you are very nervous about this conference. I wonder if we can talk about your anxiety before we talk about your class work?" This gives the student a chance to express her concerns, and it provides evidence to the student that teacher is sensitive to her needs.

Focusing on the nonverbal behavior gives additional information about students to the teacher. Teachers need to train themselves to be cognizant of nonverbal messages. Often students send nonverbal messages about how they are reacting long before they send verbal messages. For example, experienced teachers can tell when the class hour is over without having to look at their watches. Students begin to close their books and shift in their seats when the class hour approaches.

Students will often express their inattentiveness nonverbally before they express it verbally. The sensitive teacher makes a note of this and incorporates the message in his/her teaching. He/she may need to change the pace or level of the lesson. Whatever the reason, by attending to the message, teachers may be able to ward off more disturbing verbal behavior.

Monitoring students' nonverbal listening behavior may provide the teacher with valuable information. Students as listeners send nonverbal signals to their teachers about their involvement. Some students nod their heads occasionally to indicate their attentiveness. Others doodle with pencils and pens to indicate their lack of interest. Still others will lean back in their seats with their arms folded to indicate their disinvolvement with their teachers.

Teachers should not become defensive when they pick up nonverbal signals of disinvolvement in students. A typical teacher remark to this situation is, "Joey, I want you to sit up in your seat and listen to what I am saying." This statement presumes that Joey is at fault for not listening and he has to adapt his behavior. A terribly boring lesson could be the reason for inattentiveness.

The teacher who responds as cited previously probably acts defensively in situations like this because he/she interprets the student's behavior as being disrespectful. This in turn is evaluated as a blow to the teacher's self-esteem. A more productive approach might be to observe the behavior and then try to assess accurately the reasons for it. In any case, if the teacher thought that the issue should be dealt with, a more direct and less defensive response could be, "Joey, I sense by the way that you're seated that you are not very interested in what I am saying. That concerns me, could we discuss it?" This approach has the possibility of discussing the problem in a less defensive *posture* because it does not put either person in a defensive position.

A final important consideration of nonverbal behavior is *personal distance*. Each person has a unique distance between him/herself and others with which he/she feels comfortable. The distance varies with individuals and situations. Some people like to be very close when communicating while other people feel quite uncomfortable when communicants are close together. A general guide is that between 1 1/2 to 3 feet is comfortable for most people. Invading another's personal space makes individuals very uncomfortable. This may result in their backing away or putting up their hands as if to ward off the invader. A sensitive teacher notes the nonverbal behavior of students and is sensitive to their individual needs for personal space.

SUBCULTURAL DIFFERENCES
IN NONVERBAL BEHAVIOR

Methods of communication are determined, in a large measure, by social context. An important component of social context is culture. Culture in turn is a composite of a system of customs, beliefs, and values. An individual's culture shapes language and actions.

Subculture may have value orientations different from the main culture. Components of subculture include race, ethnic group, social group, and regional location. These components of subculture determine much of the verbal and nonverbal communication styles of people. In some cases, subculture orientations to communication and what that subculture deems as an appropriate communication style may be at variance with the main culture. When this happens a good chance exists for misunderstanding to occur.

Most differences between subcultures are to be centered on three aspects of society. Shuter (1979) classifies these aspects as age, sex, and activity. Age aspects refer to how certain subcultures value the young, middle aged, or old. For example, Chinese-Americans are taught to venerate their elders. The sex aspect refers to the equality or inequality of relationships between males and females accorded individuals in the subculture. Many Hispanic subcultures place a premium on maleness or machismo. Other subcultures (e.g., Chicano, Italian-American, Puerto Rican) also give males a dominant role in society. The activity aspect refers to whether a culture is a *doing* or ; *being* one. A doing culture emphasizes punctuality, productivity, and efficiency. A being culture views self-enhancement and human interaction as being very important. The United States can be classified as a *doing* culture. Puerto Rico and most Hispanic cultures can be listed as *being* cultures. The way each views time is different. Hispanics use time as a means to enhance personal relationships. In business transactions much time is devoted to getting to know the individual before talk of business can ensue. This sometimes drives American business executives to distraction. *Doing* cultures often perceive this as frittering away precious time, and in some cases, indolence.

Over the years subcultures have developed their own language patterns which may deviate appreciably from the main culture. Because of barriers between subcultures in our society, opportunities for learning different cultural patterns of communication are limited.

> Complete with its own words, meanings, even grammatical rules, an argot is often misunderstood by those outside of the subculture. Only by familiarizing oneself with the language differences can misunderstandings be diminished and conflicts reduced. (Shuter, 1979, p. 145)

Specific examples of nonverbal behavior differences among various subcultures are often revealing. Time value, eye contact, and touch will be examined for Black, Asian-American, native-American, and Hispanic peoples. These areas will be treated superficially to offer an appreciation of the variety of differences among subcultures. Interested readers may want to explore subcultural differences further by reading some of the additional references cited at the end of this chapter.

Time

How individuals manage and value time is learned through the socialization process. Subcultures in the United States have different views about punctuality and constraints time places on individuals. Hispanics, native Americans, and Blacks have similar perceptions about time which differ from the main culture. Generally, appointed times are not interpreted as exact times in these subcultures. What is important is how time is spent interacting with others. Social gatherings in these subcultures tend to be open-ended with respect to time.

Communication with others is extremely important as an indication of hospitality in many subcultures. Time spent over meals is both an end in itself and a means to enjoy personal relationships. This process consumes considerable amounts of time. Abruptness in dealing with people is frowned upon and viewed as being inhospitable.

Individuals from the main culture often misjudge the motives of subcultures that have laissez-faire attitudes toward time. They may impugn laziness or irresponsibility to native Americans because of what seems to be an attitude of nonchalance toward time. The carefree attitude of Hispanics toward time is looked upon by some as indolence.

Eye Contact

Looking into the eyes of another is taboo in Navaho subcultures (Hall, 1969). To look directly at another is to display public anger toward that person. In practice, Navaho adults often discipline children nonverbally. A simple stare is considered a reprimand as it is an indication of anger and disapproval.

Contrasted with this are people with German and English heritages who are taught to "look people straight in the eyes." This attitude would be met with confusion by most native Americans, Hispanics, and some Black subcultures.

For Puerto Ricans to look directly into the eyes of authority figures is considered disrespectful. The Black subculture also shares this attitude. In studies reported by Shuter (1979) Blacks maintained direct eye contact when speaking but decreased the amount considerably when listening. It appears that for Blacks listening and direct eye contact are incompatible. Understandably, for a teacher to remark to a Black child, "You look at me when I am talking to you," would be very frustrating for that child.

Touching and Personal Space

Physical contact and dramatic gestures in communication are common to several cultural subgroups. Mexicans, Italians, and Jewish-Americans are famous for their emphasis on touching and gesturing in communication. Members of these subgroups usually engage in exaggerated hand gestures to illustrate and elaborate their meanings in communication. The distance taken by these participants in conversation is much closer than that taken by people from the dominant culture. In many cases, what feels to be a comfortable distance between communicants to Mexican-Americans would be a violation of personal space to Anglos. On the other hand, Anglo styles of communication appear to be cold and uncaring to Mexican-Americans. Misunderstandings occur more frequently when nonverbal communication is appraised only from an individual's personal cultural frame of reference.

Blacks have a high rate of touching. The elaborate ritual of "giving skin" or "give-me-five" attests to the importance of personal contact for Blacks. Shuter (1979) gave a brief description of some body postures of Blacks that are unique to that subculture. His descriptions include "peeping" (girl watching) and "wolfing" (bragging). These gestures and postures are distinctive of the Black subculture; and if viewed by whites from a nonblack perspective, misunderstandings may occur and inappropriate meanings and motives may be assigned to these behaviors.

SUMMARY CHART FOR TEACHER
NONVERBAL BEHAVIOR

Classifications of teacher nonverbal behavior have been constructed by several researchers. Working from classification systems can give insight to the effects of nonverbal behavior exhibited by teachers. Love and Roderick (1971) have devised a classification system that produces a method of assessing how nonverbal behavior is related to important characteristics of effective teachers. Morganstern (1974) has adapted their classification; and Form 3.1 includes some important features of this system. Form 3.1 illustrates positive and negative examples of nonverbal behavior associated with each category. By incorporating nonverbal behavior similar to the positive examples given in the table and by eliminating nonverbal behavior given by negative examples, the reader can guide his/her nonverbal behavior so that it becomes more effective in teaching.

The next rating scale to be discussed is best used in a one-to-one student-teacher encounter though it can be adapted to a classroom setting. The observer rates the teacher's nonverbal behavior only. For each teacher response (columns on table) the observer will place a number (1, 2, 3, 4, or 5) for each of the four categories: A. Eye contact; B. Posture; C. Voice; and D. Topic following. For example, if in the first exchange with a student (or peer trainer), the teacher was natural and relaxed,

Form 3.1

Nonverbal Observation Form

CATEGORY

1. *Accepts or praises student behavior—teacher behavior directed toward student(s) that tends to enhance, reinforce, please, or suggest positive feedback regarding a student behavior.*

POSITIVE EXAMPLES	**NEGATIVE EXAMPLES**
The Teacher:	The Teacher:
a. Displays affirmative head shakes and/or smiles	a. Displays negative head shakes
b. Pats students on the back (or other physical non-verbal gestures of acceptance such as placing hand on shoulder or head of student or putting arm around student)	b. Frowns (at student)
c. Clasps or other hand signals that signify acceptance	c. Turns away from student when positive feedback is expected

2. *Displays student ideas—*any visual teacher behavior involving the display of students' written, spoken, or pictoral ideas.

POSITIVE EXAMPLES	**NEGATIVE EXAMPLES**
The Teacher:	The Teacher:
a. Writes and/or puts students' comments on the board	a. Collects student work and discards it in waste can
b. Holds up a student's project and displays it to class members and/or passes it around the class	b. Does not use student works as model for other students

Form 3.1 Continued

CATEGORY

3. *Shows interest in student behavior*—the teacher creates an atmosphere that displays an interest in student behavior.

POSITIVE EXAMPLES	NEGATIVE EXAMPLES
The Teacher:	The Teacher:
a. Establishes and maintains eye contact with student	a. Avoids eye contact with student or makes darting and quick eye contact
b. Goes through work or material that is on student's desk	b. Avoids involvement when students are working independently

4. *Moves to facilitate student-to-teacher interaction*—body movements of the teacher signals approachment as opposed to withdrawal behavior regarding students. (Body movements are distinguished from simple, smaller gestures of hand, arms, and neck.)

POSITIVE EXAMPLES	NEGATIVE EXAMPLES
The Teacher:	The Teacher:
a. Moves physically into the position of a group member (steps toward or away from a group in a gesture to "pull a response" from the group)	a. Remains seated behind desk during teaching
b. Uses whole arm and hands to signal student to respond	b. Turns back while soliciting responses

5. *Focuses student's attention on important points*—those gestures or body movements of the teacher intended to reinforce, stress, or direct the students' thoughts and attention to important objects, persons, or ideas.

POSITIVE EXAMPLES	NEGATIVE EXAMPLES
The Teacher:	The Teacher:
a. Uses a finger or pointer	a. Stands motionless while communicating

Form 3.1 Continued

CATEGORY

b. Employs a nonverbal gesture with a verbal statement to give it emphasis. (For example, when talking about a third point, teacher raises three fingers.)	b. Paces back and forth distractingly

6. *Demonstrates and/or illustrates*—teacher's nonverbal movements serve to clarify, exemplify, or explain.

POSITIVE EXAMPLES	NEGATIVE EXAMPLES
The Teacher:	The Teacher:
a. Performs a physical skill	a. States verbally (only) the correct procedures for an activity
b. Illustrates a verbal statement with a nonverbal action, e.g., in a discussion of probability, the teacher flips a coin	b. Gives explanations without use of nonverbal behavior

his/her eyes were focused on the student, and his/her voice showed caring and involvement while following the topic in context of the student's response, he/she would be rated in column 1 as 5, 5, 5, and 5. The illustration in Form 3.2 is how this rating would appear for the first interchange.

Form 3.2

Attending Behavior Report

TEACHER (TRAINER) _____   RATER _____   DATE _____

For each teacher response place a number from 1-5 in the appropriate teacher response column under each of the four major categories of attending behavior.

Response

1 2 3 4 5 6 7 8 9 10 11 12 13 14 15 16 17 18 19 20

A. EYE CONTACT
1. No direct eye contact with student or glare
2. Shifting eye contact
3. Eye contact is generally appropriate, but some shifting
4. Appropriate eye contact
5. Comfortable, inviting focus of eyes when talking   5

B. POSTURE
1. Constant movement that is distracting
2. Some distracting movement or posture
3. No noticeable movement or distracting posture
4. Comfortable, natural posture
5. Consistent posture that encourages talk   5

C. VOICE

1. Mostly distracting and unpleasant
2. Often distracting and unpleasant
3. Often appropriate with some distracting qualities
4. Generally appropriate
5. Pleasant and warm showing caring and involvement   5

D. TOPIC FOLLOWING

1. Introduces new topic with no relation to previous content
2. Moves to topic with little relation to previous content
3. Moves toward new topic after referring to previous content
4. Generally stays with pupil in content
5. Stays with pupil in content   5

TOTAL 20

COMMENTS OR SUGGESTIONS

*Rating example where a teacher had, during the first response, good eye contact, comfortable posture, pleasant voice and stayed with the topic content.

SELF-TEST, CHAPTER 3

Instructions for multiple choice questions. Encircle *letter* of best answer.

1. Attending skills are a part of

    a. empathy.
    b. genuineness.
    c. respect.
    d. all of the above.

2. When a message contains inconsistent verbal and nonverbal components most people

    a. trust nonverbal behavior.
    b. trust verbal behavior.
    c. choose neither behavior to trust.
    d. trust nonverbal behavior about as often as they trust verbal behavior.

3. Communication patterns

    a. are similar across the world.
    b. are similar across any particular country.
    c. may vary with the particular subculture.
    d. are stable through generations.

4. One of the following would be indicative of a "doing" culture.

    a. long meals with ample opportunity for discussion.
    b. parties that do not begin and end at their appointed times.
    c. business and social relationships that blend.
    d. the idea that ends justify means.

5. One of the following is true about classroom participation.

    a. has a random pattern.
    b. forms a pattern mostly to the teacher's right side.
    c. is related to the eye contact pattern of the teacher.
    d. depends on the student's disposition.

6. Which choice best describes eye contact?

    a. can be a device to maintain involvement.
    b. has varying meanings with some subcultures.
    c. is one of the most powerful nonverbal messages available to people.
    d. All of the previous.

7. The distance between people at which they feel comfortable talking is called

    a. conversation distance.
    b. personal space.
    c. life bubble.
    d. communication index.

8. Which is an example of paralinguistic behavior?

    a. Eye contact.
    b. Rate of speech.
    c. Crossed arms.
    d. Smiling.

9. Native Americans have which of the following views about eye contact?

    a. Eye contact is maintained equally with all members of the tribe.
    b. Women are not to use direct eye contact with males.
    c. Adults seldom use eye contact with each other.
    d. Children are taught to look away from adults when communicating.

10. Moving about slowly and looking sad at a funeral is an example of which of the following classifications of behavior?

    a. Situational propriety.
    b. Subcultural ambiguities.
    c. Masking.
    d. Paralinguistic behavior.

ANSWERS: 1. (d), 2. (a), 3. (c), 4. (b), 5. (d), 6. (d) 7. (b), 8. (b), 9. (d), 10. (a)

11. Discuss how sometimes sending inconsistent messages puts receivers in difficult situations.

12. Describe the relationship between attending behavior and all other communication skills.

13. Write a description of a person who is sitting in a closed body position.

14. Explain how eye contact can be used by the teacher to help maintain student attention.

15. Discuss how some subcultural groups in the United States utilize different interpretations of nonverbal behavior.

Activity 3.1 Attending and Nonattending Dyads

Objective: To understand the importance of attending (or nonattending) in effective communication.

Group Size: Any even number. Group members will form dyads.

Time: Approximately 30 minutes.

Procedure:

1. Class members separate into dyads.

2. One member of the dyad is chosen as the listener and the other the sender.

3. The sender attempts to communicate something to the listener. The listener engages in nonverbal nonattending behavior (e.g., by looking at the clock, flipping through the pages of a book, etc.). This communication attempt should be done for about five minutes.

4. After five minutes roles are reversed and the communicative exchange is enacted again.

5. The class leader stops the activity after five minutes and the focus of discussion is directed on how the sender felt when he/she tried to send a message and it was not received attentively.

6. Different dyads are formed, this time the sender communicates a message and the listener employs appropriate attending skills. After five minutes roles are reversed.

7. Leader signals the end of the activity and regroups. The results of the interactions are processed by contrasting feeling participants had when they were listened to with those when they were nonverbally ignored.

Activity 3.2 Stack Deck

Objective: To become aware of the meanings of nonverbal behavior and how a nonverbal behavior can represent several different affective states.

Group Size: Any number of groups with 6-8 members in each group.

Time: Approximately 30 minutes.

Procedure:

1. Class members separate into groups ranging in number from 6-8 members.

2. Each group is given a stack of 3x5 cards. Each card has written on it a different affective state and its behavioral description. The stack is placed face down in the middle of the group.

3. Each member, in turn, takes a card from the stack and pantomimes the affective state that he/she has drawn. The other members of the group try to identify the affective state. The pantomime continues until the affective state is named.

4. When the affective state is named, the next group member takes a turn at pantomiming.

5. After each member has at least two turns, the leader stops the activity. Small groups are brought together to process their reactions. Some groups are brought together to process their reactions. Some examples of affective states are anger, joy, boredom, frustration, anxiety, shyness, hostility, happiness, and love.

6. Some questions for discussion:

    a. Were you frustrated when your pantomimes were not quickly identified?

    b. How often did nonverbal behavior represent different affective states?

    c. What were the easiest affective states to identify?

Activity 3.3 Pictures Are Worth a Thousand Feelings

Objective: To show that nonverbal behavior can indicate a variety of feelings and to become aware of the influences of nonverbal behavior in our lives.

Group Size: Small groups of 6-10.

Time: Approximately 20-30 minutes.

Procedure:

1. A number of pictures from magazines are cut out and pasted on stiff paper. Pictures should be chosen for their expressive qualities.

2. Each participant writes his/her reactions to the pictures in terms of

    a. What feelings do the pictures portray?

    b. What feeling do the pictures convey to you?

3. Groups reassemble and the reactions collected.

4. Discuss the reactions to the pictures in terms of

    a. Were there several different feelings identified for each picture?

    b. Did participants have different reactions to the pictures?

Activity 3.4 Nonverbal Log

Objective: To increase your sensitivity to nonverbal behavior in your life.

Group Size: Does not apply. This is an individual activity.

Time: Varies

Procedure:

1. Each participant will keep an observation log of the nonverbal behavior that he/she encounters in life.

2. Format includes:

   a. an objective description of the encounter emphasizing nonverbal behaviors exhibited in the encounter;
   b. observer's reaction to the encounter are recorded (e.g., how the observer thinks the nonverbal behavior affected the participants).

3. The following is an example of a typical entry in your log.

   9/21—I entered my dorm room today and my roommate and his girl friend were talking. From the hushed tones and the way they reacted to me nonverbally I felt that I was intruding. I felt very unwanted in the situation and I left as soon as I could.

Activity 3.5 Body Rhythm Diary: Master Chart

Objective: To become aware of your particular body rhythm.

Group Size: This is an individual activity.

Time: For the 24-hour period from _____ to _____
Procedure:

1. Record your answer to each of the questions.

2. After the 24-hour period, review your recorded answers. Then in a paragraph or two write a description of your body rhythm.

Sleep and Napping

1. When did you go to bed?

2. How long did it take you to fall asleep?

3. Did you sleep well?

4. Did you remember your dreams?

5. When did you wake up?

6. Did you use an alarm?

7. Did you feel alert?

8. Did you take any naps?

      a. If so, when?
      b. If so, for how long?

Appetite and Eating

9. At what times did you experience hunger pangs?

10. When did you have

      a. breakfast?
      b. lunch?
      c. dinner?

11. At what rate did you eat your food? (slow, normal, quick)

      a. breakfast?
      b. lunch?
      c. dinner?

12. Which meal did you like the best?

      a. Which food looked the best?
      b. Which food smelled the best?
      c. Which food tasted the best?

13. When did you snack?

    a. How many snacks did you eat?
    b. Were the snacks fruit, vegetables, cookies, etc.?

14. How did you eat during the last 24-hours? (select one) no appetite, normal appetite, gluttonous appetite

Health

15. Weight before breakfast?   (weigh yourself each day)

16. Did you have any aches, pains, or discomforts?

    a. If so, what type?
    b. If so, where?

Physical and Mental Activities

17. Type of physical exercise during this 24-hour period? (golf, jogging, racquetball, etc.)

    a. When did you exercise?
    b. How long did you exercise?

18. On the whole, how would you describe yourself during the last 24 hours? (Select one) clumsy, normal, adroit

19. Type of intellectual activity during this 24-hour period? (reading, writing, study, etc.)

    a. When?
    b. For how long?

20. On the whole, how would you describe yourself during the last 24-hour period? (Select one) mentally dull, normal, productive:

21. Type of relaxing activity during this 24-hour period? (watching TV, sunbathing, etc.)

    a. When?
    b. For how long?

22. On the whole, how would you describe your activity during the last 24-hours? (Select one) inactive, normal, very active:

23. At what time did you feel:

    a. alert?
    b. tired?
    c. athletic?
    d. agitated?
    e. happy?
    f. depressed?
    g. sensitive?
    h. disoriented?

24. At what times did you want a smoke?

25. At what times did you want a drink?

26. Did you have any good fantasies?

    a. When?

27. On the whole, during the last 24-hours could you concentrate easily?

    a. Were you easily distracted?
    b. Or normal?

28. Were you more introverted or extroverted?

29. How would you summarize your mood during the last 24-hours? (happy, sad, joyous, despondent, listless, etc.)

Environmental Stimuli (during the past 24-hours)

30. What did you enjoy seeing the most?

31. What did you enjoy seeing the least?

32. What was the most pleasing sound you heard?

33. What was the least pleasing sound you heard?

34. What smell did you enjoy the most?

35. What smell did you enjoy the least?

36. What taste was most appealing?

37. What taste was least appealing?

38. What feeling (touch) was most pleasant?

39. What feeling (touch) was least pleasant?

ADDITIONAL RESOURCES

Books and Publications

Atkinson, D. R., Morten, G., & Sue, D. W. (1979). *Counseling American minorities: A cross-cultural perspective.* Dubuque, IA: W. C. Brown.

Egan, G. (1975). *The skilled helper: A model for systematic helping and interpersonal relating.* Monterey, CA: Brooks/Cole.

Hall, E. (1966). *The hidden dimension.* New York: Doubleday.

Hall, E. T. (1969). Listening behavior: Some cultural differences. *Phi Delta Kappan,* 379-80.

Mehrabian, A. (1969). Significance of posture and position in communication of attitude and status relationships. *Psychological Bulletin, 71,* 359-72.

Shuter, R. (1976). Proxemics and tactility in Latin America. *Journal of Communication.*

Vacc, N. A., & Wittmer, J. P. (1980). *Let me be me.* Muncie, IN: Accelerated Development.

Films and Filmstrips

The Eye of the Beholder. Film Library, Instruction Service Center, University of South Carolina, Columbia, SC 29208.

Prejudice: Cause, Consequences, Cures. Film Library, Instruction Service Center, University of South Carolina, Columbia, SC 29208.

Communication: The Nonverbal Agenda. Film Library, Instruction Service Center, University of South Carolina, Columbia, SC 29208.

Basic Attending Skills. Box 641, North Amherst, MA 01059.

Organizations

The organizations that are helpful would be the same as listed in earlier chapters.

REFERENCES

Hall, E. T. (1969). Listening behavior: Some cultural differences. *Phi Delta Kappan,* 379-380.

Love, A. M., & Roderick, J. A. (1971). Teacher nonverbal communication: The developmental field testing of awareness unit. *Theory into Practice, 10,* 295-299.

Mehrabian, A. (1971). *Silent messages.* Belmont, CA: Wadsworth.

Morganstern, B. F. (1974). *Rationale and training guide for a nonverbal classification system.* University of Missouri, Columbia.

Shuter, R. (1976). Proxemics and tactility in Latin Americans. *Journal of Communication.*

Shuter, R. (1979). *Understanding misunderstands: Exploring interpersonal communication.* New York: Harper & Row.

Sommer, R. (1967). Classroom ecology. *Journal of Applied Behavioral Science, 3,* 489-502.

Sommer, R. (1974). Learning outside the classroom. *School Review, 82,* 601-607.

Chapter 4

PROBLEM-SOLVING MODEL STAGE I: EXPRESSING FEELINGS

In this chapter are described and explained purposes and skills in Stage I of the problem-solving model: expressing feelings. Teacher skills for this stage are empathy, respect, genuineness, and concreteness. Each skill is divided into components for easier acquisition. Practice activities and illustrations of appropriate use of the skills are distributed throughout this chapter.

EXPECTED OUTCOMES

By studying the material in this chapter the reader should be able to

1. state the major purpose of Stage I,

2. respond to a student's concern at a minimally effective level, and

3. identify effective and ineffective communication styles.

COMBINE PROBLEM SOLVING WITH
HUMAN RELATIONS TRAINING

The vehicle chosen in this text for resolving classroom concerns is problem solving through a communication skills approach. In essence, this text combines problem-solving or decision-making technology (Horan, 1979; Janis & Mann, 1977; Steward & Winborn, 1973) with human relations training skills (Carkhuff, 1969; Egan, 1975). The approach blends features of the efficacy of problem-solving technology with the positive interpersonal aspects of human relations procedures.

A simple problem-solving model is presented in Figure 4.1. It is derived from models of Horan (1979), Janis and Mann (1977), and Stewart and Winborn (1973). this model presents the broad stages of the problem-solving approach.

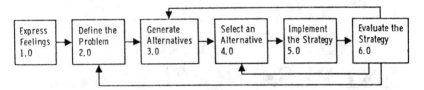

Figure 4.1. Overview of problem-solving model.

Basically, the problem-solving process involves an individual thoroughly investigating a broad array of alternatives, gathering as much information about the problem as possible, selecting an alternative, programming the requirements of the strategy, and implementing the chosen course of action. Each of these activities is represented as a block in Figure 4.1.

An effective solution to a problem depends upon how well each step is accomplished. Stages of the problem-solving model are interrelated so that unsuccessful completion of one effects succeeding stages. For example, if only a few alternatives are generated, the effectiveness of the chosen strategy is limited. Similarly, if the problem is poorly defined or not defined accurately, then the evaluation stage becomes nearly impossible to ascertain.

Effective living can be thought of as making wise decisions. This is as applicable to everyday life as it is to the classroom. The approach advocated in this text was chosen because it can provide students with skills in problem solving that they can employ in their daily interactions.

PURPOSE OF STAGE I

The major purpose of Stage I is to facilitate the process of students exploring feelings and emotions underlying their concerns. Often students, and people in general, act impulsively about events without experiencing the real emotions tied to their problems. Thus, a student may act in an angry manner when in reality he/she is feeling rejection.

Exploring feelings behind behavior is a prerequisite for developing long-term solutions to problems. Students are sometimes confused about the dynamics of their feelings. This can produce uncertainty and interfere with successful resolutions of problems. A teacher who responds effectively in Stage I helps the student to explore the feelings behind the related problem and to identify accurately his/her emotional state. Additionally, the teacher, by responding to the student on a feeling level, communicates that he/she really is listening to the student.

The skills in Stage I demonstrate to students that the teacher is capable of caring and that he/she is in "touch" with the student. Being in touch conveys the message that the teacher is there for the student's benefit and that the teacher eschews the use of power or authority to communicate with students.

Exploring feelings related to concerns is important for another reason. Often students will voice feelings initially that are not at the heart of their concern. They may do this for two reasons. First, students may not trust teachers with their concerns so they test the teacher with a "safe" concern to see how the teacher will react. Related to this type of testing behavior is the fact that some students do not reach out easily; they must be absolutely sure of the teacher's trust. Second, youngsters often are unable to identify their feelings without help. For example, if Janey came to a teacher and said, "Punish Susie, she is being mean to me!" it may be that Janey is really hurt by Susie's behavior. A teacher who responds effectively will be able to help Janey identify that she is really hurt by Susie's actions, and that punishment is not the best solution to the concern.

Sometimes to conceptualize feelings involved with concerns as forming layers is helpful. The teacher generally exposes these layers one at a time to get at the real emotions behind the concern. The teacher's sensitivity to the actual feelings behind behavior is an important aspect in communication with students. Knowing that the first concern expressed by a student may not be the most important one, the sensitive teacher does not jump in with premature solutions. Rather, he/she aids in the process of gently unfolding the layers of feelings.

COMMON BARRIERS TO COMMUNICATION
WITH STUDENTS

Many of our communication patterns have been developed over decades. Some of our current patterns actually may hinder communication. Others may be barriers to effective listening.

Activity 4.1 Communication Barriers of Students

In the following situation, Activity 4.1, try to construct a response to the situation.

Student (George) to teacher:

I'm sorry Ms. Smith I wasn't able to finish my homework. I started but my father wanted me to help him with some work around the house. I told him that I had your homework to do, but he doesn't listen; he never listens to me. Anyway, by the time I finished helping him it was time to go to bed.

If you were the teacher in this situation, how would you respond to this student? Write in the space provided exactly what you would say to him.

Later you will be asked to analyze your response to determine if it is a barrier to communication.

Common Roadblocks to
Student Communication

Several authors have categorized typical ineffective teacher responses. Gazda (1977) and Gordon (1970) have provided useful means of classifying certain kinds of responses to student concerns that present barriers to good communication. In the following list are typical teacher responses to George who was unable to finish his homework. You were asked previously to write a response to this situation. Determine if your response falls into one of the categories listed.

The Commander. This category describes the teacher who relies heavily on ordering and directing. Responses from this category often begin with "You must," "You need to." These responses tend to cut off further communication. Often students feel rejected or humiliated when they are recipients of such responses. For the situation in Activity 4.1,

"You must always do your homework regardless of the circumstances" is an example of teacher response acting as a commander.

The Inspector. This category is described by the teacher who attempts to ferret out reasons behind student problems. Statements may begin "Why did you?" While the intent of the teacher who probes, interrogates, or questions may be for the students' benefit, these behaviors often make students defensive. Additionally, teachers who have this pattern of communication desire quick solutions to concerns. Jumping into quick solutions prevents students from fully exploring feelings behind their concerns. An example of the Inspector applicable to Activity 4.1 is, "Why did you wait until the last minute to do your homework?"

The Preacher-teacher. Teachers who respond in this mode enlist a host of reasons for manipulating student behavior. Some of these reasons are "It's your duty..." "You should..." "Good students don't..." Students quickly pick up the meaning behind these messages, and they are apt to resent the attempts at manipulation. An example of a Preacher-Teacher response in Activity 4.1 is, "It is your responsibility as a son to obey your father and as a student to complete your homework."

The Advice Dispenser. The teacher who fits this category has an ample supply of advice to dispense. Unfortunately, not everyone wants advice, and premature advice giving deprives the individual from solving his/her own problems. You can distinguish the advice dispensed from others by the frequent use of lead-ins such as, "What you should do," "It would be in your interest to," "What I would do." An example of the Advice Dispenser is, "You should explain to your father the importance of homework and that you can finish his work after you complete your assignment."

The Judge. This teacher always seems to evaluate students' behavior. Responses in this category often begin, "You were not right..." "Good students do their homework..." "You need to shape up..." Obviously, communication between students and teacher is not enhanced through the use of this type of response. Another example of the Judge is, "You need to pay the consequences of your lazy behavior."

The Consoler. While statements within this classification appear to be kind, their effects may not be. Statements such as "You'll get over..." "Don't worry..." "Later you'll understand..." are common in the response repertoire of the Consoler. However, students quickly realize that teachers are responding just to make them feel better. Students may well conclude that the teacher really does not understand their concerns.

An example of the Consoler, for Activity 4.1, is, "I really feel sorry for your situation."

Teachers make many other common responses that are barriers to communication. An exhaustive list is not important, rather it is essential to recognize that some sincere genuine responses are more facilitative than others.

Activity 4.2 Roadblocks to Student Communication

In the following examples, Activity 4.2, note typical teacher responses to situations. Categorize the response by the names described previously. Write in the space provided after each teacher response the barrier type that is representative of that response. Choices are the *Commander,* the *Inspector,* the *Preacher-teacher,* the *Advice Dispenser,* the *Judge,* and the *Consoler.* After each response write in the blank the barrier to communication type that best describes the response.

Example A: Fourth grade girl to teacher

The kids are always picking on me. They never let me play with them on the playground. They say that I'm a sissy and tell me to go play with the girls.

Teacher 1. "What are you doing to make the boys call you a sissy?"

Teacher 2. "Pay no mind to the boys. If you ignore them long enough they will stop teasing you."

Teacher 3. "Don't worry about it. Someday you'll look back on this and laugh about it."

Example B: Ninth grade boy to history teacher

I don't know what to do about my algebra. I just can't seem to learn the stuff. I'm doing my homework but I can't seem to apply it in tests.

Teacher 4. "What do you think is causing the problem?"

Teacher 5. "Come on now! A smart kid like you. Why you're one of the smartest kids in your class."

Teacher 6. "From your view things always look worse than they really are. Stick with it and I'm sure you will do all right."

Teacher 7. "The first thing you have to do is go see your teacher. Then work out a schedule for yourself. Take it a little at a time."

Some possible choices for Example A are the following: Teacher 1, Inspector or Detective; Teacher 2, Advice Dispenser; Teacher 3, Consoler. Possible choices for Example B are: Teacher 4, Inspector; Teacher 5, Consoler; Teacher 6, Judge; Teacher 7, Advice-Dispenser.

Barriers seldom provide a foundation for effective communication. What they convey to students is a lack of trust, doubt about their capabilities, and disinterest in them. Communication barriers also promote dependency. In many cases barriers act to close the channels of communication to students. In almost all cases they hinder the expression of feelings that are so vital for self-exploration of concerns. In some cases students may be unaware of their actual feelings, in other cases they may deny these feelings to themselves. An effective teacher who provides the proper atmosphere can promote the necessary expression of feelings in students.

STAGE I EXPRESSING SKILLS

Certain communication skills when emitted by teachers facilitate the expression of feelings and emotions by students. These skills promote the ideal environment for accurate communication. These skills convey to students that the teacher understands their concerns, respects students ability to be responsible for their actions, and is without pretense in his/her caring. The names of these skills are empathy, concreteness, respect, and genuineness. When combined with attending behavior, these techniques have the capacity to promote exploration and expression of feelings in students.

Empathy

Empathy is a skill that communicates to students that teachers understand the students' world as they experience it. Empathy is the ability to attend and respond to students that communicates an awareness in students that their uniquely personal selves are appreciated by the teacher. Empathy is the ability to view the students' world from their "internal frames of reference." To be empathic the teacher tries to perceive the student's world as if the teacher were the student.

In order to do this successfully, the teacher must merge worlds with the student.

> When the client's [student's] world is clear to the counselor [teacher] and he can move about it freely, then he can communicate his understanding of what is vaguely known to the client [student], and he can also voice meanings in the client's [student's] experience of which the client [student] is scarcely aware. It is this kind of highly sensitive empathy which seems important in making it possible for a person to get close to himself and to learn, to change and develop. (Rogers, 1957, p. 95)

The teacher thus needs to view the student's life not in terms of the teacher's value system, but rather in terms of how the student is experiencing it. In order to do this successfully the teacher suspends his/her essence and life and for the moment lives in the world of the student. When he/she can convey to students that the teacher is able to understand the moment-to-moment happening occurring with students as seen from the students' internal frame of reference, positive change is likely to occur.

When this happens the teacher and student worlds merge momentarily. This enables students to explore their world and to identify and "own" their emotions and feelings. By exploring and expressing feelings associated with concerns, students are in a better position for self-understanding. This self-understanding in turn fosters the possibility of long-term solutions to concerns.

Empathy As a Skill. What has been discussed so far about empathy has been abstract. Ultimately the teacher needs to translate the meaning of empathy into behavior. This can be done systematically, however, it is crucial that the teacher's attitude about empathy be carried over into actual behavior. Responding empathically can be thought of as a two-step process. The first step involves discriminating the feelings and content from the student's message. The second step involves responding verbally to the student in such a way that it accurately conveys the message that you understand the student's world. The following suggestions are given for discriminating and responding.

1. *Attend* to the student's feelings.
2. *Observe* nonverbal clues.
3. *Listen* carefully to the student's message.

4. *Summarize* the main content and feelings of the student's message.
5. *Communicate* to the student understanding of the message as viewed from the student's world.

In attending to the student, the teacher puts into action the skills outlined in Chapter 3. This indicates that the teacher is involved in the interaction. By observing the nonverbal behavior of the student, important clues can be gleaned about the student's contemporary feeling state. A quick glance at the student's body posture, facial expression, and gestures can tell a great deal about the inner feelings of the student.

Listening carefully is done by trying to get inside of the student. Asking the question "How would I feel if I were the student doing and saying these things," helps to focus listening habits. In summarizing the student's message it helps to ask the question "What is the *core* of what this student is feeling and saying?"

Activity 4.3 Feelings of Students

The following examples, Activity 4.3, will aid you in sharpening your discriminating skills. In each of the vignettes, choose one or more feeling words that may be associated with the student's internal frame of reference.

Example A: Girl, age 15, to teacher

I really can't figure Janey out. She says she is my best friend, yet she talks behind my back. Some of the things she says about me are really bad.

This girl is feeling

Example B: Boy, age 11, to teacher

Hey, teacher. We won the Little League Pennant last night! I've been playing little league for three years and this is the first time that I've been on a team that has won first place!

This boy is feeling

Example C: Boy, age 17, to teacher

I can't stay in school. My folks want me to get a job and help them out. I don't know, I really like school, but my folks really need the money. I guess I'll have to drop out.

This boy is feeling

Possible choices for Example A are hurt, anger, confusion;
Example B, excited. pleased, overjoyed;
Example C, squeezed, confused, boxed-in.

Activity 4.4 Adjectives Describing Student's Feelings

In the following examples, Activity 4.4, encircle the adjectives after each vignette that accurately identify the student's feelings. More than one adjective for each vignette may apply.

Example A: Teacher to teacher

My wife and I have decided to get a divorce. There are so many complications—so many little details to take care of. It's not going to be easy to end a relationship we have had for ten years.

The husband feels a) arrogant, b) excited, c) depressed, d) confident, e) sad, f) scared, g) worried, h) strong.

Example B: Student to student

I've been at the University for more than a year now, and it's no big deal. Somehow I thought it would be different. Actually, it's just so-so.

The student feels a) let down, b) excited, c) disappointed, d) happy, e) elated, f) bored, g)) blah, h) pleased.

Example C: Student to student

This empathy training is a lot of bull. It's not going to work. I don't see how being empathic is going to help anyone. Yet, we have to practice it. I say shove it!

This student feels a) resentful, b) satisfied, c) angry, d) contented, e) happy, f) upset, g) optimistic; h) hopeful.

Example D: Student to teacher

I don't know why I have to take all those English classes. They're a waste of time. You never get to use that stuff anyway. Why do we have to take it?
This student feels a) resentful, b) put off, c) happy, d) satisfied, e) angry, f) upset, g) discouraged, h) elated.

Example E: Student to teacher

My father keeps blaming me for all the trouble in the house. I can never do anything right no matter how hard I try. Trying to please him is impossible.

This boy feels a) jubilant, b) concerned, c) empty, d) frustrated, e) at peace, f) touch, g) trapped.

Example F: Student to teacher

I just received my SAT results and I made high enough scores to get into the university. I can't believe it. I thought I really bombed the test.

This student feels a) surprised, b) upset, c) anxious, d) elated, e) worried, f) happy, g) cautious.

Some possible answers for
Example A are f) scared, e) sad, g) worried

Example B, a) let down, c) disappointed, f) bored, g) blah
Example C, a) resentful, c) angry, f) upset

Example D, a) resentful, b) put off, f) upset, g) discouraged

Example E, b) concerned, c) empty, d) frustrated, g) trapped

Example F, a) surprised, d) elated, f) happy.

Activity 4.5 Identifying Reasons for Feelings

Go through Examples A-F, Activity 4.4, and give reasons why the individual feels that way. For each example choose one of the feeling words in the list and give a reason why the person felt that way. As an illustration Example A could be done in the following way.

The husband felt *worried* because he was unsure what problems getting a divorce would cause. (In this illustration the word worried was chosen and "unsure of what problems getting a divorce would cause" was given as the reason.)

Do the same for Examples B through F.

Example B

Example C

Example D

Example E

Example F

In being empathic, communicating an understanding of how the student perceives his/her world is important. This was explained as basically a two-step process. The first step is to recognize the feeling state of the student and the second step is to respond with that information and to give a reason for the feeling as the student experiences it. This response conveys to the student that the teacher understands what the student is experiencing and accepts the student's behavior without passing judgment on it.

The following is an illustration of an empathic response by Teacher 2 to Teacher 1's message. Teacher 3's response to Teacher 1 is not empathic.

Teacher 1: "Darn these students. They make me angry enough to kill them. I knock myself out for them and they could care less."

Teacher 2: "You're really furious at your students because they don't appreciate your efforts that go into preparing your lessons!"

Teacher 3: "Oh, don't let them get you down. All you can do is try your best."

Teacher 3's response illustrates a barrier to communication while the response of Teacher 2 identifies the feelings involved in the concern. In this illustration Teacher 1 was expressing some anger because of the way students were reacting to his/her teaching. Through additional empathic responses Teacher 1 may come to understand that he/she is really feeling inadequate and is expressing anger because of this feeling. On the surface Teacher 3's response does not seem inappropriate, however it does little to promote growth and understanding in Teacher 1. Teacher 3's response is an example of what was previously labeled the Consoler. Teacher 2's response facilitates Teacher 1's expressing his/her feelings.

Activity 4.6 Responding With Feeling and Reason

In the following vignettes, Activity 4.6, four responses are given. Choose the best response for each vignette. Remember the response should reflect the core of what the other is feeling and it should provide a reason for that feeling.

Example A: Student to counselor

Hey, I'm here because Mrs. Hitchcock sent me. As far as I'm concerned I've got nothing to talk about.

> 1. She must have had a good reason for sending you here. What do you think it is?

> 2. Mrs. Hitchcock wanted you to come see me.

> 3. You're angry because you're forced to be here.

> 4. Mrs. Hitchcock usually does not send students to me unless she has a good reason.

Example B: Student to teacher

This is an awful place to go to school. No one is ever where they should be and when you finally find them they say they are too busy.

> 1. You don't like going to school here.

> 2. All schools are like this. This one is not special.

> 3. Everyone around here is on the go.

4. It hurts you to think that if you really needed help you would not be able to get it.

Example C: Student, crying, to teacher.

I'm not going to be able to return to school next year.

1. You ought to think of your future. Stay in school.

2. Why?

3. You really would like to stay in school but you can't and you're really upset by it.

4. It's kind of hard, isn't it?

Example D: Student to teacher

All you hear from that teacher is do this, do that. Get in line and be quiet. Hurry up, and begin your work.

1. Your teacher's constant nagging is beginning to make you angry.

2. What are you doing to make her say these things?

3. I guess you will have to put up with her until the end of the year.

4. Why don't you tell her where to get off?

Example E: Teacher to teacher

Well that principal has got some nerve. Where does he get off speaking to me in that tone of voice?

1. What did you do to make him so angry?

2. You're really angry and hurt to be treated with such disrespect.

3. Forget it. He has got to have someone to pick on and today it was you.

4. Yeah, he is one S. O. B.

Example F: Teacher to teacher

I love being back teaching, but my husband thinks I should stay home with the kids.

    1. I can see why it's important that you should be home with your children.

    2. You're feeling trapped because your husband wants you to stay home and you are excited about your work.

    3. Husbands can be unreasonable at times.

    4. Seems like he hasn't heard of women's liberation. He needs to wake up.

The answers to the examples are A-3, B-4, C-3, D-1, E-2, and F-2. Notice that each of these choices contains a feeling word and a reason for the feeling given in each response. These two components, feeling and reason, comprise the essence of an empathic response.

Activity 4.7 Empathic Responses

For the following situations, Activity 4.7, write an empathic response for each. Write verbatim what you would say. The first situation is completed and serves as an example.

Situation 1: Teacher to teacher

(sighs) *I've really had a tough year with the class.*

You feel upset with yourself about the way you managed your class this year.

Situation 2: Girl student to teacher

I went to a party last night at Jimmy's house. We were having a great time. The boys wanted me to smoke some pot. They said it wouldn't hurt me and that I was just chicken. But I don't know...smoking pot is a pretty serious thing.

Situation 3: Student to teacher

I just received an admission notice from State University. I'm accepted into the university! Wow, I wonder how it's going to be at college.

Situation 4: Student to teacher

That Ms. Jones shouldn't be able to get away with what she's doing. She punishes the whole class if just one person misbehaves. Why should I be punished for someone else's wrongdoing?

Situation 5: Student to teacher

Mr. Thomas, I really enjoyed your class this year. Normally, I don't like history, but in your class I even did some extra reading.

The following is an example of communication between a student and teacher where the teacher uses empathy to facilitate the student in exploring feelings. The student is aided in the exploration process by the teacher using empathy.

Larry: "You know I wish my parents would stop nagging me. They are always yelling at me."

Teacher: "You're feeling pretty angry at the way your folks are treating you."

Larry: "Yeah, they treat me like I was a baby. Larry, do this, Larry do that. Boy I'm getting pretty sick of that."

Teacher: "You resent your parents for treating you like a child."

Larry: "You better believe it! They think that this is the 1900s. I can't make a move without their approval."

Teacher: "You sound frustrated that your parents won't recognize your ability to be independent."

Larry: "You know I'm almost an adult. They're good parents, but they won't let go of me."

Teacher: "It must be an uneasy feeling to be upset with your parents on the one hand and love them on the other."

Larry: "I guess I never thought of it that way. Yes, I do love them but we have got to work this problem out."

In this example the teacher acts as a sounding board for Larry. The teacher employs all of the attending skills mentioned previously and listens to the core of what the student is feeling and experiencing. The teacher is accepting Larry and his behavior. By not judging and moralizing, the teacher creates an environment for Larry to explore and express his concerns.

Rating Scales for Empathic Response. Several experts in the field have developed rating scales for empathic responses (Carkhuff, 1969; Egan, 1975). Ratings make it possible to receive feedback on performance and to evaluate progress while practicing skills. The scale in Figure 4.2 indicates ratings and what they represent in terms of being helpful.

1	2	3	4	5
Not helpful, possible interfering with commu nication	Somewhat helpful, but still fails to facilitate good commu- nication	Minimally helpful. Capable of facilitating good commu- nication	Helpful, attends to feelings in the student	Very helpful, very accurate, encourages the student to understand his/ her concerns in the fullest.

Figure 4.2. Rating scale for an empathic response.

The following example illustrates empathic responses with ratings. The quality of the responses is noticeably different.

Teacher to teacher

I don't hate my wife, but I don't know what to do about my life. I like to be honest about the whole business, but it may not be fair to my wife. It's really an unusual situation.

Rating   Response

1   "Marriage is not an easy business these days."

2   "Sounds like you've got problems in your marriage."

3   "You are having mixed feelings about your marriage."

4   "You are feeling really confused and bewildered about what you should do about your marriage."

5   "You are feeling anxious and confused because while you're feeling your marriage is dead, you don't want to hurt your wife."

Activity 4.8 Rating Empathic Responses

For the following situations, Activity 4.8, rate each response on a scale of 1 to 5 using the criterion established in Figure 4.2. Place your rating on the space after the letter of the response. You may use a rating more than once in each situation.

Situation 1

This is a rotten course. We've had all this junk last year. That's the way it is around this lousy school.

    a.   You're going to have to stick it out.
    b.   Sounds like you don't like my course.
    c.   You're angry because the courses in the school are a waste of your time.
    d.   You're upset with my course because you already know the material.

Situation 2

Can you believe my parents! First they said that I could go to college, now they say that I can't. They are not going to pay for the expenses.

a. What did you do to make them do this?
b. You feel discouraged about not being able to go to college and angry at your parents for their decision.
c. You feel sad because you won't be able to go to college.
d. That's a tough break for you.

Situation 3

Why do you always pick on me? I want to know why it's always me and not the other kids. I think you have got it in for me.

a. Now Joey, I treat all my students the same way. Don't misbehave and you won't get picked on.
b. You think that I pick on you unfairly.
c. Either shape up or ship out. That's the way it is around here.
d. You're upset with me because you think I pick on you unfairly and that maybe I don't like you.

The ratings for each response are Situation 1: a. 1, b. 2, c. 4, d. 3; Situation 2: a. 1, b. 5, c. 3, d. 2; Situation 3: a. 1, b. 3, c. 1, d. 5. If you were within a point (plus or minus) of these ratings you have indicated understanding of how to discriminate between good and poor facilitative responses. If you were more than one point away from the rating, go back over the situations and try to understand why your ratings were discrepant.

Genuineness as a Skill

Genuineness is another behavior displayed in Stage I. Rogers (1957) believed that growth is facilitated when students interact with genuine teachers. Genuineness is shown by a teacher who is without a facade, who displays what he/she is feeling and experiencing in the relationship at the moment it is happening, and who is aware of these feelings and accepts them within the context of the relationship (Rogers, 1957). In some respects genuineness is more easily explained in terms of what it is not. Everyone has had teachers who seemed always to be wearing a mask, to be operating behind some artificial front. They appeared to be playing a role or to be saying things they did not actually feel. In a real sense they displayed outward selves that were different from their inward selves.

A tendency exists not to trust individuals who are not perceived as genuine. Their sincerity is doubtful and as a result others are hesitant to reveal themselves too deeply. That a teacher who is not genuine does not permit effective communication with students is easy to imagine. These teachers often hide behind their professional facades. They "play at" the teacher role. To imagine these teachers in activities outside the teaching role is difficult. In a sense these teachers do not come across as real people.

On the other hand, individuals who portray genuine behavior elicit trust. They somehow get the message across that they are persons who exhibit accurate pictures of self. These people encourage others to be open, not to deny selves and feelings, and to be less defensive about concerns.

A teacher who is genuine with students presents a model for them. Genuineness demonstrates to students that trust and honesty are very important ingredients in healthy relationships. Most importantly, genuineness demonstrates that individuals can make mistakes at times and still be accepted. Thus, students can present their entire beings to teachers without fear that they will be ridiculed or punished. Their flaws as well as their good points are equal parts of themselves. Carkhuff (1969) made this statement about genuineness:

> While suspending our own frame of reference, we must continue to communicate in a genuine manner. This does not mean that we dominate the helping process with our free expression of ourselves . . . what genuineness does mean is that we do not present ourselves in a phoney manner. At the very minimum, we present no facade that would misrepresent ourselves. We present no mask from a professional or other role that might make the helpee uncomfortable and unable to share herself. (p. 78)

Egan (1975) constructed a checklist for genuine behavior for counselors. By considering the helper to be a teacher, the checklist is applicable and helpful to teachers-in-training. The five points of the checklist are as follows:

> 1. Is the helper (communicator) his natural self? Does he avoid projecting a stylized role of the "teacher" that is overtly and overly "professional"? Does he avoid using professional jargon ("teacherese")?
>
> 2. Is the helper spontaneous (and yet tactful), or is there something rigid and planned about his behavior? Does he move easily with the student?
>
> 3. Does the helper avoid defensiveness, even when the student questions, challenges, or attacks him?

4. Does the helper express what he thinks and feels, with proper timing and without disturbing or distracting the student, but without putting a number of "filters" between himself and the student?

5. Is the helper open? Does he project a willingness to share himself? (p. 58)

Genuineness is practiced within the context of the communication: it is not exhibited in and by itself, but is communicated to others by the quality of words and actions. In many respects genuineness refers to the ability of a person to project him/herself as a whole. This can best be accomplished if verbal and nonverbal behavior is consistent. If what is said is congruent with what is done, the quality of genuineness is demonstrated. This in turn projects trust in students. When teachers are genuine they avoid operating with "hidden agendas." That is, what they claim as their purpose is in actuality the same as what they do. Students are very adept at discovering the manipulation tactics of adults. The genuine teacher avoids any kind of duplicity in words and deeds.

In Chapter 3, double messages were discussed at length. A double message occurs when the verbal and nonverbal components of a segment of communication are inconsistent in their meanings. The teacher who has a habit of sending double messages does not project a genuine image. Students find it very difficult to establish a trusting relationship with these teachers.

On the other hand, those teachers who are capable of projecting genuineness encourage students to reveal themselves at the deepest level. The intensity of these relationships is profound. The potential for growth in students is enhanced.

In summary, genuineness can be thought of as a process. "Genuineness, like empathy, is perceived to be a process and not a state. It is continuous, not static; continuing openness and authenticity mark the process" (D'Augelli, D'Augelli, & Danish, 1981, p. 59).

Concreteness as a Skill

Students often speak in vague terms about their concerns. This may be because they are unaware of exactly what they are experiencing or because they do not have the experience, vocabulary, or ability to define accurately their concerns. Before any long-lasting problem-solving strategies can be enacted, an accurate understanding of the concern is necessary. Being concrete aids in identifying feelings and emotions involved in concerns. This in turn facilitates establishing goals and strategies for problem solving.

Sometimes getting individuals to be concrete about their problem is difficult. Often people refuse to be concrete in order to delay dealing with concerns. If problems are vague and unidentifiable, then a person is unable to work on them.

Teachers can aid in the process of helping students be more concrete about their concerns. They can do this in two ways. First, they can be concrete in their own expression of feelings. In this manner teachers serve as models for students. In the second way teachers can reply to students in more concrete terms than those with which students responded. For example, if a student said, "I don't feel so hot today," the teacher can reply, "It sounds as if you have a headache."

In many respects concreteness means speaking about behavior, experiences, and feelings in specific terms. The quality of specificity is extremely important in effective communication between student and teacher. In Table 4.1 examples of vague and concrete experiences are given. The concrete examples facilitate understanding and clarifying of concerns. In order for students to get a "handle" on their concerns they first must be specific about their experiences, behaviors, and feelings.

Table 4.1

Examples of Vague and Concrete Statements

Vague Statements	Concrete Statements
1. "I really blew it at home today."	1. "I came home too late for supper today. My father and I got into an argument."
2. "The kids in class pick on me."	2. "The kids in class called me names such as skinny and beanpole."
3. "I really screwed things up."	3. "I put off studying for my math test until the last minute."
4. "I feel blah."	4. "I feel depressed because my boyfriend cheats on me."

Concreteness means being specific about *experiences, behaviors,* and *feelings.* In the following example specificity in these three dimensions is notable.

Vague Statement: "I'm doing okay in school, I guess."

Concrete Statement: "I'm holding my own in math and English, but I'm falling behind in history and I'm starting to panic."

Activity 4.9 Stating Concretely

For each vague statement listed, in Activity 4.9, replace it with a more concrete one. Be specific in describing experiences, behaviors, and feelings.

I don't treat my students right.

I'm feeling down today.

Students give me a hard time.

The principal turns me off.

You can take this job and shove it.

Respect as a Skill

Respect is understanding, accepting, prizing, and being in psychological contact with another. Respect is shown to a student when the teacher accepts a student as a person regardless of his/her behaviors. Respect is allowing others the freedom to be without imposing restrictions.

A distinction exists between respect and permissiveness. Permissiveness is not what is advocated in this text. It is quite possible for a teacher to disagree with a student's behavior and at the same time accept the student. It is this attitude in the concept of respect that is important. Students understand and appreciate teachers who demonstrate respect. These teachers communicate that what students feel and vocalize is important regardless of how trivial they may seem.

Egan (1975) constructed guidelines which help to assess whether a person is demonstrating respect in his/her communication style. The following criteria serve as indicators to determine the quality of respect present in a relationship.

1. Does the helper (communicator) seem to be "for" the other in a nonsentimental, caring way?

2. Is the helper obviously working at communicating with the other?

3. Is the helper dealing with the other as an unique individual and not just a "case?"

4. Does the helper avoid being nonjudgmental?

5. Does the helper use accurate empathy frequently and effectively?

6. Does the helper communicate understanding of whatever *resources* the other reveals and not just understanding his/her problems?

7. Is the helper appropriately warm? Does he/she avoid equally "coldness," the intimate type of warmth that characterizes friendship and the "canned" warmth of the teacher role?

8. Does the helper attend effectively?

9. Does the helper avoid statements and behaviors that might indicate a desire to exploit the other?

10. Does the helper find ways of reinforcing the other for what he/she does well (such as engage in painful self-exploration)?

In the following example the response notably lacks respect.

Student: "The teachers in this school have really got it in for me. I can't do anything without getting permission. If anything goes wrong, I'm the first one to catch the blame."

Teacher: "Well, John, you have nobody to blame but yourself. You've caused trouble before and now you want everything to be forgotten. You have got to pay your dues."

Teachers using responses like this resort to advice-giving and judgmental evaluation. They show little of the quality of respect that is necessary to develop a trusting relationship between student and teacher. The following is another example of a response that lacks respect because it does not demonstrate acceptance on the part of the teacher.

Student: "Well, next fall I am going to the university upstate. It's a good school, it has a great reputation in engineering. But it means leaving the people I know and making new friends. I'm going to especially miss my girlfriend Debbie. Maybe I should stick around."

Teacher: "When I was your age I didn't have the luxury of having to make that kind of decision. I had to go to night school in my hometown."

By making a response like this, the teacher dismisses as unimportant what the student was communicating. Such a response tells the student that here is a person who does not know how to listen, who cannot appreciate other people's concern, and who is quick to make judgments about others' behavior. This type of teacher quickly shuts down the channels of communication.

Respect also can be demonstrated nonverbally. Teachers can show respect by being attentive to students' concerns. They can devote their full attention to the student when communicating. Instead of grading papers while talking, a teacher demonstrates respect by putting the papers aside, by maintaining eye contact with the student, and by being fully involved in the communication. Webster (1974) described a teacher who demonstrates respect:

Respect which you actualize by refusing to accept me at less than I can be, while recognizing my right to grow at my own pace and be me. When I blow it, you do not demean me with parental consolation, well-meant advice, or suffocating over protection. With respectful silence you enter into and accept my feelings of inadequacy and embarrassment. You show respect by being honest with me. When my perceptiveness strikes a vulnerable point within you, you do not retaliate by putting me down or by refusing to express your own feelings. Instead you say, "Ouch! You're right! Although I'm uncomfortable, I appreciate you." (Webster, 1974, p. 85)

SUMMARY

This chapter elaborated the main purpose of Stage I: to facilitate students exploring and expressing their feelings about their concerns. The teacher helps in this process by exhibiting empathy, genuineness, respect, and concreteness. Each of these skills was defined and discussed in the context that a good relationship for communication is promoted best by utilizing these skills.

Opportunities were provided to assess understanding of skills. The reader is encouraged to practice skills in his/her everyday interactions. Similar to the acquisition of any skill, practice with feedback enhances the quality of the skill.

SELF-TEST, CHAPTER 4

1. The two component skills of empathy are

   a. responding and communicating.
   b. communicating and respect.
   c. respect and discriminating.
   d. discriminating and responding.

2. The focus of empathy is on

   a. the teacher.
   b. the helpee.
   c. the student.
   d. none of the above.

3. Respect is always associated with

   a. authority.
   b. power.
   c. the teacher.
   d. none of the above.

4. Being genuine most closely means

    a. being yourself in the context of the moment.
    b. being a good teacher.
    c. portraying an accurate teacher role.
    d. having to be naive at times.

5. The word most closely associated with concreteness is

    a. specificity.
    b. honesty.
    c. openness.
    d. discrete

6. Being empathic with students

    a. promotes trust.
    b. helps students express their feelings.
    c. promotes self-exploration in students.
    d. all of the above.

7. Empathy incorporates all but which of the following?

    a. Responding to the internal frame of reference of the student.
    b. Working out a possible solution with the student.
    c. Focusing on the core of what the student is saying.
    d. Being "with" the student in his/her concern.

8. The greatest problem with barriers to communication is that they

    a. are used too often by adults.
    b. work best with younger children.
    c. interfere with the process of communication.
    d. can be used by students in retaliation.

9. Concreteness helps students to

    a. develop trust in teachers.
    b. deal in abstractions.
    c. translate their concerns to specific terms.
    d. determine what is phoney or nongenuine.

10. Respect most nearly means

    a. being without pretense.
    b. being yourself.
    c. accepting others without constraints.
    d. being polite.

ANSWERS: 1. (d), 2. (b), 3. (d), 4. (a), 5. (a), 6. (d), 7. (b), 8. (c), 9. (c), 10. (c).

11. Discuss the importance of empathy as it relates to the purpose of Stage I.

12. List 10 adjectives that may be used to describe genuineness. (You may use phrases).

13. Complete the following sentence and expand the thought into a paragraph. I can show respect to students as a teacher by

Activity 4.10 Practicing Expressing Skills

A. In Activity 4.10 choose the best response that represents an empathic statement for each situation.

1. 9th grade female student to teacher

I'm supposed to give a speech in front of the class tomorrow. But I can't do it. I'll get up there and I'll freeze. I don't think I can make it.

    a. You don't really mean that do you?
    b. When you get home tonight rehearse your speech in front of your parents until you have it perfect.
    c. You're really anxious about getting up before your peers because you think you might not do well.
    d. It'll be all right, we all get stage fright.

2. Teacher to teacher

My third period class is driving me crazy. For some reason nothing goes right in there. I can't put my finger on it, but the dynamics in that class are enough to drive me up a wall.

    a. That sounds strange coming from you. You always handle your classes so well.
    b. Sounds like that class is really getting to you and you're upset because you can't figure out what to do.
    c. Give it time. It will work out.
    d. Yeah, I know. Some classes, for some reason, will drive you nuts.

3. Teacher to teacher

I have just received a letter from the Board of Education. I was informed that I had been chosen as teacher of the year. Imagine that! From the hundreds of teachers in the system, they chose me.

    a. You're surprised and pleased for being chosen teacher of the year.
    b. Congratulations!
    c. Well, you certainly deserve it. It doesn't surprise me.
    d. That's nice. I'm happy for you.

4. Parent to teacher

Now I want you to do whatever is necessary to straighten Mike out. If he needs a whipping that's o.k. Do whatever. Lord knows I can't make him mind.

    a. We don't use corporal punishment, Mrs. Smith.
    b. Sounds like you're frustrated because you cannot control Mike's behavior.
    c. We believe in firm but fair discipline here and that's what we will do with Mike.
    d. You have tried to make him behave, but it hasn't been successful.

5. Teacher to teacher

Meeting, meetings. That's all we have around here. If that principal would spent time in the classroom, he'd see what the problems really are.

a. You're upset with the principal because he isn't doing his job properly.
b. You're angry at the principal because of his frequent meetings.
c. Let it go. It's not worth getting angry about.
d. Yeah, once they become principals they forget what it was like to be a teacher.

6. Student to teacher

You're the best teacher I've ever had. I liked coming to class. You treated me like I was a real person.

a. Well, son, I treat all my students fairly.
b. Thank you, that makes my job worthwhile.
c. You're pleased that I treated you fairly in class.
d. It was nice having you in class, too.

7. Student to teacher

I don't think that I can talk about it. What happens between my girlfriend and me is too personal.

a. It would be wise to talk about your relationship with your girlfriend before the thing gets out of hand.
b. You find it difficult to talk about personal things that happen between you and your girlfriend.
c. Every relationship has problems. Talking about them to someone may help.
d. I understand how you feel, but sometimes it's good to get things off your chest.

8. Student to student with the intention of the teacher overhearing the comment.

She never lets you have time to talk. You gotta be quiet all day long. She never gives you a break.

a. You know that there are rules in this school and that they must be obeyed.
b. You feel disturbed that I do not allow you time to talk about things you like to talk about.

c. You know that we are on a tight schedule and if we spent time talking we would never finish our work.

d. Students have to be quiet to be able to finish their lessons. It would not be fair to other students if you talked.

9. Student to teacher

I really thought I was going to be elected school president. Everyone worked so hard and they all said that they would vote for me. I can't figure it out.

a. This should teach you a lesson. Never count your chickens before they hatch.

b. Sometimes these things happen. We need to learn how to face our disappointments.

c. Losing is tough.

d. You're disappointed that you didn't win and a little surprised that all that work didn't pay off.

10. Student to teacher

I have been chosen to be in the school play and I'm gonna have the lead. Wow!

a. I'm really proud of you. Congratulations!

b. It's like I've been telling you: Hard work pays off.

c. You're really excited about getting the lead role.

d. Well, isn't that great. I bet your mom and dad will really be happy for you.

11. Teacher to teacher

Year after year I am doing the same thing. It's like I'm on a treadmill going nowhere. Hell, if I had enough nerve I'd quit teaching.

a. Come on now. It isn't all that bad. You're just discouraged today.

b. Teaching can get to you, but quitting is not the answer. You've got too much invested for that.

c. You feel discouraged because teaching has become less rewarding for you.

d. Hey, knock it off! I'll buy you a drink on the way home.

12. Student to teacher

*I can't decide whether to take American History or European History.
European History is harder but Mr. Kalaf is teaching American
History and he is tough. I don't know. What would you do?*

      a. Personally, I like European History. It was my favorite
subject.
      b. Sounds like you're confused and unsure and would like
someone to make the decision.
      c. You have the ability to pass any subject that you take. I
don't think that it's going to be a problem.
      d. Ultimately, you are going to have to decide that question
for yourself.

13. Student to teacher

*Man, why not smoke pot? Adults have their alcohol and we have our
pot. All the kids are into it. What's wrong with smoking?*

      a. Seems like each age group has its own vices.
      b. Both seem equally dangerous to me. I can see your point.
      c. You can't see any difference between alcohol and pot.
      d. You're angry for us telling you what to do when we have
our own vices.

14. Student to teacher

*I can't seem to concentrate for any length of time. I sit down to study
and I read the same thing over three times. I must be going crazy.*

      a. It's not that bad. Together we can work out your problems.
      b. Sounds like you really got it bad.
      c. You feel like you're going insane.
      d. It frightens you when you try to concentrate and find that
you can't.

15. Teacher to teacher

*It's the same old story when I get home. Bitch, bitch, bitch. My wife
doesn't even let me get through the door before she begins. Sometimes
I work late rather than face going home.*

a. Sounds as if you're fed up with your wife's behavior and you're looking for some escape from it.
b. Wives can be like that. Try a little patience. Take her out to dinner.
c. I see what you're saying. Marriage can be a bummer.
d. Conditions at your home aren't the best.

ANSWERS: 1. (c), 2. (b), 3. (a), 4. (b), 5. (a), 6. (c), 7. (b), 8. (b), 9. (d),, 10. (c), 11. (c), 12. (b), 13. (d), 14. (d), 15. (a) (c)

B. For each of the following situations write verbatim what you would say to the helpee. Do not describe what you would do, rather write an empathic response for each situation in the space provided.

16. Student to teacher

I've studied this math over and over again. My parents explain it to me at home and it makes sense, but when I try to do it in class, everything flies out the window.

17. Student to teacher

Janey always picks on me. I don't do anything to bother her but she always tries to get in a fight with me.

18. Student to teacher

I can't figure it out. My grades have always been very good in other classes but in your class they are the pits.

19. Teacher to teacher, about another teacher

She just lets her students run wild. Those kids are not learning anything and my students wonder why they can't behave like hers.

20. Teacher to teacher

I've had it. If we don't get the raise we are asking for from the board, I'm going to quit. You can take so much.

21. Student to teacher

Mrs. Williams, I, er, oh, I don't know how to say this but I forgot my homework assignment.

22. Student to teacher

My dog, Joe, got run over this morning. Now he's dead. He was running with us and a car hit him.

23. Student to teacher

I guess I'm gonna have to drop out of school. My mom's been sick and unable to work. We really need the money. I hate to quit now since I'm so close to graduation.

24. Fourth grade boy to teacher

Why do we have to do this English stuff? Nobody ever talks like that anyway. So what's the use of doing it?

25. High school girl to teacher

I tried out for cheerleader and I was selected!

C. In each of the following statements rewrite the statement with more concrete terms. First underline the vague terms in the original sentence and then write a new statement using more specificity. The first one is completed as an example.

26. I'm feeling _kind of down_ today.

"I'm feeling depressed today because I got back my chemistry exam."

27. This course is for the birds.

28. I tried jogging but that's a bummer.

29. He's something else.

30. I wish that that teacher would get off my case.

D. In the following activities you are asked to rate each response to the situation on a scale of 1-5. The following scale is reproduced for reference.

1	2	3	4	5
Not Helpful	Somewhat Helpful	Minimally Helpful	Helpful	Very Helpful

31. First grader to teacher

The children at this school don't like me. They are always poking fun at me. They tease me about my clothes.

    a. You're hurt because the children pick on you especially about the way you dress.
       Children are sometimes mean to other children. I
    b. hope they haven't hurt your feelings.

c. You're very hurt at the children because they laugh at your clothes and you know that's all your family can afford.

32. Junior high school boy to teacher

My dad doesn't visit us much anymore. It used to be that he came to see us kids often and took us places. Now he just comes over, stays a few minutes and leaves.

a. Why do you think he does that?
b. Sounds like you're a little upset with your dad.
c. You're confused about how your dad is feeling towards you because he isn't coming over to see you as often.

33. Teacher to teacher

I went to see the principal today about that troublemaker I have in my third period class and she told me that I had to handle my own problems.

a. You're angry at the principal because she didn't give you support.
b. You can count on her to do something like that.
c. How quickly they forget once they get out of the classroom.

ANSWERS TO RATINGS: 31. (a) 4, (b) 2, (c) 5; 32. (a) 1, (b) 3, (c) 4; 33. (a) 3, (b) 1, (c) 1

E. The following activity incorporates a series of statements made by a student. Each statement is related to the overall concern. A blank space between statements represents a place for a teacher response. In the blank space write an empathic response so that it facilitates the expression of feelings by the student and it continues the flow of communication for the next student response., It may be helpful to read over the student statements before beginning. A complete version is included at the end. Many possible responses could be made for this activity. Compare yours with the one that is completed.

34. *Wow, what a bummer! Nothing ever goes right in my life. Everything I do turns to crap. I'm sick and tired of trying.*

35. *Yeah. The other day at work I really screwed up and I couldn't get off work until I cleaned up. Boy, was my boss angry. I felt awful.*

36. *Because I had to stay later at work, I was late for my history exam, I was all shook up and I flunked it. You know I have to pass this course if I'm to graduate.*

37. *I went over to Jim's house. He was my best friend. I found him there with Cindy, my girlfriend. I really blew up. I began shaking uncontrollably.*

38. *I don't know what to do. There is nowhere for me to turn and I'm tired of trying to make things work out. Sometimes I feel like jumping out of a window.*

39. *Can you imagine that? The two people I trusted most in the world cheated on me. I guess you can't ever trust women, but I kinda thought that Cindy was different.*

40. *My job is going to pot. I really like it, but I'm screwing up so badly that I better quit before I get fired. I can't do anything right.*

41. *I can hear my parents say "I told you so." They told me I would not be able to work and go to school. They said that I couldn't handle it. They never really have any confidence in what I can do.*

42. *If I just can get over this hurdle, maybe things will work out. I've been through rough times before. If I can just hang on.*

ILLUSTRATIVE RESPONSES: An example of responses to the nine excerpts (34 through 42) follows: Notice how exploration on the part of the student is facilitated. Your responses may not be exactly the same, however, that doesn't mean that they are not appropriate.

34. *Wow, what a bummer! Nothing ever goes right in my life. Everything that I do turns to crap. I'm sick and tried of trying.*

(Teacher response):

It sounds like you're feeling discouraged because things are going badly for you.

35. *Yeah. The other day at work I really screwed up and I couldn't get off work until I cleaned up. Boy, was my boss angry. I felt awful.*

(Teacher response):

You didn't do well at work so your boss made you stay late and you felt terrible about it.

36. *Because I had to stay later at work, I was late for my history exam. I was all shook up and I flunked it. You know I have to pass this course if I'm to graduate.*

(Teacher response):

You're agitated because you did poorly on your exam which is jeopardizing your chances for graduation.

37. *I went over to Jim's house. He was my best friend. I found him there with Cindy, my girlfriend. I really blew up. I began shaking uncontrollably.*

(Teacher response):

This made you even more depressed because you needed someone with whom to talk and you find your best friend and girlfriend together.

38. *I don't know what to do. There is nowhere for me to turn and I'm tired of trying to make things work out. Sometimes I feel like jumping out of a window.*

(Teacher response):

You feel so trapped that you can't see a way out.

39. *Can you imagine that? The two people I trusted most in the world cheated on me. I guess you can't trust women, but I kind of thought that Cindy was different.*

(Teacher response):

You didn't have much trust in women before and now Cindy's action really blew you away because you trusted her.

40. *My job is going to pot. I really like it, but I'm screwing up so badly that I better quit before I get fired. I can't do anything right.*

(Teacher response):

It's discouraging to like your job and yet do poorly at it, especially because your co-workers and boss are going to think that you're incompetent.

41. *I can hear my parents say, "I told you so." They told me that I would not be able to work and go to school. They said I couldn't handle it. They never really have much confidence in what I can do.*

(Teacher response):

You feel especially bad because you know that your parents won't understand and right now it would be nice if they could.

42. *If I can just get over this hurdle, maybe things will work out. I've been through rough times before. If I can just hang on."*

(Teacher response):

While you're really discouraged now, you have hope that if you can get through this rough period you have the inner resources to make it.

ADDITIONAL RESOURCES
Books and Publications

Berenson, D. H. (1971). The effects of systematic human relations training upon the classroom performance of elementary school teachers. *Journal of Research and Development in Education, 4,* 70-85.

Brammer, L. M. (1979). *The helping relationship* (2nd ed.). Englewood Cliffs, NJ: Prentice-Hall.

Carkhuff, R. R. (1980). *The art of helping IV.* Amherst, MA: Human Resource Development Press.

Colangelo, N., Foxley, C. H., & Dustin, D. (Eds.). (1979). *Multicultural nonsexist education: A human relations approach.* Dubuque, IA: Kendall/Hunt.

Combs, A. W., Avila, D. L., & Purkey, W. W. (1978). *Helping relations* (2nd ed.). Boston: Allyn & Bacon.

D'Augelli, A. R., D'Augelli, J. F., & Danish, S. J. (1981). *Helping others.* Monterey, CA: Brooks/Cole.

Egan, G. (1975). *The skilled helper: A model for systematic helping and interpersonal relations.* Monterey, CA: Brooks/Cole.

Evans, D. R., Hearn, M. T., Uhlemann, M. R., & Ivey, A. E. (1979). *Essential interviewing: A programmed approach to effective communication.* Monterey, CA: Brooks/Cole.

Gazda, G. M., Asbury, F.R., Blazer, F.S., Childress, W.C., & Walter, R. P. (1977). *Human relations development: A manual for educators* (2nd ed.). Boston: Allyn & Bacon.

Gordon, T. (1970). *Teacher effectiveness training (T. E. T.).* New York: Peter Wyden.

Johnson, D. W. (1981). *Reaching out interpersonal effectiveness and self-actualization* (2nd ed.). Englewood Cliffs, NJ: Prentice-Hall.

Long, L. (1978). *Listening/responding: Human relations training for teachers.* Monterey, CA: Brooks/Cole.

Rogers, C. R. (1957). The necessary and sufficient condition of therapeutic personality change. *Journal of Consulting Psychology, 21,* 95-103.

Webster, C. L. (1974). Effective counseling: A client's view. *Personnel and Guidance Journal, 52.*

Films (F) and Filmstrips (FS)

Heart of Teaching (F). Agency for Instructional Television, Bloomington, IN.

Organizations

The organizations that were helpful would be the same as listed in earlier chapters.

REFERENCES

Carkhuff, R. R. (1969). *Helping and human relations: A primer for lay and professional helpers. Vol. 2 Practice and Research.* New York: Holt, Rinehart and Winston.

Carkhuff, R. R. (1980). *The art of helping IV.* Amherst, MA: Human Resource Development Press.

D'Augelli, A. R., D'Augelli, J. F., & Danish, S. J. (1981). *Helping Others.* Monterey, CA: Brooks/Cole.

Egan, G. (1975). *The skilled helper: A model for systematic helping and interpersonal relating.* Monterey, CA: Brooks/Cole.

Gazda, G. M., Asbury, F. R., Blazer, F. S., Childress, W. C., & Walter, R. P. (1977). *Human relations development: A manual for educators* (2nd ed.). Boston: Allyn and Bacon.

Gordon, T. (1970). *P. E. T. Parent effectiveness training.* New York: Peter H. Wyden Press, Inc.

Horan, J. J. (1979). *Counseling for effective decision making.* Scituate, MA: Duxbury Press.

Janis, I. L., & Mann, L. (1977). *Decision-making: A psychological analysis of conflict, choice, and commitment.* New York: The Free Press.

Rogers, C. R. (1957). The necessary and sufficient conditions of therapeutic personality change. *Journal of Consulting Psychology, 21,* 95-103.

Stewart, N. R., & Winborn, B. B. (1973). A model for decision-making in systematic counseling. *Educational Technology, 69,* 13-15.

Webster, C. L. (1974). Effective counseling: A client's view. *Personnel and Guidance Journal, 52,* 285-289.

Chapter **5**

PROBLEM-SOLVING MODEL STAGE II: DEFINING THE CONCERN

The purpose of this chapter is to present information about skills that enable teachers to facilitate the process of students identifying and defining concerns. Problem identification is the main goal of Stage II. New skills presented in this chapter are advanced empathy, self-disclosure, confrontation, and immediacy.

EXPECTED OUTCOMES

By studying the content in this chapter the reader should be able to

1. give a minimally effective response demonstrating advanced empathy,

2. describe the importance of self-disclosure and immediacy in accurate communication,

3. confront students in a facilitative way, and

4. discuss the importance of assuming accurate ownership of a concern when appropriate to do so.

DEFINING STAGE

Classroom problems can only be solved effectively when they are defined accurately. Vague identifications can only lead to incomplete solutions. Recall that in Stage I students and teachers alike expressed their feelings about the problem. These actions served as a catharsis, dissipated anger and hostility, and provided for a cooperative atmosphere for Stage II, Defining the Concern.

In the defining stage students and teachers consider the problem from a more objective point of view. In many cases when points of view differ, the teacher helps clarify the situation so that actions can be taken for effective resolution. The first step of the defining stage calls for examining the concern minutely. From this process, the concern can be established and identified objectively.

For example, a situation in which Joey is labeled a troublemaker would not identify the concern accurately and objectively. This problem is better served if the concern can be identified more precisely. The concern may be better defined as Joey tripped Billy when Billy walked past Joey's desk. A concern defined in this manner make solutions more tenable. The problem defined as "Joey is a troublemaker" is too general. Joey could be a troublemaker in a hundred-and-one different ways, or he could be one in just a few ways. In addition, the label of troublemaker helps to shape the way Joey is perceived. In turn, perception may lead to teacher actions that may not be positive.

The second step of the defining stage is to determine who has the problem. The question of problem ownership is very important in classroom interaction. Often the teacher assumes ownership of all problems in the classroom ranging from noise level to squabbles between students.

When a teacher inappropriately assumes ownership of a problem and acts to solve the problem, it deprives students of their responsibilities in solving their own problems of living together. Thus wrongful ownership models for students a less effective way of working through solutions. Assuming appropriate ownership of and the attendant responsibility for the problem is a powerful behavior to develop in students. It reinforces the concern that an unpleasant problem is better solved when faced squarely and solutions are more equitable and long lasting when the individual who has the problem takes the initiative and the responsibility for resolving it. Teachers may not be doing students a favor when they try to solve student problems instead of having students take the responsibility of solving these problems.

Teachers are often tempted to solve student problems. After all, teachers are the adults in the classroom and the persons who have the designated authority. Students often look to teachers to solve problems and to seek answers from them. Some students have learned that having others solve problems is easier than solving problems themselves. Other students have been reared in such a way that adults have always solved problems for them. In either case, students are not learning appropriate life skills. Regardless of a teacher's philosophy of education, most would agree that students should assume the initiative and responsibility for their own problems and that facing problems is more effective than avoiding them.

Problems can be conceptualized as a falling into one of three areas of concern. Gordon (1970) has identified and described the three areas. Figure 5.1 serves to put ownership of problems in a proper perspective.

Examples of concerns that fall into the student problem area are incompleted homework assignments, grades, interpersonal relationships with peers, and attendance. Examples of concerns that fall into teacher problem area are selecting an appropriate methodology for certain instructional areas facilitating an adequate learning environment for each student, arranging appropriate resource materials, and completing certain clerical tasks. The teacher takes the initiative for solving those problems that fall within his/her domain. Teachers misappropriate their problem ownership when, for example, they take the initiative to improve a student's grades by requiring that the student remain after school each day to finish homework accurately. The area of student grades is that particular student's problem. The student must assume the responsibility for improving the situation; the teacher can be a facilitator in whatever ways as deemed necessary. This may include staying after school for help. However, the difference is that the strategy is not imposed on the student and it is the student's decision to take the responsibility for resolving the problem. When students assume ownership of their problems, solutions are apt to be long lasting.

One purpose of human relations training is to enlarge the NO PROBLEM area of the diagram at the expense of the other two areas. The relationship between the areas is such that as the NO PROBLEM area increases a subsequent reduction occurs in the other two areas. Although thinking that some point exists in which the classroom is free from problems is naive, an overall goal is to make STUDENT AND TEACHER PROBLEMS areas as small as possible and to develop an effective problem-solving strategy to deal with future concerns.

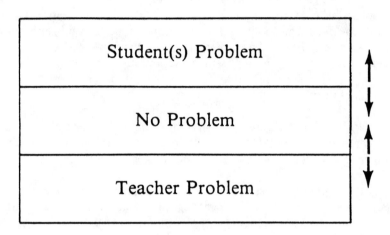

Figure 5.1. Representation of problem ownership.

Note. The diagram represents an area that contains possible classroom concerns. Student concerns include, among others, grades, vocational choice, friendships, and sexual identity. Teacher concerns include, among others, subject matter presentation, assessment, competency, and professional development. The No Problem area represents behavior that is not troublesome to students or teacher. Effective human relations training increases the No Problem area, while at the same time decreases Student Problem and Teacher Problem areas.

Good problem-solving procedures involve the ability to identify correctly a problem and to place problem ownership in the appropriate area.

In order for the problem to be defined accurately it must be understood objectively by all students. That is, if the problem is between students, the students must be able to view the problem from all sides. This does not mean that the student agrees with each side, but rather that the students understand the viewpoints of others. When this has been achieved an agreement on problem ownership will have been reached.

The teacher assists in this process by guiding students through each viewpoint and by working through a definition of the problem that is understood by all students. Teachers' skills that facilitate this process are advanced empathy, self-disclosure, confrontation, and immediacy.

Advanced Empathy

Advanced empathy differs from primary empathy in a number of ways. Primary empathy communicates an awareness of the student's *surface* content and feelings. Primary empathy helps students identify feelings and emotions with which they are most easily in touch. This skill is most appropriate for Stage I, Identifying Feelings. In contrast to primary empathy, advanced empathy attempts to identify and bring to the level of awareness buried or *hidden* feelings of students. Advanced empathy provides the student with an opportunity to experience new meanings and feelings in life. Because this type of response is apt to be threatening to students, caution should be exercised when making advanced empathetic statements. Avenues should be left open to students so that they have the option of accepting or rejecting the validity of the response.

Several ways exist to respond with advanced empathy. Egan (1975) has detailed categories of responding with advanced empathy which enhance a fuller understanding by students of their problems. This in turn creates the requisite condition for defining problems objectively. Some ways of responding with advanced empathy are disclosing feelings and content that are implied by students but which they are not fully aware; summarizing student content statements that appear unrelated; tying together themes; putting together students' experiences, feelings, and behaviors in a meaningful way; guiding students to conclusions; and providing alternative viewpoints and interpretations of students' experiences, feelings, and behavior.

Responding with advanced empathy often helps students become aware of their underlying feeling in concerns. A method that teachers can employ to help discover underlying feelings in their students is observing cues from students' behaviors. For example if a student is relating past school experiences and is outwardly expressing anger, this person may be sending out cues that he/she is really feeling hurt and rejected. Nonverbal behavior is especially important in this regard. Nonverbal behavior is more difficult to disguise and thus can be a more accurate indication of a student's actual feelings.

Voice qualities (for example, tone, inflection, rendition, and volume) also are good indicators of underlying feelings, especially anxiety. Anxiety is often expressed by rapid speech, and higher than usual pitch and volume. Rapid gestures and jerky body movements often portray an anxious person. Sometimes impulsive behavior that is not the usual repertoire of a student is a sign that the student may be under tension.

A teacher can use certain questions to organize his/her thinking for advanced empathy. Some examples of such questions follow.

1. What is the common thread in what the student has been saying, feeling, and experiencing?

2. What are the most intense feelings that the student has been expressing?

3. What can be implied rationally from what the student has reported?

4. What patterns are evident in what the student has reported?

Advanced empathy can be a powerful skill for aiding students to understand their concerns fully. However, caution should be exercised when using advanced empathy. The teacher needs the awareness that in some cases advanced empathy may create defensiveness in students. Usually, in these cases it is best to back off from the student. The student may not be ready to examine implications and responsibilities of his/her concerns.

The following examples will help to distinguish primary empathy from advanced empathy. Advanced empathy is additive in the sense that it supplies information or feedback to students that has not been available to them. This provides a basis for the student to view the concern from another point of view. Implicit in advanced empathy is an element of interpretation beyond the surface expression of emotion. For this reason advanced empathy is best emitted when the relationship between individuals is based on trust and understanding.

Because a solid relationship is needed, advanced empathy is introduced after Stage I, Expressing Feelings. The relationship is assumed to be healthy at this stage, and surface feelings and emotions that are a part of the problems have been dealt with previously. The following examples illustrate the use of advanced empathy.

3rd grade girl to teacher

In this situation the third grader (Jane) has been voicing her concerns to the teacher about her relationship to Mary. Lately, Mary and Jane have been antagonistic to each other when previously they were best friends. Jane has been talking it over with the teacher. The teacher has facilitated Jane's expressing her feelings over the situation. The surface feeling that Jane has been showing has been anger with Mary. The teacher responds with advanced empathy:

"Jane, you have expressed a lot of anger over Mary's behavior. I am wondering if you are not only angry at Mary, but that you feel a little rejected by Mary's behavior and that this is the reason for your anger."

In this example, the teacher has acknowledged the surface feelings of anger and goes beyond that to suggest that something else may be influencing Jane. This gives Jane an opportunity to view the problem from another point of view and to come to a fuller understanding of the problem.

High school boy to teacher

In this example the boy has expressed his concern over the situation that school has not been going well for him. His grades are not what they should be and he seems to have lost interest in school. He complains most often about spinning his wheels in school. However, during the interaction, the teacher picks up that this student has a tendency to engage in self-pity. The following response is an example of advanced empathy for this situation.

"Your grades are not very good this semester again and you seem to be going through a bout of depression over this. I am concerned that you

may be making the situation worse than it is by engaging in a lot of catastrophic thought patterns. You may have a tendency to place everything in a gloom and doom situation."

In this situation the teacher puts together certain information and arrives at the conclusion that the student may have a tendency to feel sorry for self. The teacher shares this observation but does so in a cautious manner.

Self-disclosure

When used appropriately self-disclosure can help students understand themselves and their actions. Teacher self-disclosure occurs when teachers relate their feelings to students. Appropriate teacher self-disclosure provides models for students and helps students to understand their own range of feelings.

Additionally, teacher self-disclosure when related to similar student concerns can give insight and understanding to students. At times teachers can share some concerns that students are experiencing. A teacher's disclosure about feelings and action about the concern aids students in their struggle to understand their world more fully.

Some cautions should be observed when using self-disclosure. A point to remember is that the focus of any interaction should be with students. Self-disclosure is not primarily for the teacher's benefit. The real value of teacher self-disclosure is the degree to which it aids student self-understanding. A common error in self-disclosure is when it is used to gain sympathy or to impress students. In such cases the motivation for self-disclosure is suspect.

The following example illustrates appropriate self-disclosure.

Student: *"I don't mean to be cruel. I say things that when I look back on them, they sound pretty stupid."*

Teacher: *"I sometimes fall into that routine especially when I am unsure of myself. I try to come off bright and cynical. In a sense, I guess to compensate for my lack of assurance."*

In this teacher self-disclosure, the teacher has offered a piece of personal data for the benefit of the student. This information may prod the student into a deeper self-understanding. It also places trust in the relationship. A mutuality must be present in order for self-disclosure to be successful. Self-disclosure presents a model which gives permission and encouragement to students to understand some of the dynamics of their actions without being self-defeating.

The following are some helpful points about using self-disclosure:

1. Self-disclosure should not divert the focus from students.

2. Self-disclosures that share feelings are more effective than reviewing one's past life history.

3. Self-disclosures are not attempts to shock or impress students.

4. Self-disclosures should not imply that students must feel and act the way the teacher did.

A description of appropriate self-disclosure is that it is a sharing of the teacher's experiences with students in a genuine climate. Appropriate self-disclosures are mature, timely, and produce student growth and self-understanding.

By being self-disclosing a teacher presents a nondefensive posture for students. What is communicated to students is that openness and genuineness are prized in human interactions. Additionally, teachers share with students their mistakes as well as their good points. This takes away the burden of being perfect from the teacher. By being self-disclosing a more realistic person is held up to students.

Hopefully, students will learn how to be self-disclosing when it is appropriate and how to help others by using self-disclosure. The power of the teacher as a model cannot be underestimated. An open and genuine self-disclosing teacher presents a valuable example for students to emulate by displaying an effective model for interpersonal communication.

Some examples of teachers using self-disclosure follow. These examples can be used to help readers formulate good self-disclosing responses.

Example A: Student to teacher

I am going to take the SAT this coming Saturday. I'm really anxious, I'm not sleeping well.

Teacher: *I sense what you're going through. When I was preparing to take my masters examination I was really a wreck. I kept thinking of what people would say if I did not pass. Is that how you're feeling?*

Example B: Student to teacher

Mr. Smith, I just got notified that I did not make the basketball cut. I really thought that I was going to make it this year.

Teacher: *That hurts. Reminds me of when I was cut from my high school football team. I made myself think that I was a failure in everything. It really meant alot to me and for awhile I thought I was destroyed. Is that how you are feeling?*

Confrontation

Invariably points of confrontation exist in everyone's life. To avoid confrontation is to leave unresolved many aspects of interpersonal relationships. Some people prefer to avoid rather than to confront others. Then, again, a lay interpretation of confrontation views the skill as aggressive and punitive.

Confrontation is often misunderstood. In some cases, vicious character attacks are justified by individuals under the guise that confrontation is for someone's own good. Nothing could be further from the truth. Confrontation has nothing to do with punishing or calling people on the carpet. *Confrontation as used in this text is an attempt to help students understand themselves more fully by pointing out discrepancies, distortions, and game-playing actions of students. Confrontation also encourages underdeveloped and underused potential of students to remedy their ineffective actions (Egan, 1975).*

Confrontation involves a certain amount of risk on the part of teachers. Teachers confronting students is sometimes difficult because the process involves the possibility of bringing negative feelings into the teaching relationship. However, growth is not possible without change. Changing behavior can be viewed as a confrontation of old ways with new ones. The effective teacher engages in confrontation in an atmosphere of concern and intimacy. This attitude is necessary in order for confrontation to be successful.

Egan (1975) has identified several aspects of student behavior that have potential for confrontation. These are discrepancies, distortions, games, tricks, and smoke screens, Each will be discussed separately with brief explanations and examples.

Discrepancies. These behaviors in students are at variance with each other. That is a student may be discrepant in what he/she does and what he/she says. Or a student may hold a view of self as being humorous, for example, that others see as sarcastic. In this example a discrepancy exists between how a person views him/herself and how others view him/her.

The following are some discrepancies that are common among students:

• Student appears one way (angry, upset) but claims that everything is o.k.

• Student holds a set of beliefs which vary from actual behavior (e.g., claims that equal treatment of persons is commendable but acts in bigoted manner).

• Student sends a message verbally that is contradicted by nonverbal behavior.

• Student claims that school is important but does not study.

Distortions. Students sometimes distort their worlds because facing reality is threatening. To lessen the threat the student may engage in viewing the world in a way that makes it safe for him/her. Rarely is this helpful to students. Great amounts of energy and time are consumed making their world safe. Providing alternative views of their world through confrontation can help students face their worlds more realistically. For example a student who assumes a hard, bitter attitude (dog eat dog world view) may be trying to protect him/herself from personal involvement. An illustration of this distortion is the student who claims that he/she is a victim of racism as an excuse for all of his/her shortcomings.

Some other examples of common distortions in students are as follows:

- The student who is obstinate but claims he/she is committed to something.

- The student who confuses pride and vanity for loyalty.

- The student who views boys as "always after something" yet dresses provocatively.

- The student who claims he/she is witty, but his/her humor is always at someone else's expense.

Games, Tricks, and Smoke Screens. *Game playing can be defined as activities performed by an individual calculated at making others responsible for his/her own needs.* Because changing behavior is not easy and, in many instances, painful, many people engage in smoke screens, games, and tricks to avoid changing their behavior. To these people continuing with ineffective behavior is more comfortable than risking change, especially when no guarantee exists that the change will be successful. In many respects, the old adage, something (even though it seems harmful) is better than nothing, applies to these individuals.

Students also engage in tactics to avoid life's intimacies. People have an amazing number of ways to avoid effective communication in their lives. The teacher who can assess game playing in students and who confronts the student gently, but firmly, provides a valuable service to the student.

A cautionary note should be made at this point. Many teachers get caught up in student game playing. Some students are very clever in seducing teachers into their tricks.

Examples of Confrontation. Notice the game playing in the following example.

Student to teacher:

I really think that you're wonderful, Mr. Abernathy. The way you get the material across is terrific. And the way you control the class. You're strong.

Admittedly, the situation is taken out of context. However, the point to be made is that teachers do not take responsibilities from some students. Some students develop the habit of blaming others for what has gone wrong in their lives. In the school situation these students are able to itemize lists of reasons why a certain teacher or other students are responsible for their problems. By confronting the student about this process, the teacher may be able to help the student view the concern from an alternative reference. However, the teacher risks having the student perceive that he/she is being rejected. Confrontation can be a risk-taking behavior. However, the benefits can be far-reaching.

In the following example the teacher confronts the student and leads him/her to view the problem from a different perspective:

Teacher: *Jim, you have been telling me about how your math teacher mistreats you for some time. I think I have a pretty good idea of what is going on. I'm wondering what you might be doing to contribute to his behavior?*

Jim: *Nothing. I don't do anything.*

Teacher: *Well, help me with this. What do you suppose he thinks that you are doing? Let's suppose he were here talking to me. What would he say about the situation?*

Jim: *He'd probably say that I cut his class often and that I don't do my homework regularly.*

The example demonstrates how the teacher leads a student to an alternative reference through confrontation. By using this procedure the teacher gently guides the student from an idiosyncratic point of view to a more global one. This is necessary before full understanding can take place. However, the potential for students to become defensive during confrontation is high. The helpful teacher observes behavior in students to ascertain whether the confrontation is producing reactive behavior in his/her students. By being perceptive, the teacher can couch the concern in tenuous terms to make it less confrontative. Terms such as "could it be," "a possible explanation," and "let me run this by you for your consideration" are a few of several leads that make confrontation more gentle.

The following examples illustrate different areas of confrontation with appropriate teacher responses.

(Situation where the teacher notices a discrepancy between verbal and nonverbal messages.)

Student: *Hey, it doesn't bother me. Water off a duck's back. I'm not angry about it.*

Teacher:*Jerry, you say you're not angry, but you're talking very loudly. Your shoulders are scrunched up and you are clenching your fist. What you are saying with your words and what you are saying with your body come across to me as two different meanings. I'm wondering if you still have some anger left over from your argument with your father.*

(Situation where a discrepancy exists between verbal and expressed behavior.)

Student: *Ms. McArthur, I don't have my homework assignment finished. I did it last night, but my dog chewed it up.*

Teacher: *I understand how that might be upsetting to you, Jack. On several occasions you have made commitments to have your homework finished regardless of circumstances. I'm caught between accepting what you said about your homework and your previous statements on your commitments.*

(Situation where the student is resisting constructive actions to his/her problems.)

Student: *I guess I wasn't feeling too well. Anyway you have it in for me. I can't do anything right in your class. I can't help it. I just act crazy in class.*

Teacher: *When you continually make excuses for yourself, it makes me upset. I get a little angry because your behavior blocks me from reaching you. I'm not sure what you want from me and I find that I am frustrated. I wonder what purpose your behavior has for you.*

(Situation in which a student is unaware of influence of his/her behavior on another student.)

Student: (to another student) *You're a jerk and you're really dumb. Why don't you get lost.*

Teacher: *Sam, are you aware of what you are saying to Mark? Do you understand how it comes across to him? It would be more meaningful for us if you would describe what he does and how it makes you feel. Could you try saying it again without being harsh and judgmental?*

Summary of Confrontation Skill. In summary, the following points about confrontation are delineated.

1. Confrontation is a useful skill a teacher can use when discrepancies exist in students behaviors.

2. Discrepancies may exist

   a. between two feelings which are discordant.
   b. between what a student feels and what he/she thinks.
   c. between what a student thinks and how he/she acts.

3. If a discrepancy concerns a student's feeling, thinking, and acting, anxiety will be experienced by the student.

4. The experienced anxiety may be reduced by

   a. changing one or both parts of the discrepancy to make them congruent. (This can be aided through confrontation.)
   b. redefining the discrepancy so that it doesn't appear to be related. (This is a psychological defense mechanism called compartmentalization. While it sometimes reduces the anxiety, it is rarely effective on a long-term basis.)
   c. Distorting information important to one or both parts of the discrepancy. (This is another defense mechanism called denial. Similar to compartmentalization, it is not always effective.)

Sometimes confrontation is best delivered on a one-to-one basis. This is especially true when the content of the confrontation does not concern the whole class or it is such a personally intense matter that it should be conducted in private. Johnson (1980) has incorporated a step-by-step approach to this type of confrontation. It has uses in teachers' personal as well as professional lives.

The teacher should structure this type of confrontation so that ample time is available for the conference. As with any kind of confrontation the purpose is to enhance the effectiveness of the student's growth. To this end the focus of concern should be on the student. Unless the student perceives concern and caring he/she will become defensive.

Confrontation involves a certain amount of risk on the part of the teacher. Thus, the purpose of confrontation should not be carried out for a sense of retribution, rather it should be for genuine resolution. For this reason the teacher assesses whether he/she has any emotional ties with the situation and whether these are under control. If one is angry, confrontation should be avoided.

Component Skills of Interpersonal Confrontation. Following is a list of skills and definitions that are necessary for effective confrontation. While avoiding a cookbook approach to problem solving is important, the order that the steps are presented is also important. The reader is encouraged to review these steps several times before practicing a confrontation.

1. *Personal Statements.* Messages that tell the student how the confronting person is feeling, doing, and thinking (self-disclosing). The use of personal pronouns is frequent (I, me, my, etc.), *"I* feel upset about bringing this subject up." *"I'm* a little uncomfortable about this, but *I* think that it is very important to *me."*

2. *Relationship Statements.* Messages that reveal thoughts and feelings about the student in the relationship. Use of personal pronouns is frequent (immediacy), for example, "I have come to *appreciate your friendship* and *enjoy your company."*

3. *Behavior-description Statements.* Messages that accurately describe the observable behavior of the student. Statements facilitate validation (concreteness), for example, "Mary, you say that you're angry with Jim, yet *you always smile* when you talk about what makes you angry."

4. *Description-of-your-own Feeling.* Messages that contain personal statements about feelings concerning the confrontee's behavior (personal statements), e.g., "I felt *rejected* when you said that you would call if you couldn't make it to supper on time and you didn't.

5. *Understanding Responses.* Messages that respond to how the student has reacted to the confrontation (empathy), e.g., "You feel as though *I'm out of line* for bringing this up." These responses are especially useful if the student has become defensive.

6. *Perception-check-of-other's Feelings Statements.* Messages that check out the student's reaction in order to assess whether confronter's perception is accurate. These messages express neither approval nor disapproval but are used to make sure that the feelings of the student are understood, e.g., "I get the feeling that you're annoyed by your mother's nagging. *Is that right?*" This response requires that the student provide information about the teacher's perception.

7. *Interpretive Response.* Messages used with interpretive confrontation that cast hypotheses about motives and feelings of the student (advanced empathy), e.g., "You're demanding that I do what you say, *maybe because you want to show me that you are the boss.*" Be aware that this type of response may cause a defensive reaction. Be prepared to emit an understanding response (number 5).

8. *Constructive Feedback.* Messages that provide constructive feedback to help the individual to become aware of the effect of (and other's interpretation of) his/her behavior, e.g., "You often react to my physical height whenever we get into a heated argument. I get *angry* because I think that it is *unfair.*"

If the teacher suspects that the student is becoming upset over the confrontation or is becoming defensive, the teacher can respond empathically. For example, the teacher may say, "John, you are feeling upset with my bringing this matter up. Can we talk about this?" The teacher and John can discuss this issue, however, the teacher refocuses back to the confrontation issue when this matter is resolved. The possibility also exists that the student is using "hurt" behavior as part of a game-playing strategy to avoid actions.

The sensitive teacher weaves previously learned skills into the interaction whenever appropriate. He/she is self-disclosing, genuine, empathic, and concrete whenever necessary. Too often confrontation is thought to be a harsh encounter. It does not have to be. The astute teacher senses when to back off and when to refocus. After all, confrontation is for the benefit of the student. It is not to be confused with punishment.

Immediacy

Immediacy refers to the context of the relationship between student and teacher. Immediacy is viewed as the relationship in the "here and now" time context. Sometimes dynamics in a relationship interfere with the successful progress of finding a solution. The troubling dynamic may have nothing to do with the problem in question.

A rather blatant example of such a case would be if a person was bothered to the extreme by blue eyes and he/she were communicating with someone who had blue eyes. The fact that blue eyes were discomforting to the individual will affect the quality of the communication regardless of what the focus of the problem was. While this example is unrealistic, it does serve to illustrate the immediacy concerned with the here and now or present relationship between two communicants. Often immediacy occurs between two people who do not share common value systems or experiences. Blacks and whites may not be able to communicate well not because of the problem that may be between them, but simply because the race difference causes a problem in immediacy.

Problems in immediacy must be dealt with before any real progress can be made. Sometimes raising the issue is enough. If a participant is uncomfortable in a situation because of a race difference, he/she may get beyond this by saying, "I guess I am feeling uncomfortable because you are Black. I know that it is my problem and it has nothing to do with our discussion, but I am wondering if we can deal with this?" By being genuine and self-disclosing the person experiencing the problem of immediacy has taken steps to deal with it.

Another area of immediacy sometimes occurs when working with handicapped students. People sometimes are embarrassed or do not know how to act with the handicapped. If the handicap involves disfigurement, it may further complicate the problem. In this case getting the problem out in the open and getting it resolved is the best course of action.

Immediacy also refers to keeping the communication in the present time context. This text takes the position that it does little good to dredge up past histories to bring into the dialogue. This often creates a defensive posture by the recipient. Teachers are often guilty of presenting a student's history of conduct in front of the class regardless of the present situation. This only serves to diffuse the issue and create resentment in students. The teacher should facilitate focusing the problem by keeping examples and dimensions keyed to the here and now context when working on a concern.

SUMMARY

The major objective of Stage II is defining the concern. A problem is well defined when all participants appreciate the different opinions that are involved in the concern. The individual who can only appreciate one point of view about the problem is not in a very strong position for effective problem solving.

Skills that help with this process are advanced empathy, self-disclosure, confrontation, and immediacy. These skills place the teacher in a role that goes beyond the support and emphasis of Stage I.

A problem is well defined when everyone can agree to it. Problems that are stated objectively, that is, without judgments and values, is apt to be more acceptable. Thus, defining Joey's behavior as "lazy" is not as productive as defining it as "homework completed at a 60% rate." Defining a problem as "he is a slob" is not as effective as "he does not put his clothes in the appropriate place." The important point to be made is that there are people with problems not problem people. The teacher who understands this distinction is in a better position to facilitate the resolution of student problems. More is written about this important aspect of problem solving in Chapter 6.

SELF-TEST, CHAPTER 5

1. Advanced empathy differs from primary empathy because it is

    a. more accurate.
    b. more interpretive.
    c. more meaningful.
    d. more helpful.

2. The main goal of defining the problem

    a. is for students to express their feelings about the problem.
    b. is to come up with a solution.
    c. is to have student view the problem from many perspectives.
    d. none of the above.

3. Self-disclosure gives the teacher an opportunity

    a. to reveal something intimate and private about him/herself to students.
    b. to provide a model for openness for students.
    c. for the teacher to be vulnerable to students.
    d. to demonstrate to students how problems should be solved.

4. Confrontation enhances the teacher's position because

    a. It involves more risk than other skills in the previous stage.
    b. It should be used only with older children.
    c. It works best on male students.
    d. It provides an opportunity for students to vent their feelings about the concern.

5. Which of the following is true about confrontation?

    a. he/she can ventilate his/her frustrations with students.
    b. it affords the teacher an opportunity to get even with students.
    c. students need to be shown where their deficiencies are.
    d. none of the above.

6. One specific purpose of advanced empathy is

    a. to solve a student's problem.
    b. to make students comfortable.
    c. to help students view problems from an alternative frame of reference.
    d. to uncover surface feelings about the problem.

7. Which describes a disclosing person most accurately?

    a. One who is defensive.
    b. One who readily relates personal information to strangers.
    c. One who can reveal intimacy at appropriate times.
    d. One who is always ready to help people with their problems.

8. Which is *not* an area for possible confrontation?

    a. Values and beliefs.
    b. Behavior that is contrary in individuals.
    c. Feelings and behaviors that are inconsistent.
    d. Thoughts and actions which are opposites.

9. Being able to accurately identify who has responsibility for solving concerns is

    a. related to how one views who has the problem.
    b. mainly the concern of the teacher.
    c. not as important as the teacher delegating responsibility to students.
    d. overrated in terms of effective problem solving.

10. Which of the following is probably not a problem for confrontation?

    a. Student who habitually comes to class late.
    b. Student who wears his hair different from what you consider good taste.
    c. Student who claims to believe one way but acts contrary to the belief.
    d. Student who wants good grades but doesn't always finish his/her homework.

ANSWERS: *1. (b), 2. (c), 3. (b), 4. (d), 5. (a), 6. (c), 7. (c), 8. (a), 9. (a), 10. (b)*

11. Discuss the importance of being self-disclosing in the teacher-student relationship.

12. What is meant by owning the problem? What special implications does problem ownership have in teaching?

13. Discuss the difference between effective confrontation and aggressive "telling the person off."

Activity 5.1 Confrontation Responses

Choose the best example of confrontation response from the following:

1. Student to teacher (student smiling): It really makes me angry when I think about what she said to me this morning.

    a. You're really upset about this incident.
    b. Why don't you just forget it. It will all blow over in a few days.
    c. You smiled when you said that you were angry. I wonder how that fits in with what you're saying?
    d. Being angry can really take up a lot of your energy.

2. Student: I could care less about what happens to my mother. It doesn't make any difference to me. She could drop dead and I wouldn't care.

    a. Sounds like you're pretty upset with your mother.
    b. You don't really mean that. You're just angry at her now. You really love her, but you're angry and hurt this moment.
    c. A son should not talk about his mother that way. He must love his mother. It isn't correct for you to speak about her that way.
    d. I hear you say that you don't care, yet I see how you keep trying to reach out to her. You have told me often how much you wish that she would respond to you. I wonder if you really care for her more than you are willing to admit.

3. Student (a 15-year-old boy who has been quarreling with peers): I'm well-liked by the fellows. You see, I'm laid-back, but just don't push me around. Nobody tells me what to do. They know not to fool around with me.

> a. You say that you get along with the guys, but at the same time you say that the guys had better watch out for you.
> b. You sound like you're a pretty tough kid. I wonder if you're as tough as you say you are.
> c. That doesn't sound like a very good attitude to me. Sounds like you're out to prove that you can't be pushed around.
> d. I guess you're saying that you don't like to be told what to do and that you won't stand for it if some guy comes up to you and tells you what you can and cannot do.

4. Student (an unassertive person): I can handle myself now and not get taken advantage of in most situations.

> a. It must feel pretty good to get a handle on your concern.
> b. I'm pleased to hear you say that.
> c. People have no right to take advantage of you. I'm glad to see that you have finally stood up to them.
> d. If you are an assertive person, could you help me out to understand how you get into the situations that you told me about?

5. Teacher to teacher (young teacher who has put off her wedding date three times): I really love him a lot. I can't see living my life without him. We've made so many plans for our future, I can't wait to get started. It's been bad luck that we had to postpone the dates before.

> a. You sound really excited about getting married. That must be a wonderful feeling.
> b. You've postponed your wedding before, but you say that you really want to marry Bob. I may be wrong, but I'm not sure that you really want to marry him.
> c. Marriage is a serious commitment. It should not be a decision easily made. Making a marriage work these days is tough work.
> d. I think that you should either do or not. You can't continue this way.

Activity 5.2 Advanced Empathy

Choose the alternative that demonstrates advanced empathy for each of the following situations.

1. Student: I'm not sure I can handle this class. It might be a little too much for me.

    a. Most of us think that way when they enter a new course.
    b. The class looks almost too tough.
    c. If you stick with it, I'm sure you will do all right.
    d. You may be feeling scared about this course because you think that you don't have the ability.

2. Student: The girls won't let me play in their games. They always call me names and nasty things. I hate them. I hate their guts.

    a. You mean to tell me that the girls won't let you play in any games.
    b. Hating doesn't solve the problem. It never does any good.
    c. Sounds like you're really angry at the girls.
    d. I wonder if you're angry at the girls because they are rejecting you.

3. Student: It's so hard to make a decision when you don't know what to do. I'm tired of going to school but the kind of job I want requires a college degree. I wish that I didn't have to go to college.

    a. Tough choices are hard to live with—but you have to make a decision.
    b. You seem to want it both ways: A good job without putting the effort into it. I'm wondering how realistic that is?
    c. Well, what kind of a job do you want?
    d. I guess that is difficult but 10 years from now you will be glad that you chose college.

4. I have a choice between American and European history. European history is harder, but Ms. Green, who teaches American history, is really tough.

  a. That's a difficult decision.
  b. I think that you'll find both interesting.
  c. It seems to me that your choice is based on a criterion that needs to be examined. How do you think a course should be chosen?
  d. You don't have too much choice, do you. You're going to have to make a decision.

ANSWERS: 1. (d), 2. (d), 3. (b), 4. (c)

ADDITIONAL RESOURCES

Books and Publications

Janis, I. L. (Ed.). (1982). *Counseling on Personal Decisions: Theory and Research on Short-term Helping Relationships.* New Haven: Yale University Press, 1982

Films

Formulating the Counseling Goal. American Association for Counseling and Development. 5999 Stevenson Avenue, Alexandria, VA 22304.

Identifying the Problem. American Association for Counseling and Development, 5999 Stevenson Avenue, Alexandria, VA 22304.

REFERENCES

Egan, G. (1975). *The skilled helper: A model for systematic helping and interpersonal relating.* Monterey, CA: Brooks/Cole.

Gordon, T. (1970). *P. E. T. Parent effectiveness training.* New York: Peter H. Wyden Press.

Johnson, D. W. (1980). Attitude modification methods. In F. Kanfer & A. Goldstein (Eds.). *Helping people change* (2nd ed.). Elonsford, NY: Pergamon Press.

PROBLEM-SOLVING MODEL STAGE III: GENERATING ALTERNATIVES

Chapter **6**

Skills required for generating alternatives for solutions to problems are presented in this chapter. Before a teacher begins the process of generating alternatives, a number of conditions must exist. Successful problem-solving techniques are only as effective as the degree to which certain requirements are met. The problem must be defined and expressed. Undefined and unexpressed problems are bleak prospects for problem solving. Both teacher and student must have the desire to resolve the problem. Solutions cannot be imposed on people if they are to be long lasting.

EXPECTED OUTCOMES

By studying the material in this chapter the reader will be able to

1. discuss conditions that must be met before effective generating of alternatives can take place,

2. describe the role of the teacher in the process of generating alternatives, and

3. list and explain skills that facilitate successful conclusion of generating alternatives.

Ch 6   Problem-Solving Model Stage III   157

PRECONDITIONS FOR CHANGE

Problem solving involves changing behavior. To some, change creates anxiety because it entails a certain amount of risk. Individuals become comfortable in old ways even though the ways may not be very effective. To ask people to change is to ask them to risk giving up old ways for new ones. This is not always accomplished easily. For some, the fear of not knowing what changes will bring is greater than the discomfort of remaining in the same situation without change. Oftentimes this fear is ungrounded, nevertheless, the person acts as though it were true.

The presence of certain conditions facilitates risk taking. *Trust* is a major consideration in this process. A trusting environment conveys to students that risking change is all right. The risk of the unknown may be frightening to some; however, a trusting atmosphere can help assuage the fear. The perceptive teacher is aware of the profound effects that trust has on students. Trust always gives permission to venture. It conveys to the student that no matter what the outcome of attempts, results will still be accepted. Without trust behavioral change is next to impossible.

The teacher engenders trust by being consistent, open, and self-disclosing. Additionally, trust involves *mutuality*. Teachers trust students. Teachers can share with students an incident in their lives in which they were vulnerable and had to risk trying to change. Teachers need to acknowledge how threatening the process was and how rewarding it can be. Trust can be demonstrated by being self-disclosing and nondefensive. By providing a model of trust the teacher demonstrates how it is done. By risking with students, students witness that risk taking can be worthwhile, and personal growth is largely a matter of how much risk one is willing to take.

Student motivation to change behavior is contingent on a number of factors. Home, background, economics, and experiences have ramifications on a person's motivation to change. However, in the school context, trust in the teacher may be the greatest agent to enhance motivation to change in students. Thus, engendering trust and mutuality in the classroom will be repaid many times over.

Another important ingredient in problem solving is *intentionality*. That is, each party must desire an equitable solution to the problem. Power struggles, competition, and the like reduce the chance of successful problem solving. When intentionality exists everyone involved has a vested interest in seeing the problem solved. However, intentionality is not imposed on students. For obvious reasons this would be counterproductive.

Chances of failure and backsliding also are reduced if intentionality is present. Similar to motivation, intentionality is enhanced through trust and respect. In this atmosphere teacher and students work together to solve a mutual concern. Problems are not viewed as win-lose situations, rather they are perceived as something that exists currently which is impeding mutual effectiveness, and its removal benefits each one involved. This attitude separates an effective from an ineffective classroom climate.

Trust, respect, risk taking, and intentionality are related variables in the process of change. Without adequate amounts of each, individuals are less apt to engage in effective problem solving. Rather, they are often defensive and suspicious, intent on protecting their own interests. Energy that is diverted into these activities leaves little for more productive ones. Teachers who are sensitive to this dynamic realize that building trust into the teacher-student communication pattern depends on the quality of the relationship. Skills previously cited in this text—empathy, genuineness, self-disclosure, and so forth—promote, maintain, and enhance the quality of the relationship. Adversary roles are lessened when the emphasis is on mutuality and the relationship is based on trust.

WORKABLE PROBLEMS

Often problems are stated in such a way that they become an endless struggle to solve. A reason for this is that the problem was never defined specifically enough. When the definition of the problem is not clearly understood, generating possible solutions is extremely difficult. Most problems that go unsolved are stated vaguely. For example, if a teacher declared, "We have got to do something about our classroom behavior!" it may appear to be a well-defined problem. However, the manner in which the problem is expressed is so vague a thousand and one different acts could be included in "our classroom behavior." Unless a more specific statement is made, resolution of the problem is unlikely. Also, in this situation the task is never completed in so much that the endpoint is not stated. Motivation for students would be difficult because no beginning or end to the problem is defined.

Criteria for Judging
Workability of Problems

In the following example, one teacher is talking to another. Teacher A is disturbed with her classroom management. She says to Teacher B, "I am not satisfied with the way I handle my classroom." In order to move to more concrete specifications of problems certain criteria can be employed. Egan (1982) has developed a number of criteria to judge whether a goal or a problem is workable. Some of these may be helpful to teachers.

Workable Problem Definitions

Workable problem definitions are stated as outcomes which need to be distinguished from processes or strategies. For example, a person may claim that he/she needs additional training in teaching. This is not a problem, rather it may be a strategy for becoming a more effective teacher. Similarly, a problem can be stated by outcome as the desire to lose ten pounds; a strategy would be to join Weight Watchers. Confusing strategies with outcomes makes problem solving more difficult.

Concreteness. Problem definitions that have potential for successful resolution are stated concretely. Vague problems are unsolvable. "I want to do better in school" is much too general. "I want to make three A's and two B's" is more concrete. Vague statements such as, "I would like to become a better teacher," "I want to relate to my wife in a more effective way," or "I want to become a better person," need to be translated to more specific terms. Often the reason the problem is stated vaguely is that the person does not have a clear grasp of the problem. The process of expressing feelings in Stage I may help to translate vague notions into concrete terms.

Measurable. To be able to determine whether a problem has been solved is important. One way to do this is to state the problem in such a way that it is verifiable. The overriding concern for this criterion is "How do I know when I have achieved the resolution to my problem?" The teacher who states that he/she would like a better relationship with his/her class has no way of knowing if the goal is ever accomplished. However, if the problem is worded such that fewer than four student reprimands per day constitute an improved relationship, judging the effectiveness of strategies is possible. Initially many individuals have a tendency to be reluctant at stating problems this way. There seems to be a cold approach to this method. However, positive results often make converts of people.

Implicit in this criterion is some measurement of current status of the problem. In the case mentioned previously the teacher would need to know how many reprimands were given on typical days. The adage, "If we don't know where we are and where we are going, how do we know when we get there?" applies for this criterion. Some authors call this baseline data.

Realistic. Unlike Candide, views of problems must be grounded in reality. That the problem chosen can be solved and that its solution depends on the reasonable efforts of all people involved is essential. To ask individuals to participate in solving problems that are beyond their ability is to invite frustration and failure. The problem chosen, no matter how precise and measurable, is unsolvable if it is beyond the means of the people involved. This must be assessed realistically. Sometimes expectations have to be lowered in light of reality.

Basically, a problem is realistic if student and teacher resources are adequate to the task and if the external environment does not prevent the problem from being solved. Many concerns become problems when they are not grounded in reality. Parents who insist that their child go to medical school when the child does not have the ability may be generating a problem. The parents' wishes for the child are not realistic, and they may see the child in their own image rather than what he/she actually is. This view can cause a great deal of frustration for both parents and child. The child may take these frustrations to school where they become a problem for the teacher. Solving the problem cannot revolve around getting the child into medical school. Other aspects are more realistic to the problem. Parents may need to readjust their view of their child's capabilities and more importantly to accept their child as a worthy person in their readjustment.

Checklist for Determining Workability

Before beginning to generate alternatives for solving problems, a few questions can be asked to help ensure that the stage has been properly set. The following set of questions serves as a guide and can be used as a checklist (Egan, 1982).

1. Is the problem in workable units?
   a. Is the problem stated in definite terms?
   b. Is the problem within control of the persons involved?

2. If several problems exist, has a priority list been arranged? The following are some criteria for arranging priorities.

    a. Crisis situations are to be given emphasis.

    b. Only problems that are under control of the persons involved should be listed.

    c. Problems that can be handled relatively easily should begin the list, more severely related problems can follow. The rationale behind this is that in complicated situations establishing some progress first is helpful. Choosing relatively easy problems can engender optimism in the problem-solving act.

    d. Problems that will benefit the most students in the classroom should be chosen. Less priority is given to those problems that, when solved, only benefit a few.

    e. Choosing problems that can be solved in a relatively short period of time also is helpful.

BRAINSTORMING: A STRATEGY FOR GENERATING ALTERNATIVES

Brainstorming, a technique borrowed from industry, has some important implications for problem solving. Basically, brainstorming is used to enlarge the possible alternative solutions to problems. Subsumed under the concept that two heads are better than one, a classroom full of heads may be better than one depending on level of knowledge pertinent to the problem.

The real possibility exists that an original solution to a problem may be generated through brainstorming. Horan (1979) reported that the Sylvania flash cube was thought up during a brainstorming session.

While the main purpose of brainstorming is to generate as many alternatives as possible, another benefit derived from the process is that brainstorming affords the opportunity for many individuals to become involved in the process of problem solving. When students are involved in the process of problem solving, they are more apt to be motivated to contribute to the successful resolution of the problem. The very nature of brainstorming invites participation. It can be very enjoyable, and it is a useful strategy for increasing involvement and commitment in solutions. Similar to other components of problem solving, brainstorming can be incorporated in students thinking so that it can be used easily outside of the classroom. Learning, in the final analysis, rises or falls in value to the degree to which it can be generalized outside of the classroom.

In many respects, brainstorming owes its success to the old adage that two heads are better than one. Yet, it is more than the additive effects of having more people helping with the solution. The interaction among people in the brainstorming sessions motivates them to offer more suggestions, to commit to change, and to offer creative solutions to problems.

Conditions for Effective Brainstorming

A number of conditions are necessary for effective brainstorming. The teacher has the responsibility to ensure that these conditions are present. Horan (1975) and Egan (1982) have developed lists of necessary conditions for effective brainstorming.

Suspend Judgment/Criticisms. During brainstorming care must be taken not to criticize alternatives. Free and open generation of possible solutions are encouraged. Criticism of alternatives, no matter how justifiable, is inappropriate in this process.

Exhibiting subtle clues conveying criticism is as effective as direct verbal messages. Raised eyebrow, rolling eyes, or shocked facial expressions are powerful nonverbal cues that signify disapproval. Conditional phrases, such as "yes, but also" get the message across that certain kinds of responses are not welcomed. These behaviors should be avoided in brainstorming.

Teachers facilitate responses from their students to explore realistic and supposedly unrealistic alternatives in this phase, encourage students to become uninhibited, and implore students to give the first response that comes into their minds. Teachers reward students for the *quantity* of their contributions. Other considerations regarding the alternative will come later.

Freewheeling/Letting Yourself Go. The previous description is of an almost free association process to generating alternatives. "Off the wall" solutions are encouraged. An open, nonjudgmental classroom environment is needed for this process to succeed. If a student suggests that one way that the class can become quieter is to sew shut the students' mouths, this becomes a legitimate member to the list of possible alternatives.

Caution should be offered not to encourage novelty for classroom's amusement sake. While originality is encouraged, some students may offer bizarre solutions for amusement value. The sensitive teacher knows the value of balance between fun and foolishness. However, risk is taken when originality is promoted that some abuses may occur. Sometimes humor helps to reduce the tension associated with solving serious problems. A competent teacher provides a model for this behavior. Humor can be a powerful tool in promoting successful resolutions to problems.

Quantity Is Desirable. The more alternatives offered, the better are the chances that an effective solution to the problem will be found. Additionally, some evidence exists that effective solutions are generated in the later part of brainstorming sessions (Egan, 1982). The teacher motivates students through encouragement to generate as many alternatives as they can. This process is facilitated by the teacher prodding the class to produce as many alternatives as possible. After the brainstorming process has progressed for a time, participants will begin to govern the quality of alternatives offered and those to be considered.

Piggybacking/Combining. By blending together different solutions, additional solutions can be created. Teachers can model this behavior to students so eventually they will begin to combine and synthesize previous alternatives to form new ones. Thus items on the brainstorm alternatives list serve as stimulus for producing other items. At this point a contagious feeling of excitement may develop as alternatives are generated.

Clarifying/Expanding. Using statements that ask students to clarify suggestions often create new possibilities. A simple expression, "Can you give me an example?" may prompt the student and his/her peers to offer still other solutions. Clarification should not be confused with criticisms. Clarification is asked in such a manner that the student understands the request is for everyone's benefit. The teacher who suspends judgment and criticism, encourages freewheeling/letting go, sustains quantity as desirable, promotes piggybacking and combining, and promotes clarifying and expanding sets the conditions for productive activity.

The previous five conditions create readiness for brainstorming. The important features to remember are quantity is stressed and participation valued. Vested interest helps to ensure that students will commit themselves to implement chosen strategies. Students can more easily make this commitment if they have some part in the problem-solving process. Forced strategies and solutions do not often motivate students. Participation in the process invites responsibility, and commitment results from being invested in process.

Strategies and Skills
Important in this Stage

Recording Alternatives. Several strategies and skills help to facilitate brainstorming. One is for the teacher to use a flip chart or chalkboard to record alternatives. This action serves several functions. It provides an accurate record of what transpired during the brainstorming session. By recording alternatives participants view their contributions, and the record keeping process also ensures that alternatives are not forgotten or lost.

Filling up the chalkboard or flip chart is visual evidence of brainstorming. Students enjoy seeing their teacher writing rapidly on the chalkboard trying desperately to keep up with responses. Traditional classroom procedures for responding may be suspended. Students are encouraged to offer suggestions spontaneously. To do this they simply shout the alternatives. Some teachers may find coping with this difficult. However, if the classroom spirit reflects an intention to find an effective solution, the added motivation may outweigh the inconvenience of the noise level as long as it does not disrupt other classes. The teacher should demonstrate that he/she also enjoys the process. The teacher's nonverbal behavior can convey this easily.

The record keeping aspect of writing the alternatives in view of the class also provides the mechanism for cataloging range of possibilities. Later in the session as the evaluation stage takes over, alternatives can be visually eliminated from contention by erasing or crossing them out. This serves as a concrete act of elimination, and it provides an image that the list is being shortened.

Prompting. Several other teacher skills promote the generation of alternatives. Prompting is one such skill. Prompting can be thought of as serving a kind of pump-priming function. It encourages students to continue with brainstorming. Much like an auctioneer, the teacher may prod the class to further efforts. Responses such as "What other alternatives do I hear?" "Who's got another one?" or "We're not finished yet, are we?" help to quicken the pace of the session.

Egan (1982) has itemized six kinds of prompts that help in this stage. While the teacher does not offer any alternatives of his/her own, by asking the following questions students may be spurred on to think of new and different alternatives.

1. What persons can help us achieve our solution?

2. What models or examples can help us achieve our solution?

3. What places or resources can help us achieve our solution?

4. What things (apparatus) can help us achieve our solution?

5. What organizations can help us achieve our solution?

6. What existing programs can help us achieve our solution?

Time Limits. Often setting a time limit for the brainstorming session is a good idea. To generate an ample number of alternatives does not take long. Depending on the age level and the problem involved, 10 to 30 minutes will usually suffice. Obviously more difficult or unusual problems may require more time; and usually younger children are not as apt to have as many alternatives as teenagers or adults. Setting time limits to serve as closure on the activity is one method of beginning and ending the brainstorming session. This avoids the process of suffering a slow death.

Reinforcement. The teacher can also issue reinforcement as the class engages in generating alternatives. Caution should be exercised in this activity. What is being reinforced is the *process* of generating alternatives, not a particular *idea.* Comments such as "We are really cooking now!" and "I like the way the list is growing" focus on the overall session rather than on an individual's alternative. Thus, the teacher reinforces students' involvement in the brainstorming process rather than any one alternative.

Metaphorical Thinking. Horan (1979) included training in metaphorical thinking as a way of developing creative solutions to problems. Bionics, the drawing of analogies between biological mechanisms and technological design, is a form of metaphorical thinking. Fish are able to use the oxygen locked up in water. Does something in this have implications for technological discoveries? Another procedure for training in generating alternatives is to have students envision themselves to be the problem object. The question asked in this case would be, "What would make me change if I were the problem object?"

The final form of metaphorical thinking is rooted in fantasy. The question asked in this type would be, "How can the problem solve itself?" An example of this would be the problem of dead batteries. The problem can be solved if the batteries could be made good again. Thus, the concept of rechargeable batteries would come to mind, when "how can the problem solve itself?" is asked.

Probing. Teachers can use probing as a method of stimulating generation of alternatives. Probing can prod students into coming up with creative ways of solving problems. Probings are based on certain kinds of questions. The familiar who, what, where, and when questions provide a basis for probing. The teacher seeks to find out from students:

Who do we know that can help us with our problems?
Who has had similar problems and has found effective solutions?
What individuals can be used as resources for us?
What strengths or resources do we have that will help us?
Where have we seen or experienced a problem like this before?
When is the best time to accomplish the solution? (Egan, 1982)

Summary of Brainstorming Technique

By prompting, probing, and challenging the teacher keeps the motivation level high in the process. Remember that the emphasis is on the quantity of response, not quality. Evaluation comes later. The teacher encourages participation to involve as many students as possible.

Students need to have a sense that they have a genuine part in the problem-solving process. This vested interest in the problem will pay dividends because students will work harder for equitable solutions when they have evidence that they share duties and responsibilities.

The teacher has an important role in the process of involving students in problem solving. Students become very sensitive to the idea that teachers have their own solution to problems and that teachers only listen politely to what students think and never really intend to utilize student input. This attitude has a dampening effect on students' motivation to solve problems.

Good problem-solving behavior may be thought of as wise choices of alternatives. However, if the possible number of alternatives is restricted, the quality of problem solving is left in doubt. After all, the solution is only as good as the alternatives presented. This is why getting as many alternatives as possible is important. Restricted number of alternatives produce restricted solutions.

When all possible alternatives are generated, the next step is to evaluate each as a strategy for solving the problem. At this point the teacher provides feedback about the process that occurred during the brainstorming session. Certain topics can be reviewed. Discussion on results of brainstorming can become the focal issue for the class. Reviewing such issues as whether all class members participated, or were there any impediments to the process provides valuable information for the class. It is anticipated that this information will be helpful when the class engages in brainstorming in the future. Review should center on the *brainstorming process,* not on any one alternative. The intent is that the review is being undertaken so that the class can function more effectively during brainstorming at another time.

SELF-TEST, CHAPTER 6

1. Changing behavior is difficult because

    a. enough good advice is never available.
    b. risk-taking behavior is involved.
    c. students are younger than teachers.
    d. the natural tendency is to choose the easiest way.

2. Which of the following skills does not promote risk-taking behaviors?

    a. Mutuality.
    b. Trust.
    c. Empathy.
    d. Self-disclosure.

3. Which of the following is *not* a characteristic of a workable problem?

    a. Concreteness and specificity.
    b. Outcomes that are measurable.
    c. Valuable results.
    d. Realistic problems.

4. If several problems exist, which is the best suggestion?

    a. Arrange problems according to difficulty list.
    b. Choose problems that will benefit most students.
    c. Choose problems over which you have the most control.
    d. All of the above.

5. Which of the following is *not* an activity designed to enhance brainstorming?

    a. Freewheeling
    b. Piggybacking.
    c. Clarifying.
    d. Criticizing.

ANSWERS: 1. (b), 2. (c), 3. (c), 4. (d), 5. (d)

6. Discuss why for some people changing their behavior is difficult?

7. What are some conditions that the teacher can create that promote students to engage in behavior change?

8. Describe the activities that teachers can initiate to enhance brainstorming.

9. What are criteria for judging whether a problem is workable?

10. Describe the role of prompting and probing in generating alternatives.

Activity 6.1 Brainstorming Alternatives for Self

1. Think of five concerns that are evident in your life today.

2. Write concerns behaviorally and arrange in order according to the guidelines presented in this chapter.

3. Use the concern that appears at the top of the list and generate a list of alternatives.

4. Ask another person if he/she has had or other persons if they have had a similar problem and what alternatives were suggested. Add these suggestions to your original list.

Activity 6.2 Brainstorming Alternatives for a National Problem

Think of a problem that concerns the United States (unemployment, inflation, budget deficits, etc.) and brainstorm possible solutions for one of the problems.

ADDITIONAL RESOURCES

Books and Publications

Clark, C. H. (1950). *Brainstorming.* New York: Doubleday.

Egan, G. (1982). *The skilled helper.* Monterey, CA: Brooks/Cole.

Horan, J. J. (1979). *Counseling for effective decision making.* North Scituate, MA: Duxbury Press.

Janis, I. L., & Mann, L. (1977). *Decision making: A psychological analysis of conflict, choice, and commitment.* The Free Press.

Nezu, A., & D'Zurilla, T. J. (1981). Effects of problem definition and formation on decision making in the social problem-solving process. *Behavior Therapy, 12,* 100-106.

Films

Creative Problem Solving: How to Get Better Ideas. CRM/McGraw Hill, 110 Fifteenth Street, Del Mar, CA 92014.

Problem Solving Strategies: The Synectics Approach. CRM/McGraw Hill, 110 Fifteenth Street, Del Mar, CA 92014.

REFERENCES

Egan, G. (1982). *The skilled helper: A model for systematic helping and interpersonal relating* (2nd ed.). Monterey, CA: Brooks/Cole.

Horan, J. J. (1975). Coping with inescapable discomfort through "in vivo" emotive imagery. In J. D. Krumboltz & C. E. Thorenson (Eds.). *Counseling methods.* New York: Holt, Rinehart, and Winston.

Horan, J. J. (1979). *Counseling for effective decision making.* Scituate, MA: Duxbury Press.

Chapter 7

PROBLEM-SOLVING MODEL STAGE IV: SELECTING AN ALTERNATIVE

Information is presented to help teachers and students decide which alternative of those they have generated is the best solution for their problem. Because a successful resolution can only be as good as the strategy chosen, wise decisions in choosing options are very important. Strategies and skills that facilitate the selection process will be highlighted.

EXPECTED OUTCOMES

By studying the material in this chapter the reader will be able to

1. discuss the teacher's role in selecting an alternative,

2. construct a balance sheet for evaluating alternatives,

TEACHER'S ROLE IN
SELECTING AN ALTERNATIVE

When selecting an alternative, choose the alternative that most if not all members of the class agree as being the best. Students become adept at learning how to please teachers and to respond to teachers in a way that pleases them. In some cases, students may be choosing alternatives more toward pleasing the teacher than for themselves. Whether this atmosphere is conducive to effective problem solving is doubtful. The sensitive teacher is aware of this phenomenon and acknowledges the influence the teacher role has in class decision-making activities.

In an effective classroom a norm is developed that makes students' functioning more important than pleasing the teacher. The whole class and its welfare should be more important than any one individual. Students and teachers alike must be invested in furthering the class' progress. This unity is the basis for mutuality. Mutuality, simply explained, means a group can accomplish more than any individual on his/her own. This concept does not obviate that the classroom is comprised of individual students but recognizes that individuality must be melded with group cohesiveness to strike a delicate balance. Akin to the United States society, schools endeavor to maintain individualism on the one hand and unity on the other. The success of this delicate balancing act is crucial to student development.

The teacher role is to encourage individual responsibility to the class in fostering unity. This can be done expeditiously by presenting oneself as a model. The teacher accomplishes this by actively seeking input from as many students as possible, by weighing each student response without prejudice, and by listening to students and being genuine in the professional role. By genuineness the teacher demonstrates that each student has input to the class function and has a responsibility for maintaining an effective environment.

The teacher permits students to make choices and choose strategies. Clearly, at times choices will be made that are not the best. However, this in itself is part of the learning process of the problem-solving approach. The evaluation stage will provide evidence as to the utility of the strategy. This evidence is fed back into the problem-solving paradigm. Thus students use the evaluation phase as evidence of their effectiveness in choosing a strategy. Adjustments are made based on information received. This adjustment demonstrates the learning process of the problem-solving model that can be transferred easily to life outside the classroom. Students are apt to learn more effectively if they experience the consequences of their choices.

In many instances the teacher is the facilitator in the selection process. Verbal and nonverbal components of the teacher's messages are constantly monitored by students. Teachers can lend unknown support to certain alternatives by their verbal and nonverbal messages. Thus, a teacher monitors his/her actions as a facilitator, however, this does not mean the teacher cannot ask questions, seek clarification, and present information about alternatives. The teacher interacts with the class in a neutral manner in which the chief concern is to gather data to help students make wise choices. The supportive questioning and challenging format that is used by the teacher with the expressed purpose of advancing remediation of common concerns is a healthy sign of an effectively functioning classroom.

SYSTEMATIC APPROACH
TO PROBLEM SOLVING

The diagram of the problem-solving model presented in Figure 4.1 is an oversimplification. It presents a skeletal structure that can be expanded to include a detailed approach to each stage. For example, the stage that is the focus of this chapter is selecting an alternative (Block 4.0 in Figure 4.1). This stage can be developed to include a variety of smaller, more detailed steps. A representation is shown in Figure 7.1.

Figure 7.1 represents a systematic procedure for selecting an alternative to a problem. When individuals make a decision a process of some sort is gone through to arrive at a strategy. However, individuals sometimes go about the process in a disorderly way. This introduces potential sources of error into the selection process because idiosyncratic tendencies of individuals may confound the situation. Examples are when an impulsive person may not exercise his/her ability to generate a variety of options, when a person commits the process to memory which invites possible error, or a person may select an alternative that obviates, or is in conflict with certain value systems because the conflict was not considered before making the decision.

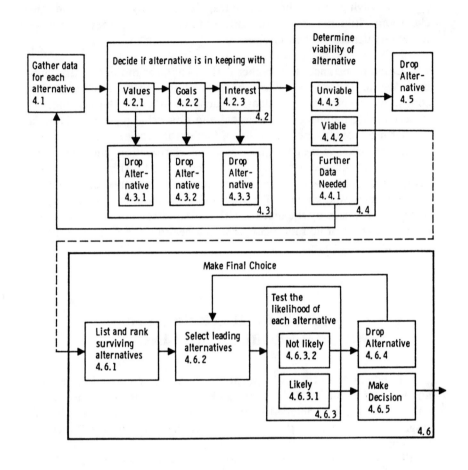

Figure 7.1. Expanded version of "Select an Alternative" stage.

The quality of problem-solving behavior can be enhanced by a systematic approach. Obviously, a systematic approach will take more time than approaches that tend to have a more impulsive quality. In the classroom this becomes a crucial variable because so many individuals are involved. Time spent on systematic problem solving must be balanced with efficacy. Teachers often complain that they do not have enough time in the day for teaching. Much of their time is engaged in disciplinary actions. A problem-solving approach to classroom interaction, while taking more time initially, may be more effective in long-term results.

The problem-solving approach teaches a very important life skill—a process for solving concerns. Rather than being punitive, the problem-solving approach provides a strategy for solving concerns in the future. Time spent on problem solving has a positive aspect, thus contrasting it to time spent on discipline, which has a negative aspect. As students become more skillful in the problem-solving process, the amount of time it takes will decrease.

In addition, the problem-solving approach is preventative. Disciplinary approaches are usually crisis-oriented, thus they have little generalizing effect; the teacher must continue to deal with student behavior on a case-by-case method. Constant disciplinary action exacts a psychological toll from both students and teachers. Stress, fatigue, and irritability are some of the by-products of individuals engaged in disciplinary procedures. Problem-solving approach places the problem in a positive light and provides a strategy for remediation.

Teacher actions are less apt to be seen as punitive when the problem-solving approach is used. Responsibility for behavior rests with students and teachers alike. Thus, a more positive approach to discipline is fostered by the problem-solving method. The approach does not cast teachers and students in adversarial roles, rather it provides the structure for cooperation in solving problems.

SELECTING THE BEST ALTERNATIVES

Choosing the most appropriate alternative for a given problem is often seen as the most difficult aspect of problem solving (Egan, 1981; Horan, 1979; Janis & Mann, 1977; Stewart & Winborn, 1973). In reality, the actual final choice process is not as difficult as are the steps that go into the procedure. For many, the most difficult aspect is gathering pertinent information for each of the alternatives. In order to make a wise selection, all important data should be known about each alternative. Much information may be gathered, but it may not all be useful. This sifting out of information is time consuming. Another problem is assessing information quickly. Some decisions are more temporal than others. An advantage to problem solving with an entire class is that the teacher has all the students as a resource. Students in the class can be assigned different alternatives to research. By working in small groups, much of the time for this activity can be reduced. Thus, the problem-solving model utilizes skills learned in the classroom about working in small groups and gathering information.

With the advent of microcomputers and library information retrieval systems the information gathering process can be shortened considerably. Recent innovations in both of these areas soon will be filtering into the classroom.

According to Figure 7.1 an alternative can be selected by following a systematic method. After the pertinent data are gathered for each alternative, the next step is to examine alternatives to see if each is consistent with the class' values, goals, and interests. The major question to be answered focuses on whether the alternative is in keeping with positive values, goals, and interests of students. For example, in a situation in a classroom in which a student's belongings were missing, an alternative of spanking each child until the culprit is discovered would not be consistent with the group values, interests, and goals. The question to be answered is, "To what degree is this alternative consistent with learning positive values, goals, and interests?" A related consideration questions whether the means, regardless of their efficacy, produce positive skills and strategies that can transfer outside of the classroom. If the response is negative to this query, the viability of the alternative is doubtful; and strong consideration should be given to eliminating that alternative from contention.

DETERMINING VIABILITY
OF ALTERNATIVES

The next step is to determine which alternatives are viable for further consideration. Some alternatives will be so "far out" that they will be eliminated quickly from contention. Other alternatives may need more information, while some are obvious contenders. This status is displayed graphically in Cell 4.4 of Figure 7.1.

CRAVE System for Ranking Alternatives

Some writers in the field of decision making have devised strategies for ranking alternatives. Egan (1981) devised the CRAVE system for evaluating the viability of options. In his system, five criteria variables are used. CRAVE is an acronym for control, relevancy, attractiveness, values, and environment. Each of the five criterion is assigned a score ranging from 0 to 5 for each alternative. Thus, any given alternative may have a total score from 0 to 25 points. An explanation for each criterion follows.

Control. Alternatives that score high on this criterion indicate that class members had a great deal of control over the actions needed. In the example where a clean classroom is the problem and assigning specific duties to class members is an alternative, the alternative could be scored 5. In the example of making the school playground more enjoyable by purchasing additional equipment, the alternative is not within the control of the students; thus its score would be zero.

Relevancy. High ratings for this criterion would be determined by the effectiveness of the strategy. Those alternatives that appear to be very capable of accomplishing the resolution of the problem, regardless of their attractiveness, would score high on this criterion.

Attractiveness. This criterion addresses the issue of how much appeal a certain alternative has for class members. Some alternatives are more attractive than others and they have more motivational value. This is an important feature in choosing an alternative. However, attractiveness should not be weighted more heavily than other criteria.

Values. The major point to address in this criterion is the degree to which the alternative is within the values and moral standards of class members. An obvious example over an alternative that would be scored zero is when classroom noise is a problem and one of the alternatives is to throw all the boys out of the second story windows. Another example is if the class members would like to purchase some equipment but they do not have the funds. An alternative suggestion may be to steal the money. This would be rated zero. An alternative which suggests having a bake sale may be rated 4 or 5 on this criterion.

Environment. Considerations important for this criterion are objects and individuals in the problem environment that may interfere with alternatives. If planning a surprise party for one of the teachers is an alternative, and interaction with this teacher is frequent, then the rating for this alternative would be low. If the classroom environment is relatively free of major obstacles for implementing the alternative, then the rating would be high.

A composite sheet for the CRAVE procedure aids in the screening process. A grid can be constructed similar to Table 7.1 in which alternatives are coded and listed in the first column. Scores are given for each of the five criterion variables. A total rating for each alternative is obtained by summing the ratings, and this value is placed in the total column. The total values are then used as a basis for ranking alternatives.

Scoring the criterion for CRAVE can be more reliable if each criterion is rated across alternatives before proceeding to the next criterion. That is, the procedure is to rate the Control (C) criterion for each alternative before proceeding to the Relevancy (R) criterion. In this manner, the relative value for a given criterion can be compared among the alternatives. Thus the field of the alternatives becomes the standard for ratings. Values one through five are made relative to the poorest or best alternative for a given criterion. This method is more reliable because to rate each alternative on all five of the criteria first and to then remember the best alternative for each criterion would be difficult.

BALANCE SHEET FOR
RANKING ALTERNATIVES

The decisional balance sheet developed by Janis and Mann (1977) offers another approach for selecting the best alternative for a problem. Applied to the classroom, four main categories make up the balance sheet grid. These categories can be filled with positive and negative entries for each alternative. These four categories adopted for a classroom are

1. utilitarian gains and losses for the classroom;

2. utilitarian gains and losses for important others in the school and community environments;

3. class members approval or disapproval; and

Table 7.1

A Grid for the CRAVE System for Selecting an Alternative

Alternative	Control C	Relevancy R	Attractiveness A	Values V	Environment E	Total T
1						
2						
3						
4						
5						
6						
7						
8						
9						
10						

Note. Each alternative is assigned a score ranging from 0-5. Totals are determined by summing the ratings.

4. approval or disapproval by important others in the school and community environments.

An explanation for each of the categories follows.

1. *Utilitarian gains and losses for the classroom.* Considerations for this category focus on benefits or negative consequences accrued from a particular alternative for class members. If a group were deciding on where to take a field trip, considerations would be the knowledge gained from the different trips, the time spent away from school, the enjoyment of each trip by the class as a whole, the expenses of each alternative, and what must be given up to assure that the trip is possible.

2. *Utilitarian gains and losses for important others in the school and community environments.* This category includes all expected benefits or negative consequences for important people in the school and community environments. In the field trip example, considerations for this category might be the effect (positive or negative) on the other class groups in school, the involvement for parents, and the predictable benefits or negative consequences for the community. Parents' providing transportation, lunches, and supervision may have to be taken into consideration for this category.

3. *Class members approval or disapproval.* Considerations within this category center on concepts that students hold for the classroom regarding moral, ethical, and legal values. Processing this category is difficult unless students are able to identify with the class and all students are able to view the class as adhering to a particular identifiable set of standards. The class environment represents certain kinds of behavior and values, and students are able to acknowledge behavior, values, and attitudes which coincide or clash with those of the class.

Certain questions can be asked under this category: "Will the class members be proud if this choice is made?" "By making this choice is the class adhering to its standards?" "To what degree does making this choice improve the integrity and standards of the class?"

For some problems this category has little value, while for others it may have tremendous implications. For example, if the class were raising money for a scientific field trip on electronics and an alternative for the trip was visiting the local town's video arcade, some questions may be raised about this alternative in relation to the class standards.

4. *Approval or disapproval by important others in the school and community environments.* The difference between categories 3 and 4 is the point of reference. Category 3 concerns class image; category 4 concerns significant others (teachers, principal, and parents) and the community (neighborhood, church, and parents). Questions to be asked are: "Is this action in keeping with the school's image?" and "Would our parents approve of this choice?"

The balance sheet format lends itself to application on a chalkboard, flip chart, or overhead projector. Table 7.2 is an example of a balance sheet to be used to consider alternatives for class field trip. Alternatives are placed in columns for the four categories.

Pluses and minuses are assigned to the list of pertinent questions for each category. For example, a number of questions should be included for Category 1, gains and losses for the class. The questions become the foundation for assigning positive or negative balance for Category 1 on each of the alternatives. Pertinent questions are devised for each of the categories. Duplicating the questions for student use is helpful. Placing questions on four panels of chalkboard is another method of keeping criteria for judgment in view of class.

Having each alternative on a separate worksheet where more space can be utilized also can be helpful. Student worksheets can be condensed and transferred to the master balance sheet after the initial scoring of alternatives. At this time a ranking of all alternatives is necessary. The balance sheet with pluses and minuses does not offer a quantitative method of ranking. The CRAVE system, however, does. The quantifiable aspects of the CRAVE system can be combined with the balance sheet method to facilitate ranking alternatives. Each of the four categories can be rated from 1 to 9 points. If an alternative seems to satisfy all of the pertinent questions for a category, it receives an 8 or 9. If it does not seem to meet the criteria for the category, then it receives a 1 or 2. The points for all four categories are summed to obtain a total value for each alternative. At this stage to rank the alternatives according to their numeric values is relatively easy. (CRAVE system is explained on pp. 183-5.)

As with the CRAVE system, reliability and rating accuracy can be improved by rating all of the first categories for the alternatives and then going on to the second category. This provides the class with a relative standard to make the 1 through 9 assessments.

Table 7.2

Sample Balance Sheet (Used for Considering Class Field Trip)

Alternatives	Anticipated Gains or Losses		Anticipated Approval or Disapproval	
	+ or − incentive values	For class	For significant others in school environment and community	For class	For significant others in school environment and community
1. Go to the University Planetarium				
2. Go to Murphy's All Electronic Game Room				
3. Go to the electric company's nuclear reactor plant				
4. Go to the city's Museum of Natural History				
5. Go to the World's Fair				
6. Go to Disney World				

SELECTING LEADING ALTERNATIVES

After alternatives are ranked and the class agrees that no new considerations need to be discussed, selecting the leading or most promising alternative becomes a relatively easy task (refer to Figure 7.1, Box 4.5). No criteria are set for the number of alternatives that should be kept in contention. Sometimes one alternative stands head and shoulders above the others. In this situation to continue with the elimination process would be useless. This alternative is clearly the class' choice and the decision should be made by the class to implement it.

Possibly two or more alternatives may be equally attractive. These alternatives can be weighted against each other to help determine the best alternative for the class.

At this stage the teacher's role becomes crucial. By virtue of his/her own past experiences, the teacher may be in a better position to render a judgment or to bring in additional pertinent information. Prompts and open-ended questions are methods teachers can use to solicit additional information for alternatives.

A list of prompts can be helpful in this process. A few are listed here to illustrate their nature.

1. Are people who can help us with this problem willing to help?

2. Were there any similar situations that we can recall that will help us with this problem?

3. To what places have we gone that would be helpful with this problem?

4. What materials or things could be helpful with this problem?

The teacher may possess knowledge that may add or detract from an alternative. It behooves the teacher to introduce pertinent information into the situation. Care and tact are necessary in order not to influence unduly an alternative by the weight of teacher comments.

Having the entire class involved in the decision-making process invests the students in the process, thus helping to make each student commitment solid. The second advantage is that the teacher can distribute alternatives to groups in the class to gather more information if needed. The group can work in research units dividing responsibilities among members of the unit. Skills learned in other subject matter areas can be integrated into that process. Cooperation with other teachers in different subject matter areas also can be helpful. Library skills can be utilized in this process in a meaningful way. Other teachers may have skills that will aid students in acquiring additional information.

When all the information is collected, the choice can be made of which alternative appears to be the best in view of all the others. The additional information may be enough to provide clear evidence that one alternative stands out above the others.

Conversely, perhaps no alternative is sufficiently attractive that consensus is possible. In this case, even more information may be needed, old alternatives may be re-examined, or previous stages can be repeated to insure that they have been completed adequately. The problem may have been defined too broadly or not defined accurately. Occasionally, gathering information uncovers material that reveals pertinent information on the problem such that the problem has to be redefined. In such cases recycling to Stage I is necessary. However, having been through the process once and having the benefit of additional information will expedite progress through the stages.

Sometimes individuals stick to a problem that has been poorly defined because much effort has gone into the process. These people are reluctant to let go of the defined problem when in reality redefining the problem would be better. Teachers can facilitate the process of giving up alternatives.

EPILOGUE

In this chapter major procedures on selecting an alternative were presented. In essence, the question raised is "What course of action should the class embark on to resolve the problem?" The teacher acts as a moderator, record keeper, and synthesizer during the process. The efforts of the teacher are directed to aiding students toward the very best alternative for the class. This may not be the best alternative for the teacher, and the teacher must be able to distinguish between the alternatives without prejudicing one or the other.

The teacher must judge whether skills and behaviors called for in the alternatives are within the class members' capabilities. While some benefits are derived from just attempting tasks that are beyond the capabilities of the class, a point of diminishing returns does exist. The teacher weighs this fact in his/her mind before an alternative is chosen. The question is, "Can my class members implement the requirements of this alternative?" If the answer is "no," the next question becomes, "Is the learning from failing to be able to carry out the alternative more beneficial to the class members than the discouragement that it may produce?" Teachers understand the necessity of allowing students to fail and to learn from their failures by having students process their mistakes. They also are aware that motivation is severely curtailed when repeated attempts at resolving problems are not successful. This decision is not an easy one to make, but it lends itself to the problem-solving paradigm. That is, the teacher can weigh the advantages and disadvantages of the class attempting an alternative that is likely to fail. The balance sheet and the CRAVE system can be aids in making this decision.

SELF-TEST, CHAPTER 7

1. The problem-solving model presented in this chapter

    a. works for classroom concerns most effectively.
    b. applies to work problems in mathematics.
    c. can be used outside the classroom as well.
    d. is best applied at the high school level.

2. The most important feature of the problem-solving model is

    a. it presents strategies in a systematic way.
    b. its new approach.
    c. its borrowed features from computer technology.
    d. its reliance on the teacher to solve problems.

3. When a teacher realizes that an alternative selected will not work, he/she should

    a. discourage the class from using it.
    b. remain silent.
    c. let the class go on while commenting on it.
    d. evaluate the consequences of the alternative for the class.

4. The relationship between stages of the model can best be described by which of the following?

    a. There is a great amount of independence between stages.
    b. The degree to which one stage is successfully completed helps determine the success of the next stage.
    c. For some problems, stage I can be skipped.
    d. There is no particular order to the stages.

5. Which of the following steps will probably consume the most time?

    a. Deciding if alternative is in keeping with class member interests, values, and goals.
    b. Gathering data and information for each alternative.
    c. Selecting leading alternative.
    d. They are all about the same time.

6. Which choice best describes the relationship between problem-solving approach and traditional disciplinary approaches?

    a. Disciplinary approaches are usually more lasting.
    b. Problem-solving and disciplinary approaches have the same underlying assumptions.
    c. Problem-solving-solving approach always works.
    d. In the problem-solving approach the teacher role is less antagonistic.

7. Ranking the alternatives

    a. is best left up to the teacher.
    b. can be done by a few techniques that employ quantification.
    c. requires some of the students but not the entire class.
    d. is the last stage in the problem-solving model.

8. Discuss how the importance of class unity affects problem solving.

9. Described the role of the teacher during the process of ranking alternatives.

10. What are the criteria for the CRAVE system?

ANSWERS: 1. (c), 2. (a), 3. (d), 4. (b), 5. (b), 6. (d), 7. (b)

Activity 7.1 Using the CRAVE System

1. Assume that you are a smoker who wants to quit the habit. Generate a list of alternatives for this problem.

2. Use the CRAVE system to rank the alternatives generated.

Activity 7.2 Using the Balance Sheet Format

1. Assume you are a person who is overweight. State a behavioral sentence that will define your problem.

2. List at least seven alternatives that you can use to solve the weight problem.

3. Using the balance sheet format, rank order the alternatives listed in No. 2 of Activity 7.2.

4. Select the alternative for the weight problem by using the steps in Figure 7.1.

ADDITIONAL RESOURCES

Books and Publications

Branca, M. D., D'Augelli, J. F., & Evans, K. L. (No Date). *Development of a decision-making education program. Study I.* Additions Prevention Laboratory Report, The Pennsylvania State University.

Clark, C. H. (1958). *Brainstorming.* New York: Doubleday.

D'Zurilla, T. J., & Goldfried, M. R. (1971). Problem-solving and behavior modification. *Journal of Abnormal Psychology, 78,* 107-26.

Janis, I. L., & Mann, L. (1977). *Decision-making: A psychological analysis of conflict, choice, and commitment.* New York: The Free Press.

Stewart, N. R., & Winborn, B. B. (1973). A model for decision-making in systematic counseling. *Educational Technology, 69,* 13-5.

Wallace, W. G., Horan, J. J., Baker, S. B., & Hudson, G. R. (1975). Incremental effects of modeling and performance feedback in teaching decision-making counseling. *Journal of Counseling Psychology, 22,* 570-2.

Other resources appropriate for this chapter can be found at the end of Chapters 1 through 6.

REFERENCES

Egan, G. (1981). *Exercise in helping skills.* (Revised edition). Monterey, CA: Brooks/Cole.

Horan, J. J. (1979). *Counseling for effective decision making.* Scituate, MA: Duxbury Press.

Janis, I. L., & Mann, L. (1977). *Decision-making: A psychological analysis of conflict, choice, and commitment.* New York: The Free Press.

Stewart, N. R., & Winborn, B. B. (1973). A model for decision-making in systematic counseling. *Educational Technology, 69,* 13-15.

Chapter 8

PROBLEM-SOLVING MODEL STAGES V AND VI: IMPLEMENTING AND EVALUATING THE STRATEGY

This chapter includes the content and skills necessary for implementing and evaluating strategies—Stages V and VI of the problem-solving model. All the necessary groundwork has been laid for problem solving in the previous stages of the model. Implementing and evaluating stages are now appropriate. To claim that all strategies will be successful in solving all problems is impossible, however the degree to which preparatory stages have been mastered predicts with reasonable accuracy the probability of successful problem solving. Thus the preceding stages can be viewed as a foundation for these remaining two.

In this chapter will be presented pertinent material for the last two stages of the model: implementing alternative and evaluating the process. Important skills of both stages will be presented.

EXPECTED OUTCOMES

By studying the material in this chapter the reader will be able to

1. write three paragraphs on the necessary precautions of teacher awareness before embarking on the strategy,

2. list guidelines for evaluating substeps in a strategy, and

3. write pertinent questions to be asked when evaluating a strategy.

CAUTIONS BEFORE EXECUTING
A STRATEGY

For some problems the strategy chosen is relatively uncomplicated and implementing the requirements poses no difficulties. Other strategies are more complicated and the implementation of the strategy may present difficulties. Teachers need to be aware that some strategies are more easily selected than implemented. If strategies are especially complicated, students may become discouraged. For this reason the strategy chosen should be able to be completed in a reasonable time frame. Guidelines for the time frame depend on a number of factors. One is the degree of difficulty that the problem entails. Obviously, more difficult problems may take longer than easier ones. Another factor is the age of the students involved. Older students can tolerate longer time periods than younger students. Younger students may need more immediate results of their actions to prevent them from becoming discouraged.

At this stage, the reader may have discovered that terms have been changed slightly. The word alternative is no longer used. It has been replaced by the use of strategy. Because the stage for implementation has begun, the selected *alternative* becomes the *strategy* to be employed.

A strategy that is vague, not thought out or not well planned, can be frustrating for students and teachers. Motivation levels drop quickly under these conditions. Ambiguity causes uncertainty, and an uncertain climate is less effective for problem solving. Planning includes sequencing steps necessary for the strategy to work and specifying the roles and obligations for people involved.

Some students resist the effort that is necessary to program the strategy. They tend to be impulsive and want to start out without a clear idea of where they are going. Others resist because it means changing their behavior. To some students changing behavior can be very threatening. The perceptive teacher is aware of these students in his/her classroom. Empathy by the teacher helps to promote the climate that encourages the student to make a commitment to change. Still other students may not want responsibility of working on the problem. Often they have been successful in getting others to solve their problems. They hope that some other person will take over the concern for them. These students often fail to realize the connection between their actions and the consequences actions have on themselves and others.

Problem solving is not a panacea for all students. In many cases it involves much work. Students may begin enthusiastically, but become frustrated and discouraged when positive results are not forthcoming. When the newness wears off, students may become bored with the strategies. Many will want to give up and return to their ineffective ways of behavior. However, teachers who follow the steps outlined in this chapter will be able to assist students in overcoming some of the difficulties in this stage.

PROGRAMMING A STRATEGY

Whether a strategy is implemented with efficiency depends on how well pre-intervention planning took place. Clearly, precise programming stands a better chance of success than programming that fails to account for the necessary steps of completing the strategy. However, exercise caution in becoming too detailed in planning the strategy. Students and teachers alike often resist plans that deal in minutia. Knowing the balance between overinvolvement in details and sketchy plans comes with experience, however certain factors need to be considered. Age of the students, nature of the problem, and pressing time factor are three important factors.

Figure 8.1 presents an overview of the steps involved in executing a strategy. This is an expanded version of the overall model which appeared in Chapter 4. Similar to procedures for selecting an alternative discussed in Chapter 7, the implementation stage contains several substages. Each of these substages can be analyzed for essential requirements. In reality, a thorough component analysis for every step is undertaken for the implementation stage.

Making students aware of procedures before they embark on executing the strategy has a number of advantages. By giving students an overview of what is expected, they can make sense out of the process. In addition, concrete information is provided about the problem-solving method. For students old enough to handle written material, handouts of appropriate flow charts which outline the steps and their requirements provide a score card that they can follow. Involvement is likely to be increased when students are aware of where they are going and how they are getting there.

Each of the steps of Figure 8.1 can be expanded into several substeps. For example in block 5.1, Determine Intermediate Requirements, the process for this step is similar to the general problem-solving model, slightly revised. Thus, the substeps become defining the requirements, brainstorming different approaches for carrying out the requirements, and evaluating the approaches in order to arrive at the most appropriate one.

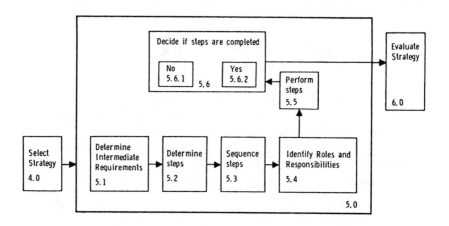

Figure 8.1. Expanded version of "Implement the Strategy" stage.

DEVELOPING PROCEDURAL STEPS
TO IMPLEMENT STRATEGY

Problems have a better chance of being resolved successfully if they are attacked systematically. Often people embark on solutions without really knowing where they are going. This is especially true for individuals who tend to be impulsive about their problem-solving strategies. They are apt not to take the time to think out the consequences of their chosen strategy. In some cases solutions tried may actually make the problem worse.

A feature of the problem-solving model advocated in this text is that a mechanism is provided for dealing systematically with problems. The systems approach forces the individual into a process that takes into account anticipated actions and consequences.

After a strategy is chosen, procedures for implementing the method need to be developed. An approach to this is to engage in task analysis, that is, to divide the strategy into component parts. Students may not view this as a necessary part of the plan. They may want to jump into action. However, initial enthusiasm may quickly turn into discouragement if students begin to flounder. This consequence can be disastrous when multiplied by a classroom of discouraged students. Planning at this stage can avert serious negative consequences.

The major consideration for separating a strategy into its component parts is determining what steps are necessary in order to implement the strategy. If having a bake sale is a chosen strategy for raising money for a class project, the following components may develop.

1. Securing goods to sell

   a. bake our own
      1) ingredients
      2) baking equipment
   b. have goods donated

2. Determining time and place of sale

3. Determining price of items

4. Determining materials needed

5. Scheduling individuals to sell goods

6. Arranging for advertising

7. Displaying baked goods

8. Cleaning up after sale

9. Accounting for net gains

Brainstorming can help in generating possible steps needed in order for the strategy to be successful. The teacher continually monitors the class by asking the class, "If we took all these steps, would we be able to . . . (have a bake sale)?" "What is missing in our steps?"

At this point steps may not be in order. Sequencing steps comes at a later time. Not all steps will be usable. The next task for the class is evaluating the steps.

Criteria for Judging Procedural Steps

In order to determine which procedural steps should be included, certain criteria are addressed. Egan (1982) identified a set of characteristics for subprogram (strategy) steps. These are related to criteria that were established earlier for evaluating alternatives. Some important considerations are clarity, relatedness, manageability, and time frame.

Clarity. Every student involved in the problem needs to have a clear idea of what the step means in terms of his/her responsibilities. Having a vague notion of what a step might involve invites errant behavior. Students cannot be expected to execute their responsibilities if they do not have a meaningful view of what is expected of them. If the responsibilities are numerous, specify tasks by writing them as a checklist. The checklist provides the group with a reference point and students need only to refer to the list when they experience confusion.

The teacher leads the discussion to arrive at clear understanding of what is expected. Questions can be asked similar to "What activities are necessary in order to complete this step?" "After completing all the activities would we still need to do anything more to complete the step successfully?"

Relatedness. Steps of a strategy must be related to one another. All the steps must "hang" together to complete the strategy in the most efficient method. Flow charts help to arrange steps and to determine the relationship of one step to another.

Manageability. A strategy that appears to be an effective solution is not guaranteed to work if the class is unable to carry out the requirements. Certain questions are important for assessing this characteristic: "Are the requirements within the class' control?" "Are resources available that will help meet the requirements?" These questions and others evaluate the group's ability to carry out requirements. If the class is unable to meet the requirements, the questions also assess the class' ability to muster outside resources. Affirmative answers to these questions indicate that the step, or in some cases, the strategy, is a viable one. In the bake sale example, class members need to determine if they are able to make their own goods. If they are not able, they need to determine others who can.

Another consideration in assessing manageability is whether the step is too large or too small. Steps that are too large may require too much of the class. Large steps often sap the motivation level of students. They may become disorganized or resistive because they cannot match their personal resources to the requirements of the task.

Steps that are too small become tedious. Again the effect may be resistance on the part of students. Overly detailed steps become "stupid" to students. They resist carrying them out, often claiming they are being treated like small children. By being vigilant, teachers can avoid making the mistake of having steps that are too small. An obvious solution to this problem is to combine as many small steps as possible.

Time Frame. Some strategies consist of steps that have time requirements that are satisfactory to the class, while others do not fit well with the needs of the class. In the bake sale example, if the gym is not available for two months and the money needs to be collected in 40 days, the time match is not good. Other time frame concerns need to be considered. Solutions should fit within acceptable time limits of the people involved in the problem. Some problems are so severe that time becomes a very crucial problem. When working with older students, delays in solutions are not as important as they are with younger children. Younger students have difficulty managing future time, and it poses a burden on them if solutions are outside of their meaningful time frames.

Common Concerns in Constructing Strategies

Janis and Mann (1977) recognized that some problems crop up in the process of implementing strategies. Egan (1982) echoes these authors from a counseling point of view. Some individuals have the tendency to avoid positive actions to problem solving. Because they have not been successful with problem solving in the past, they are reluctant to embark on strategies. Often, they have given up on trying to solve their own problems, and they are quite willing to have the teacher or other students take over their responsibilities. This is what Adler (1963) called the "discouraged" child. Ineptness is one of their most used strategies. The teacher needs to be alert not to be pulled into this scheme and reinforce the "helpless" behavior of these children.

Another potential problem that was mentioned earlier was presenting a mass of details to students. Commonly expressed, "You cannot see the forest for the trees," too many details can mask the main objective of the strategy. In a real sense, one can get lost in details and not really move any closer to the problem's solution. Activities that are detailed appeal to some because they represent a form of resistance. To others details become overwhelming, and pupils become disheartened. There exists yet another possibility, that students will view too much detail as demeaning and lose interest in the strategy.

For some individuals decision making involves sadness and even depression. Sometimes when people make a very important decision, especially one that requires some financial obligation, they experience a sense of remorse. They wonder whether they have made the correct decision or if they got a good deal on their purchase. They ruminate and cause themselves much concern over their decisions. One way of getting a person out of this morass is to get him/her moving into implementing the decision. Active involvement in the process can push a person into forgetting about the remorse associated with deciding upon a particular strategy.

GETTING STARTED ON
IMPLEMENTING THE STRATEGY

Egan (1982) wrote about tactics and logistics as methods of executing the chosen strategy. *Tactics* refers to the ability to change a plan to conform to the immediate situation. *Logistics* is the ability to bring to bear resources to implement the strategy. In the baked goods example, if it suddenly rained the tactic would be to find an alternative place to house the bake sale. A large tent may be the appropriate tactic. Being able to secure the large tent for the bake sale would involve logistics. These two factors play an important role in executing strategies.

Inevitably strategies will encounter unforeseen consequences. That strategies will be implemented as smoothly as they are planned with pencil and paper is unlikely. Circumstances arise that may cause the strategy to be modified. If teachers and students are not aware of this, they may become discouraged and give up, or they may adhere blindly to a strategy despite evidence that suggests the need for adaptation. Force field analysis, check and think steps, the application of learning principles, and sanctions are techniques that the teacher can use to help avert a strategy from failure and to help students maintain their motivation in carrying out the plan (Egan, 1982; Janis & Mann, 1977).

Force Field Analysis

Force field analysis is a procedure for identifying forces that may hinder a strategy and forces that may aid in its successful completion. The idea behind the theory is that if one can anticipate some potential pitfalls and resources to deal with them, then the individual will be prepared to deal with pitfalls if they do occur.

Brainstorming can be used to identify both restraining and facilitating forces. After potential restraining events are identified, coping methods utilizing facilitative resources can be planned to deal with restraining events should the need arise. This procedure has at least two advantages. By anticipating negative events potential disarray and confusion in students are prevented. When students encounter an obstacle which has been previously anticipated, they will have a plan to cope with it. Also, by pre-planning, a sense of resourcefulness is developed. Students can feel confident that they have options should something go astray. In addition, preplanning develops a perspective that while strategies may look very attractive in the classroom, plans may not always work out as anticipated.

In the bake sale problem, foul weather, a threatening force, could occur. If this is recognized and other alternatives (facilitative forces) are identified, then the foul weather may not be a disaster for the sale. A large tent could be available along with specified individuals responsible for erecting it. By anticipating this consequence and providing solutions to it, the chance that the bake sale can take place is enhanced.

Check and Think Steps

In the process of implementing any strategy, questions can be asked at three points: the beginning, during, and at the conclusion of activities. Before the implementation of the strategy, certain roles and responsibilities can be checked to help ensure that everything is properly organized. During the strategy crucial aspects can again be checked out. Finally, wrap-up check points can be evaluated. Together, the three check points provide a continuous feedback mechanism for the class. Modification can be made when necessary. This procedure helps ensure some control over the development of the strategy and it makes the class active participants in the process.

Learning Principles

By the appropriate application of learning principles, teachers can guide students attempts to carry out strategies. Rewarding the class as it performs tasks adequately encourages the class to push forward. Often the final goal is so distant that students become disinterested in the process. The teacher can help prevent this phenomenon from happening by dispensing extrinsic and intrinsic rewards at each step of the strategies. The teacher also can call attention to class progress when it is appropriate and commend the class on its progress. As the class begins to see its progress and feels good about the gains accomplished, the long-term goal will appear more approachable.

Because the overall strategy has been separated into steps, these steps become natural benchmarks for evaluations. As these points are reached the class can take stock of its progress. The teacher adds to this by reinforcing positive feelings generated by the class, thereby increasing the incentive to continue.

Sanctions

While sanctions (punishments/response costs) can be detrimental when used as the only patterns of interaction, they can be effective when combined with positive reward systems. Important considerations for use of sanctions follow:

1. Sanctions should be known before the strategy is started. Everyone should be aware of the "rules of the game." For example, if a certain task is not completed by a certain date, free activity time may be withdrawn. On the other hand, if the task is completed, free activity time may be increased.

2. Sanctions should be severe enough to have an effect, but not so severe that it destroys incentive. To have the class stay after school one hour everyday for two weeks may be an unrealistic sanction.

3. Sanctions should be applied immediately and consistently. Exceptions to sanctions should be made rarely. Inconsistency in applying sanctions can cause difficulty with students. Some will view inconsistent behavior as prejudicial actions; others will view it as a weakness in the teacher.

EVALUATING THE STRATEGY

Evaluation in problem solving can be considered as a twofold process. *Formative evaluation is the process of assessing the strategy while it is in progress. Summative evaluation is assessing the strategy after it is completed.* Results of each are used differently, thus they serve different purposes.

Formative Evaluation

Formative evaluation can be thought of as a monitoring process. Information gathered through formative evaluation provides a basis for instituting changes in the strategy if warranted. Often solutions fail because they are not managed and monitored effectively. Feedback is not given to participants to provide indices of their progress. A typical result is that strategies are often abandoned or gradually forgotten. This factor is especially crucial in complex problems where a strategy may have to be implemented for a long period of time. Anyone who has ever tried dieting knows the difficulty of staying with a diet strategy.

Monitoring the process can be effective in keeping a strategy on track. Some formal procedures are helpful for assessment in this area. Techniques borrowed from single-subject designs can be very useful. The concept of measuring behavior before the strategy begins (baseline) and assessing it periodically fits in with single-subject procedures. A weight loss strategy is ideal for this type of assessment. Weight before dieting (strategy) can be considered as the baseline. Daily weighings monitor the strategy and become the *formative aspect* of evaluation. The final goal of the weight loss strategy, for example, losing 15 pounds, is what is considered for *summative evaluation*. The continuous monitoring of the program can provide information on the effectiveness of the strategy as it is being implemented. Changes can be instituted if it appears that the strategy is not effective.

Monitoring also provides incentives. As the participants record their progress they become involved more deeply. In our weight loss example, simply recording one's weight periodically encourages compliance to the strategy.

Certain types of problems do not lend themselves to single-subject methodologies as easily. In the bake sale example setting up this type of design would be difficult. However, a number of crucial steps in the bake sale need to be completed if it is to be a success. This can be built into a flow-chart format or a checklist arranged sequentially. Thus, progress can be measured in terms of whether or not certain tasks have been completed.

Summative Evaluation

Summative evaluation aids in answering the question, "To what degree has the chosen strategy been successful in reaching the goal?" The answer generated from this type of question provides evidence of effectiveness of the strategy. This might be viewed as the final question. If the answer is positive and the problem is resolved, then the strategy is terminated. At this point building an evaluation timetable into the problem-solving process can be helpful. Formalizing the procedure helps to ensure that evaluation will take place.

In the evaluation session the strategy can be assessed in terms of class roles and responsibilities. This can be a time of learning for the class from its success or failure. Summative evaluation can be viewed as a debriefing session with the intent of generating information. Final evaluation should not be a fault-finding session. The spirit of "what can we learn from this experience?" should prevail.

If the summative evaluation indicates that the strategy had little or no effect on the problem, recycling is in order. The class needs to return to the list of surviving alternatives. At this point, another strategy can be chosen. Or, as often happens, new information is acquired as a result of attempting to solve the problem, and new strategies are possible. The alternatives are viewed from this prospective and a new ranking is generated. From this ranking the best alternative is chosen using the procedures learned in Chapter 7 of this book.

The experience and information gained from implementing the strategy may result in re-evaluation of the problem. Perhaps the problem was not identified accurately enough. Maybe the goal was beyond the capabilities of the class. This and other information gathered from summative evaluation is fed back into the systematic problem-solving process where it influences subsequent actions.

Incorporating Previously Learned Skills. Evaluation statements should reflect skills learned earlier. They should be concrete and contain specific information. Vague statements laden with generalities do not provide useful information and may contribute to floundering. Statements should be behavioral descriptions as well. Descriptions are to be backed with observable evidence. Students' responsibilities that were defined previously provide the basics for these descriptions. Value-laden terms such as lazy, irresponsible, and aggressive do not help much. To replace these terms with behavioral observations such as, "Jack did not complete his task 7 out of 20 times," or "Mary had four fights with Susan during a two-week period," is more appropriate. Consequences of these behaviors as they apply to the strategy should be pointed out. Did the behaviors add or detract from the strategy? In what ways could behavior have been modified to advance the strategy? Again, these evaluations are made not to attribute blame to individuals, but to enhance the problem-solving skills of the class. The teacher is sensitive to the probability that the evaluation could turn into a gripe session. By modeling appropriate behaviors and calling attention to the rules of giving feedback (Chapter 2) the teacher can facilitate productive evaluation.

Checklist for Evaluation. The following checklist provides a basis for evaluating strategy. The checklist can be used to identify the positive and negative aspects of the strategy as well as a basis for making modifications.

1. *Defining the Problem*

a. Was the problem defined so that all individuals understood it?
b. Was the problem defined accurately?
c. Was the problem defined behaviorally?
d. Was the problem defined so that its solution was within the class's resources?

2. Exploring the Problem

a. Were all individuals' feelings about the problem expressed?
b. Were feelings expressed accurately ?
c. Were some feelings overrepresented while others underrepresented?

3. Generating Alternatives

a. Were enough alternatives generated?
b. Were the alternatives viable?
c. Was the quality of the alternatives very high?

4. Selecting an Alternative

a. Were the criteria for evaluating the alternatives clear?
b. Was the ranking of alternatives accurate?
c. Was additional information needed in order to make a more accurate ranking?

5. Executing and Evaluating the Strategy

a. Were the responsibilities of each person clearly identified?
b. Were restraining and facilitative forces accurately anticipated?
c. Were modifications made in the strategy when appropriate?

One advantage of working with a class is that steps can be assigned to subgroups in the class. Appropriate subgroups can be formed after the problem has been defined and feelings explored. Working with class subgroups can shorten the time factor. This is especially true for information gathering activities. The disadvantage to working with subgroups is that coordination and management become more important. The teacher's role becomes one of being a focal point for all the activity. The possibility that the monitoring function can be completed less successfully is increased. However, the varying nature of several subgroups working together toward a goal has intrinsic educational value, especially because it is a skill that can be applied easily outside of the classroom. Students learning how to work effectively in groups have acquired a very important life skill. In contemporary society this skill is becoming increasingly important.

WORKING WITH PROBLEMS
ON AN INDIVIDUAL BASIS

At times problems do not concern the entire class but may involve as few as two students. In such cases, to have the entire class work on the problem is not always in the teacher's best interest. Also, the nature of the problem may be so personal that exposure to the class could present additional concerns.

However, the problem-solving *process* remains the same. The teacher facilitates the two or more students through the stages in basically the same manner that the class goes through, however some considerations may differ when working with an individual student.

Chances are good that the nature of the problem is personal, and it may not be appropriate to share with the class. This being the case, the teacher is sensitive to the time and place where the problem solving takes place. Certainly, for some problems the setting for solving problems should not be the center arena. However, for other problems, depending on their nature, other class members may be able to contribute to the solution. To have the consent of the individuals involved in the problem is advisable before seeking help from other students in the class.

When only a few students are involved in the problem, teacher impartiality takes on increased significance. The teacher needs to monitor his/her nonverbal behavior so as to make the moderator role credible. The teacher must be alert to conditions that are one-sided or issues that become represented disproportionately.

Contracting specific responsibilities in writing is a technique that can be adapted for use in individual problem solving. In this procedure the teacher draws up a contract whose conditions, responsibilities, and consequences are understood by participants. These are written and checked with each student involved. The teacher assesses whether or not the requirements and responsibilities are clear. Then the participants sign the contract, acknowledging they are committed to carrying out the strategy within the agreed upon conditions. The main advantage of the contracting system is that it specifies the required behavior. Because each student has a copy of the contract and has acknowledged that he/she understands what is involved, less likelihood exists that the strategy will break down.

PROBLEM SOLVING
AS A LIFE SKILL

Problem solving is a valuable life skill. Everyone engages in problem-solving behavior in one form or another, some more effectively than others. Facilitating problem-solving behavior in individuals enhances their prospects of living more effectively within their environments. Chances are individuals who have effective problem-solving skills will accomplish more in the major arenas of life, including academic, social, and personal aspects. The feature that problem-solving methodology is applicable outside of the classroom makes it a very attractive technique. When students begin to apply this technique outside of the classroom, teachers can be confident that they have made an impact.

The position taken in this text is that if a systematic approach to problems can be learned, then the chances are enhanced that effective reduction of problems will be forthcoming. If effective living can be translated into the ability to make wise decisions and to resolve problems then the systematic approach advocated in this text has a contribution to make.

SELF-TEST, CHAPTER 8

1. Write the five major steps of the problem-solving method used in this text.

2. Discuss the differences between summative and formative evaluation.

3. What is the role of evaluation in problem solving?

4. What does recycling mean in the evaluation stage?

Activity 8.1 Applying Stages I Through VI

1. Think of a problem that is taking place in your own life.

2. Write a behavior description of the problem.

3. Identify your feelings concerning the problem.

4. Think of at least seven alternatives for solving the problem.

5. Rank order the alternatives and select the most promising one.

6. Determine the responsibilities and requirements of that strategy.

7. Anticipating the restraining forces that may prevent you from implementing the strategy.

8. Devise alternative plans to meet the restraining forces.

9. Construct a set of questions that can serve as a basis for evaluation of the strategy.

ADDITIONAL RESOURCES

Books and Articles

Adler, A. (1963). *The problem child.* New York: Capricorn Books.

Egan, G. (1982). *The skilled helper: A model for systematic helping and interpersonal relating* (2nd ed.). Monterey, CA: Brooks/Cole.

Janis, I. L., & Mann, L. (1977). *Decision-making: A psychological analysis of conflict, choice, and commitment.* New York: The Free Press.

Films and Filmstrips

Materials appropriate for Chapters 2-6 are useful for this chapter.

REFERENCES

Adler, A. (1963). *The problem child.* New York: Capricorn Books.

Egan, G. (1982). *The skilled helper: A model for systematic helping and interpersonal relating* (2nd ed.). Monterey, CA: Brooks/Cole.

Janis, I. L., & Mann, L. (1977). *Decision-making: A psychological analysis of conflict, choice, and commitment.* New York: The Free Press.

Chapter **9**

VALUES: YOU CANNOT ESCAPE THEM

At one time in the country, the home played a dominant role in the education and development of children and youths. Young people learned a sense of responsibility and importance of doing an honest day's work for an honest day's pay. In large part, children learned that they had a responsibility for the welfare of the rest of the family and that this sense of welfare extended to the community level. It was not uncommon 25 years ago for boys and girls to participate actively in many community-wide efforts: cleaning and caring for school grounds, church yards, cemeteries, and other tasks. In participating, they felt a social sense of gratitude.

The situation has drastically altered in the present accelerated, industrialized, technical, urbanized, interdependent, and scientifically oriented social system. As society has changed, so has the individual's social role. Children and youth no longer help to produce goods and services similar to their parents; they are passive consumers in most situations. They no longer feel a sense of responsibility for the welfare of the family or the community. In the wake of such a loss, the school must assume an increasingly central role in helping to impart concepts to students by providing work experiences and service projects to involve students in situations and to help them interact with adults in the community while solving problems.

In the late 1800s and early 1900s the American community also played a major role in educating boys and girls and in developing their value concepts. Citizens in communities, though close knit, nonetheless had a high degree of independence together with a respect for the well-being of all community participants. If an individual living in a typical rural community or small town had an accident and was incapacitated for a period of time, then neighbors would offer consolation and assistance. If crops needed planting or harvesting, the community members would pitch in so that the individual would not be seriously hampered, financially or occupationally, by his/her mishap. If he/she were in a small business or industry, neighbors would carry on his/her responsibilities as though he/she were doing the job him/herself. This community situation no longer prevails.

Today, people are on a more impersonal relationship with one another. It is common for people not to know the name of those who live across the street. Even in a rural community, it is no longer improbable for people living a short distance from one another to know relatively little about each other. This social estrangement is a relatively recent phenomenon and it is affecting the earlier value systems which developed out of largely agrarian culture and which have undergirded American democracy and other democracies throughout the world. How do diverse subjects such as changing values in roles of the American home and community, and basic concepts which have shaped our country relate to the American school's role of preparing the individual student for social adequacy? In essence, the school has become a central force in coping with social stresses and changing values and reinforcing basic concepts as the American home and community have grown more fragmented. Contemporary society advocates education for everyone. We live in a society also in which education is the key for many to escape poverty and despair. Times are anxiety-ridden. Ideological differences divide international conference tables. National conflicts—mainly class and racial—tear at our unity. High juvenile and adult crime rates eat into our security. We pollute the air, water, and food supplies to an alarming degree. Our relationships and attitudes toward other people—not only in the nation, but throughout the world—are growing increasingly inhumane.

Under these stresses, it is absolutely necessary that we revitalize education and reinforce our commitment to a democratic way of life through educational experiences which prepare a student to cope with the society in which they will live rather than prepare them for a society which has long since passed. Value clarification is one way to help us move in this direction.

The major purpose of this chapter is to present information about values and values clarification for school children. More importantly, we hope to help one understand what values are and what influences the development of our values.

EXPECTED OUTCOMES

By reading this chapter, the reader should be able to discuss:

1. definition of values,

2. relationship of values and behavior,

3. explain the valuing process, and

4. explain benefits of value clarification activities in the classroom.

At the conclusion of the chapter can be found self-test instrument and practice activities. These materials will help the reader assess how much has been learned from the chapter, and can be helpful in applying the content of the chapter to the classroom setting in a meaningful way.

IMPACT OF VALUES

One can not escape values. Within every structure of our society value statements predominate and give meaning. They are in our schools, homes, churches, governments,—everywhere values exist.

If, for example, an examination of the organization of schools was made, one would find value statements. Rules and regulations include value statements. Teachers make value statements in the classroom by the style they use to interact with students. In fact, every actor on the educational stage—teacher, coach, counselor, administrator, student family, media, peer group—is up to his/her earlobe in values. And yet criticisms and misunderstandings seem to exist among, at least, some groups in the general public about value clarification. These criticisms have led to questioning whether values clarification should be taught in our schools. Today, more than ever, young people are faced with many decisions. Young people are confronted with many areas of confusion and conflict which are value-laden. How can schools, or more importantly teachers, help students cope with such issues as friends, love, sex, male/female roles, race, poverty, pollution, war, nuclear power, energy, health, money, politics, religion, and so forth?

VALUE CLARIFICATION

Value clarification is one of the most important responsibilities of the classroom teacher. This is true for those who teach such traditional academic courses as English, mathematics, science, history, and social science. We would like to embrace the definition of values as "convictions or beliefs which prescribe or determine acceptable or preferable behavior in relation to needs or goals" (Strickland, 1978, p. 428).

What Are Values?

The term "value" is often used with two meanings which are linked but which need nonetheless to be distinguished. In ethics, as in economics, value essentially means worth. As we approach an understanding of values in the classroom we would like to think of values with a different thrust. Values are the crucial questions we put to living and to life's problems, not only explicitly by raising philosophical questions, but also implicitly by the way we live. Values can be described as behavioral biases, which mold and dominate the decision-making power of a particular individual (Peters, 1962). Therefore, values affect decisions as well as actions. Egan (1975) emphasized the importance of the relationship between values and action by stressing that "a value is a value only to the degree that it is translated into some kind of action" (p. 94). Peterson (1970) described common characteristics of values. The first two are quoted and the third is paraphrased.

1. Values are hypothetical constructs that are inferred. They are criteria upon which choices are justified.

2. Values represent the desirable in the sense of what one "ought" to do.

3. Values act as motivational forces. Values provide standards that do not momentarily arise in any given situation but offer directions in a variety of circumstances. (pp. 51-53)

Smith (1962) offered five functions of an individual's value system. The five are paraphrased as follows:

1. Supplies the individual with a sense of purpose and direction.

2. Supplies the basis of individual action, and of unified, collective action.

3. Serves as the basis of judging behaviors of individuals.

4. It enables the individual to know what to expect of others as well as how to conduct him/herself.

5. Establishes a sense of right and wrong. (p. 373)

Human values also can be translated into skills similar to those of reading, spelling, and computing. Accordingly, values can be learned just as one learns other skills. Learning takes place among students when skills are taught in an environment which considers the basic needs of the learner. Therefore no skill can be taught in an atmosphere which fails to take account of each student's basic needs for safety, belonging, love, respect, and self-esteem, as well as individual's needs for information, knowledge, and wisdom. Perhaps the apathy and alienation which have pervaded schools indicate the lack of satisfaction of those basic needs.

An important function of schools is to fill these needs, and in filling them to produce individuals who are not apathetic: individuals who have a sense of themselves and purpose and direction in life. The school has the function of producing self-actualizing people, to use Abraham Maslow's phrase.

Maslow (1970) theorized that basic human needs fall into certain categories. Physiological needs for food, warmth, and shelter; needs for safety and security; need for belongingness; need for love; needs for respect and self-esteem; and need for self-actualization. These needs form a natural hierarchy of perceived importance to the individual. That is, when the individual is primarily concerned with meeting his/her physiological needs, he/she has little time or energy to be concerned with or even have awareness of the higher order needs of belongingness or love.

As the lower order needs are satisfied with increasing ease, they become less important, and the individual changes his/her focus to the next higher need. In other words, lower needs must be met, at least partially before higher needs can be realized. When a person, for example, feels safe and secure from physical or psychological threats, he/she ceases to think about safety needs and begins to take security for granted. Instead, attention and energies are directed towards the next step in the hierarchy; gaining a sense of belongingness, becoming an accepted member of a group. Another good example of the school personnel understanding and providing for basic human needs was the federally funded program, which began in the 1960s, providing breakfast for economically deprived children. It is almost impossible for hungry children to concentrate on learning when their basic need for nourishment has not been filled. The meeting of this basic need has provided at least part of the answer to better education for deprived children.

As suggested in the previous examples, when lower needs begin to be satisfied with increasing ease, they become less important and the individual moves up the ladder through the hierarchy of needs until all basic needs are satisfied. Only at this point can the person turn energies toward self-actualization. Maslow used the term self-actualization, however, he made it quite clear that genuine self-actualization also is social in nature. The term does not imply "doing your own thing," the self-actualized person sees him/herself as a social agent who is constantly changing and improving.

The socially self-actualizing person is creative, self-motivating, tolerant, efficient, spontaneous, and energetic. This person is a fully-functioning individual who acts on inner resource and finds within self a need to contribute to society. In summary *the socially self-actualizing person is acting on a foundation of human values.*

An individual's needs and values are very much related, because to a large extent values are defined by and, in many ways, help to satisfy needs. If something is very important to us as a need, value is high. As in the previous example the child who sits in a class hungry could not care less if the world was flat or round. Sicinski (1978) has proposed a four-level hierarchy of needs, while this model is not as complex as Maslow's (1970), it is more closely related to value development and problem solving. Much like Maslow's basic needs, on the first level of Sicinski's (1978) model are the fundamental needs. On the second level are those needs that if not satisfied interfere with the individual's ability to perform some social function. For example, an individual may not be able to appreciate the ballet or art because his/her aesthetic needs were never properly developed. Third are those needs that when not satisfied, interfere with general social functioning—that is those needs which make the person socially maladjusted. A person, for example, whose needs for belongingness, for friendship, was never satisfied when young may not be able to make friends later as an adult. Finally, the fourth level of needs are those that when not satisfied, interfere with the individual's emotional development and growth. These are the socially dysfunctional needs. According to Sicinski's (1978) model, systems of values are developed to help a person orient him/herself to satisfying these different levels of needs.

VALUES CONFLICT

Conflict generally is viewed as a tendency to perform two or more incompatible responses at the same time, resulting in emotional, mental, and/or physical stress requiring modification. Furthermore, conflict can be functional (constructive) or dysfunctional (destructive). According to Deutsch (1973) this difference is important. Conflict resolution choices are influenced by the context in which the conflict is perceived.

Some of the advantages of functional conflict are the exposure of issues, improvement of the quality of problem solving, increased emotional involvement, increased creativity, clarification of objectives, increased cohesiveness, and the establishment of group norms.

Dysfunctional conflict is characterized by a tendency to isolate, divert energy, weaken morale, obstruct cooperative action, increase differences, and cause psychological trauma. At its worst, dysfunctional conflict can even arrest or delay a child's social-emotional growth (Palomares, 1975).

A variety of models for classifying have been presented in the literature. Two of these will be presented in this section.

Psychologists have developed a typology of conflict that can help us understand further what a conflict is. As we indicated previously, a *conflict occurs whenever we are faced with a choice that involves the pairing of two or more competing motives or goals.* The four main kinds of conflict situations are called approach-approach, avoidance-avoidance, approach-avoidance; and double approach-avoidance (Dollard & Miller, 1950). Each differs from the others with regard to values an individual associates with either a goal object or given set of options.

An *approach-approach* conflict occurs when an individual is faced with a choice between two positive, equally attractive, but mutually exclusive alternatives. For example, Bernard, a junior high school student, has a choice of taking band or art during the sixth period, two courses given at the same time and both of which he would like to take. This is a relatively easy kind of conflict with which to deal; because both result in something wanted. However, making a decision usually requires giving up one alternative, and giving up something valued is usually very difficult.

An *avoidance-avoidance* conflict involves making a choice between two or more unpleasant or negative alternatives. If choices are equally undesirable, conflict may be very intense and frustrating. Sometimes escape is used as a resolution or the person tries to avoid making a choice. While Bernard is making his decision, Jack who hates science, is completing his program in teacher education at the state university to fulfill the requirements for graduation and is faced with the choice of selecting a science course. Jack has narrowed his choice to either chemistry or physics, both of which would be very unpleasant to him; the very reasons he has delayed making a decision until the last quarter of his senior year. Vacillation is typical behavior in this type of conflict; that is the individual approaches one goal, then the other. The closer the individual gets to each alternative, the stronger the avoidance response.

An *approach-avoidance* conflict involves a choice which the individual attaches both positive and negative values to a given future possibility. It attracts and repels at the same time. The undesirable points are not wanted, but they accompany the desirable ones. A young woman may want to get married and have children but yet be repelled by some of the negative consequences such as giving up or delaying her career, sacrificing her freedom and autonomy. This conflict is usually characterized by much ambivalence. The person often feels bewildered, apprehensive, discontented, inadequate, and/or useless.

Double approach-avoidance is the same as described previously except that two or more possibilities are involved, each having positive and negative characteristics. Most conflicts fall into this category, because most of our choices have both positive and negative features. A young man, for example, may be looking for a used car. He finally locates two used cars which are in line with his budget. Each car has qualities that he likes but each car also has qualities that he dislikes. In a situation such as this one, an objective third party is needed to mediate this type of conflict because the frustration and intensified feelings resulting from it may interfere with the use of good cognitive processes (Dollard & Miller, 1950).

The teacher's role with conflicted students is essentially that of a clarifier. By exhibiting the relationship skills of Stage I of the problem solving model the teacher aids the student to assess the conflict accurately. Sometimes, all that is needed is for the teacher to provide a supportive role while the student resolves the situation.

UNDERSTANDING MORAL DEVELOPMENT

Different kinds of conflicts with different kinds of actions are involved in resolutions. The primary concern in this chapter is with value conflicts that involve moral dilemmas and ethical decision making that focus attention on moral values—especially their development and the way we make moral decisions.

Moral development affects not only individual decision making, but also feelings about and relationships with other people. Researchers have found, for example, that as individuals reached higher levels of moral development and moral reasoning they felt more positively about other people in general, had a more optimistic view of mankind. Understand -ing how moral sense develops helps to understand how one relates to others.

Many theories of moral development exist, each explains how moral decisions are made, and how these decisions have meaning. These theories, to some extent, also explain our behavior, although an important difference exists between moral reasoning and actual behavior. The three theories to be considered are social learning theory, Piaget's theory of moral judgment, and Kohlberg's theory of moral development.

Social Learning Theory

Social learning theory, developed most comprehensively by Albert Bandura, explains that one learns morality through the processes of modeling and conditioning.

Modeling is an important technique used by behavioral scientists. In this process, the individual models him/herself after another's behavior or actions. It is not necessary for the individual to perform in any particular way in order to learn from modeling. Bandura and Mischel (1965) argued that the major mechanisms in moral behavior are *imitation* and *social reinforcement*. Bandura and others have conducted numerous empirical studies to support the position that children learn moral (and social) behavior through modeling.

The most famous of these experiments demonstrates that aggression is learned by modeling, or imitation as it is sometimes called. In an early experiment, when nursery school children watched as adult play aggressively with an inflated doll, hitting and shouting "sock him in the nose," children were more likely to hit the doll when they were left alone in the room with the toy than were children who did not observe this aggressive play (Bandura, Ross, & Ross, 1961). When the aggressive behavior was shown on film, subjects were just as likely to imitate it (Bandura & Mischel, 1965). Modeling of aggressive behavior is not simply limited to children. In a more recent experiment it was shown that adults do act more aggressively after witnessing aggressive behavior (Baron, 1974). In one interesting study, Brown, Corriveau, and Monte (1977) found that college student viewers became angry and aggressively aroused after watching a television show in which a couple were being mistreated by the police and a judge. Thus, at all ages and in many different contexts, our values and behaviors are affected by what we see and thus, what we imitate.

There is still another view of the social learning perspective; one which suggests that moral behavior is learned from early interactions with others and from the responses others attach to certain behaviors. Moral behavior is therefore learning through the various conditioning processes. Alexander (1969) summarized this behavioral view on moral development:

> Moral behavior can be defined as a response system developed as the result of perception of the pleasure and satisfaction occurring in other persons. It is likely that in early childhood, perhaps by the age of three years or earlier, the child comes to understand that some behavior brings parental approval and praise and other behavior brings disapproval or perhaps even disgust and anger...The child during his first five years, however, can differentiate only minimally among types of behavior that might be termed "moral"...the moral significance of behavior is only realized at a later age.

decisions, the children may be slower in moving towards the next stage, a *morality of cooperation.*

Piaget called the morality of this period *heteronomous morality.* The word heteronomous means that one is subject to another's strict governing, including prescribed rules, laws, and regulations. This again refers to the constraint that dominates the child's moral thinking.

As the child grows, intellectually, socially, and emotionally he/she moves closer toward what Piaget calls *autonomous morality*—a personal, individual morality, based more on cooperation than on constraint. The autonomous morality is not independent of the heteronomous morality, but a consequence of it; that is, the child must first learn the rules and pressures of real living in order to learn ways to break free of them when it becomes necessary. Characteristics of moral thinking at different levels are shown in Table 9.1. The words used are those frequently substituted for constraint and cooperation—restraint and participation.

Like his cognitive theory, Piaget's theory of moral judgement consists of stages of development, with each stage providing a prerequisite to the stages which follow. Three basic ideas are used to construct his theory. He relates each of these ideas—rules, realism, and justice—to patterns of behaviors and reasoning. Each basic idea will be discussed individually to better understand the moral transition from heteronomy to autonomy.

Piaget's finding on how children learn about rules helps us to understand the point at which a child begins to learn that there are right behaviors and wrong behaviors. When very young children first begin to play in a group one immediately observes that each child acts without any awareness of rules. The child's play is usually motor activity; simply pleasurable, often spontaneous in nature. At approximately two years of age the child begins to learn rules by imitating others at play, usually other children. Children at this stage are still egocentric; that is, "even when they are playing together, [they] play each one 'on his own' (everyone can win at once) and without regard for any codification of rules" (Piaget, 1932, p. 27).

When a child reaches age seven or eight, he/she begins to seriously "play to win," and becomes concerned with the codification of rules, although these rules are still rather vague. At the age of eleven or twelve,

The fact that the child does not understand the significance of moral behavior does not mean that the so-called "moral learnings" do not occur in early childhood; it simply means that the child does not differentiate moral behavior form any other taught behavior. However, a child does begin the internalization of emotional responses of others in association with actions labeled "good" and "bad." (p. 96)

On the one hand, we can see that the social learning theory view of moral development is a comprehensive one that helps explain moral development in terms of different learning processes. But on the other it is apparent that it does little to help to understand the complex cognitive processes of moral reasoning or how we go about making moral decisions.

Piaget's Theory of Moral Judgment

Jean Piaget's observations of children led him to a comprehensive theory of moral development. In 1932, Piaget published *The Moral Judgement of the Child,* a landmark study that elaborates a theory of moral judgement using much of the same methodology that characterizes his other research; namely, close observations of natural spontaneous behavior, experiments, and interviews with children. Piaget's moral theory in many ways parallels his position on intellectual growth, and he is very careful in explaining the interrelationship between cognitive reasoning and moral reasoning. Just as in Piaget's cognitive theory, in which the child progresses from simple, automatic behaviors to more complex, organized behavior, so too, in his moral theory does the child progress from naive beliefs and simple motor behaviors to more sophisticated, hypothetical, abstract reasoning.

As we begin to understand the direction that cognitive and social progress take and by which Piaget explained moral development, a process emerges for the developmental progress that characterizes the learner's transition from a fixed-rule oriented perspective to a relativistic, rational morality that transcends the narrow limitations of rules. The first type of morality, characteristic of young children, which Piaget called a *morality of constraint,* is based on fear of punishment; on the belief that we do not do wrong because we are told not to do it. In describing this stage, Jantz and Fulda (1975) explained that children view adults as authority figures who are to be obeyed. During this stage, adults need to consider the constraints they place upon children. Children need guidance during this period and it would be unfair if adults did not stipulate some guidelines for children to follow. However, if the adult totally restrains children by making and dictating all moral

Table 9.1
Summary Characteristics of Levels of Moral Thinking

Concept	Morality of Restraint	Morality of Participation
Control	Duty is obeying authorities	Mutual agreement
	Good defined by obedience to rules	Lessening of adult constraint
	Rules or laws not analyzed	Rules can be modified
Justice	Letter of the law	Restitutive justice
	Anxiety over forbidden behavior	Concern for inequalities
	Concern for violation of game rules	Concern for social injustices
	Punitive justice	Spirit of law considered
	Any transgression is serious	
Responsibility	Objective view	Subjective view
	Intentions not considered	Motives considered
	Egocentric position	Rights of others to their opinions respected
	Judgements in relation to conformity to law	Judgments by situation
Motivation	External motivation	Internal motivation
	Punishment by another	Disapproval by others
	Rewards by another	Censure by legitimate authorities followed by guilt feelings
		Community respect and disrespect
		Self-condemnation
Rights	Selfish rights	Rights of others
	No real concept of right	No one has right to do evil
	Rights are factual ownership	A right is an earned claim on the actions of others
		Concept of unearned, universal rights
		Respect of individual life and personality of others

Note. from R.K. Jantz and T.A. Fulda, "The Role of Moral Education in the Public Elementary School," *Social Education,* January, 1975, p. 28. Reprinted with permission of the National Council for the Social Studies and R.K. Jantz and T.A. Fulda.

however, the child begins to recognize more systematically differences between right and wrong, as defined by the rules of the game. "Not only is every detail of the procedure in the game fixed, but the actual code of rules to be observed is known to the whole society" (Piaget, 1932, p. 30). It is at this point that the child has developed to a large extent the adult's sense of what rules are and what function they serve.

When the child first learns rules, he/she sees them as fixed principles, which are stipulated by higher authorities. Moral behavior is dominated by constraints, by rules that he/she has learned to obey. Even when disobeying rules, the child does not question the validity of the rules, which appears to be beyond challenge.

The first signs of adult-like moral reasoning occur when the child goes from uncontrollable behavior to what Piaget called a "morality of constraint." By the age of ten or eleven, the child begins to see that rules can be fixed by agreement, that they can be changed, that they can be questioned. The child may still abide by the rules, but is willing to negotiate new rules. Piaget called this the "morality of cooperation," because the child's moral behavior now involves his/her will and cooperation that was absent in the earlier stage.

The second feature of Piaget's theory of moral judgement is when the child moves from moral "realism" to moral "relativism." When children first realize the concepts of wrong and punishment, they think in absolute terms rather than in relative, situational terms. That is, everything is either black or white, right or wrong. The child regards the objective consequences of an act rather than the subjective circumstances surrounding it. In other words the child is unable to see that shades of gray exist in interpreting any circumstance. In a series of experiments, for example, Piaget told a group of children two short stories and invited them to comment. In the first story, a little boy accidently broke fifteen of his mother's cups as he was on his way to dinner. In a second story, another little boy broke one cup as he was trying to sneak jam from the cupboard while his mother was out of the house. When the children were asked which of these two little boys were more mischievous, they answered the first was because he had broken more cups. Piaget called this type of reasoning "moral realism," and it is characteristic of children to about seven years of age. There are three characteristic features of moral realism. First, the child under the influence of moral realism views "any act that shows obedience to a rule or even to an adult, regardless of what he may command [as] good; any act that does not conform to rules is bad'' (Piaget, 1932, p. 111). The second feature is closely related to the first, the child values the letter of the law over the spirit of the law. The third feature under moral realism is children weigh an act strictly according to the circumstances and ignore the intentions and extenuating circumstances. As the development of moral judgment progresses in children, they develop a sense of "moral relativism" that enables them to consider extenuating circumstances - such as motivation, accident, and intentions in their moral judgements.

Piaget's third idea in his theory of moral judgement is the concept of justice which becomes the highest principle of morality. At an early age, the child has an idea of imminent justice which is the belief that justice is inherent in the order of things and that evil acts inherently produce evil consequences. One author (Pulaski, 1971) referred to this principle as the idea "that knives cut children who have been forbidden to use them" (p. 86). The sense of justice becomes more sophisticated as children mature. They recognize that rewards and punishments can be distributed in different ways or what Piaget called distributive justice. The development of the sense of distributive justice undergoes various transformations. Early in the child's development, up to the age of eight, the child considers right and just whatever rewards or punishments the authority figures wish to dispense. During the period between the age of eight and eleven, the child believes that all "bad" acts should receive the same punishment, regardless of circumstances. A boy who lies out of noble motivation should receive the same punishment as one who lies out of malice and deceitfulness (Belkin, 1975). At about the age of twelve, the child begins to recognize the principles of equity and fairness and develops what Flavell (1963) described as a kind of "relativistic egalitarianism in which the strict equality will sometimes be winked at in favor of higher justice" (p. 294).

Kohlberg's Theory of Moral Development

Kohlberg (1968) developed his theory much like Piaget, by interviewing children and adolescents and studying their responses to certain hypothetical situations. In this research he was especially interested in the process that young people used in arriving at moral decisions as opposed to evaluating the decisions themselves. The results of his research indicated that moral thinking moves through three levels of development namely the *preconventional,* the *conventional,* and the *postconventional levels.* Each of these three levels include two related stages as illustrated in Table 9.2. In other words, there are six specific stages in all. Kohlberg's levels of moral development are presented next.

Table 9-2   Kohlberg's Stages of Moral Development

Moral Problem Presented to Subjects

In Europe a woman was near death from cancer. One drug might save her, a form of radium that a druggist in the same town had recently discovered. The druggist was charging $2,000, ten times what the drug cost him to make. The sick woman's husband, Heinz, went to everyone he knew to borrow the money, but he could only get together half of what it cost. He told the druggist that his wife was dying and asked him to sell it cheaper or let him pay later. But the druggist said, "No." The husband got desparate and broke into the man's store to steal the drug for his wife. Should the husband have done that? Why? (Kohlberg, 1969, p. 379)

Preconventional Level

Stage 1:
"If you steal the drug, you will be sent to jail, so you shouldn't do it."
"If you don't steal it, then you'll get in trouble for letting your wife die."

Principle: Avoidance of negative consequences

Stage 2:
"If you get caught, you'll probably get a light sentence, and your wife will be alive when you get out."
"Your wife may not be around to appreciate it, anyway, and it's not your fault if she has cancer."

Principle: Act to your own advantage, using the principle of quid pro quo

---

Conventional Level

Stage 3:
"No one will condemn you for stealing the drug, but they will hold you responsible for her death if you don't."
"By stealing it, you'll bring dishonor on your dying wife, and everyone will think you a thief."

Principle: Act according to how you think others will approve or disapprove of your actions

Stage 4:
"Your duty is to your wife, and therefore you must steal the drug for her."
"Your duty is to obey the law, and you should not steal the drug.

Principle: Adherence to law and order

Postconventional (Principled) Level

Stage 5:
"The fact that you feel you have a right to violate the law does not actually give you the right to do so."
"The druggist is abusing his license to hold a public trust, and therefore has violated his implicit obligations to the society in which he works."

Principle: The rule is a social contract which can be changed by agreement

Stage 6:
"I live by the principle that to save a human life takes priority over all matters of property, and therefore feel no compunctions about taking the drug."
"I live by the principle that property is sacred and cannot by expropriated, and will therefore let my wife die."

Principle: An organized set of values which the conscience acts as the basis for decision making

---

Note. From Gary S. Belkin, *Practical Counseling in the Schools, 2nd Edition,* 1975, reprinted with permission of Wm. C. Brown Company Publishers, Dubuque, IA.

Preconventional Level. At the first level, the child begins to interpret good and bad in terms of rewards and punishments. Kohlberg used Piaget's term "heteronomous" to designate Stage 1 of the preconventional level. In Stage 1, the child reasons according to the principle of avoiding punishment by showing complete obedience to parents and other authority figures. The fear of punishment plays an important part in the determination of behavior. At this stage of development the child is egocentric. Little interest is expressed in how others feel about his/her behaviors or about how these behaviors affect others except for those who might issue rewards and punishments.

In the Stage 2 of the preconventional level, called the "Stage of Individualism and Instrumental Purpose and Exchange," morality is governed by the principle of self-satisfaction. The child may respond to the satisfaction of the needs of others for whom one cares. Reciprocity, at this stage, is a matter of "you scratch my back and I'll scratch your back." Kohlberg referred to the social perspective of this stage as "individualistic" in the sense that the child recognizes him/herself as a unique decision-making individual among others.

Conventional Level. At the second level the child begins to conform to the rules of conduct of the family, group, and community. In addition, the child is concerned with maintaining rules and expectations not simply out of fear, but rather out of a sense of identification with and loyalty to persons and groups involved. While in the first stage, for example, a person may pay his/her taxes for fear of going to prison if he/she doesn't, in this stage the belief that paying taxes is the right and lawful thing to do would be a more important factor in the decision.

At Stage 3, "The Stage of Mutual Interpersonal Expectations, Relationships, and Interpersonal Conformity," the child demonstrates what Kohlberg called the "good boy/good girl orientation. What this means in effect is the child internalizes values of his/her parents and believes that 'good' behavior is that which pleases or helps others and is approved by others...one seeks approval by being 'nice'" (Kohlberg, Colby, Gibbs, Speicher-Dubin, Power, 1978, p. 26). Therefore, the individual is primarily motivated to gain the approval of others. Consequently, the child will conform to stereotyped images of what is natural behavior, and for the first time will evaluate the behaviors of others by their intentions.

During the second stage of the conventional level (Stage 4), which Kohlberg called "The Social System and Conscience Stage," the individual is oriented toward fixed rules and the concept of obedience to authority. The individual believes at this point that the social system defines the roles and rules of behavior and conduct. During this stage there is a tendency toward maintaining the social order, and it is therefore referred to as the law-and-order-stage.

Transitional Level. Kohlberg's in later research (Kohlberg, Colby, Gibbs, Speicher-Dubin, & Power, 1978) suggested that there was a transitional level between the conventional and postconventional level. In the transitional level moral reasoning was postconventional but still not completely principled. During the transitional level, which overlaps the stages at the end of the conventional level and at the beginning of the postconventional level, individuals are able to see themselves as persons outside of a recognized social order and they make decisions without any strong commitment to society, even though they recognize its existence. They have become aware of relativity of different social standards and can therefore justify behaviors within different parameters. At the postconventional or principled level, the ability to reason morally has not yet reached its highest possibilities.

Postconventional Level. The postconventional level is known as the principled level and is the highest level of moral reasoning. At this level, the person acts according to autonomous moral principles, which have validity apart from the authority of groups or persons who hold them and also apart from the individual's identification with those persons or groups. In other words, obedience to authority and social recognition are secondary to the higher values and principles that are recognized as paramount by the individual. In Stage 5, "The Stage of Social Contract of Utility, and of Individual Rights," the individual demonstrates a social-contract orientation, generally with legalistic and utilitarian overtones. Kohlberg (1968) explained that "Morality is based on upholding basic rights, values, and legal contracts of a society, even when they conflict with the concrete rules and laws of the group" (p.24). The right action is defined in terms of general rights and in terms of standards that have been critically examined and agreed upon by the whole society. A clear understanding exists of the relativity of values, opinions, and laws which can be changed. There is emphasis on the legal point of view, but also on the possibility of changing the law rather than freezing it in terms of Stage 4's law and order type thinking. The kind of moral reasoning during this stage corresponds roughly to Piaget's morality of cooperation, as opposed to a morality of constraint.

The final stage (Stage 6) of Kohlberg's theory of moral development is the "Stage of Universal Ethical Principles." At this stage, the individual is oriented toward the decisions of conscience in accordance with ethical principles, which are rational, organized, and intended to be applied universally. Rules at this stage are "universal principles of justice, of the reciprocity and equality of human rights, and of respect for the dignity of human rights as individual persons" (Kohlberg et al., 1978, p. 26).

Moral development occurs through the sequence of these stages beginning with the child's naive moral outlook and progressing gradually during the years of pre-adolescence and adolescence into a complex, ethical, moral system. Although many persons never reach these higher levels, Kohlberg believed that through structured exercise, such as those conducted in the classroom, the level of moral reasoning can be raised by at least one stage.

VALUE CLARIFICATION IN THE CLASSROOM

Many models exist for values clarification. The first and most comprehensive however was developed by Raths, Harmin, and Simon (1966). This group perhaps should be acknowledged as the founders of values clarification programs in the schools. Raths et al. (1966), like Piaget and Kohlberg, saw a direct integration between cognition and valuing. Cognition is directed toward decision making. Within the school setting, the two are combined in the curriculum and in teacher's presentations and attitude. The goals and processes of values clarification according to the model are to help children:

1. make free choices whenever possible;

2. search for alternatives in choice making situations;

3. weigh the consequences of each available alternative;

4. consider what they prize and cherish;

5. affirm the things they value;

6. do something about their choices; and

7. consider and strengthen patterns in their lives.

As the teacher helps students use these processes, he/she helps them find values. (p. 213)

As a teacher, you may help your students find their own answers by values clarification, which has a twofold approach: guidance in analyzing, refining, and holding to values; and indirect encouragement of an appreciation of the viewpoints of others.

The valuing process incorporates three processes of valuing, choosing, prizing, affirming, and acting.

Raths et al. (1966) related seven steps for helping students work successfully through the valuing process to decisions. The seven steps paraphrased are as follows:

1. Choosing freely. If a value is forced on you, you are unlikely to accept it consciously with your values.

2. Choosing from alternatives. Your freedom of choice is greater if you are given several values from which to choose.

3. Choosing after considering the consequences. An intelligent system of values is not accepted impulsively; it requires thought and prediction of what will result from any choice you make.

4. Prizing and cherishing. You should respect your own values and view them as part of you.

5. Affirming. Once you have arrived at values, you should be willing to announce and publicly defend them, sharing them when that is appropriate.

6. Acting upon choices. Your values should be apparent from your actions.

7. Repeating. If you act on your values, you should do so consistently; if your actions are inconsistent with your values, then your value system needs reexamination. (pp. 28-30)

These processes collectively define valuing. The end results of the valuing process are called values. Value clarification methods are intended to take students through those seven subprocesses. When using this model the teacher is not concerned with the particular value outcomes of any one person's experiences, but rather, the teacher is concerned with the process that students use to obtain their value.

Simon, Howe, and Kirschenbaum (1972) provided teachers with seventy-nine classroom activities for practice in subprocesses.

• For *prizing,* they suggested that the teacher ask students to list "twenty things you love to do," which may range from reading comics to surfing or traveling abroad. When the lists are complete, the students place symbols, intended to be self-revealing, beside each activity. A letter "R" indicates an element of risk—emotional, physical, or intellectual—in the activity. The symbol "N5" denotes an activity in which the student had not engaged five years earlier. An "F" means that the student's father indulges in the same activity and shows that father and student shared certain interests. A "P" marks an activity that the student publicly affirms. Students compare and discuss their lists and the teacher, well into the discussion, reads his/her own.

• For *choosing,* the teacher asks students to draw a flight of steps or a ladder with "the kind of person I'd like to be like" at the bottom and "the kind of person I'd most like to be like" at the top. Again, students compare lists and defend their choices.

• For *acting,* the teacher outlines a situation and ask what students would do. Some possible situations are presented.

You are driving along the highway alone on a rainy day. In front of you is a hitchhiker dressed in hippie garb holding a sign lettered with the name of your destination. What would you do?

You are driving on a two-lane road behind another car. You notice that one of the wheels is wobbling more and more. It looks as if the nuts are coming off one by one. There's no way to pass the driver because cars are coming in the other direction in a steady stream. What would you do?

You are walking behind someone. You see him take out a cigarette pack, withdraw the last cigarette, and put it in his mouth, crumple the package, and nonchalantly toss it over his shoulder onto the sidewalk. You are twenty-five feet behind him. What would you do? (Simon et al., 1972, p. 33)

VALUE CLARIFICATION IN PRACTICE IN THE CLASSROOM

Swick and Ross (1979) pointed out the educational process must involve learners in identifying, organizing, implementing, and continually assessing their moral choices via a moral system of living. Further, they suggested using values clarification activities in the classroom, within the context of subject matter and also within the context of a specialized affective education program. Kay (1975) emphasized the need "to advance the cultural evolution of mankind" toward "compassionate reasoning." His emphasis in moral education is that children must learn to love one another because love is a strong basis for positive moral action.

Other researchers present goals of moral education somewhat differently, but the general agreement is that moral education as a goal and values clarification as a process are integral elements in the successful education of the individual.

In a variety of ways moral development theory can be applied to school situations, especially in terms of resolving conflict situations and going beyond the law-and-order-stage that is characteristic of much thinking in the classroom setting.

One important role the teacher must assume when including value clarification in the classroom is that of facilitating the discussion of moral issues. A moral discussion is defined as any purposeful conversation about moral issues. Most moral discussions are stimulated by moral dilemmas which present situations for which the culture offers support for a number of situations.

Beyer (1979) has proposed a program for conducting discussions on moral issues in the classroom. The program consists of five main stages. In the first stage the dilemma is presented. It may be a hypothetical dilemma or a real one. A dilemma which is most effective is one which has some relevance to the class or to a member of the class. An example of a dilemma that can be used in a class was one of the three presented previously.

An important part of presenting the dilemma is clarifying the facts and defining the key terms. This part is usually done when students raise questions about the situation, sometimes making it more specific.

During the second stage, the students take sides on the action by taking positions, pros and cons, on what the characters have done or should have done.

Students are then divided into small groups and engage in discussions about the reasoning used to qualify the actions they suggested.

During the group discussion, participants clarify their thinking and work through logical ways of justifying themselves to others.

The fourth stage is the point that the entire class is lead in discussion. This gives students an opportunity to report the reasoning which supports their positions and to hear reasons given for positions others have taken, to challenge these reasons, and to hear others challenge their own reasoning. The final stage is closing the discussion which gives the students the opportunity to reflect on what they have learned and to review their own processes of moral reasoning.

When conducting moral discussions in the classroom with students teachers should listen to students explain their values but should not offer judgements of right or wrong.

Beyer's (1979) model is useful for teachers when incorporating value clarification in the classroom. It is a well organized and flexible method of making moral discussions purposeful and more than just conversation.

Value clarification is one of the most important goals of instruction. It contributes to intellectual, cognitive and personal growth. Castell and Stahl (1975) presented six important reasons why the classroom teacher should stress value clarification in the classroom.

• Value clarification enhances the ability of students to communicate ideas, beliefs, values, and feelings.

• Value clarification enhances the ability of students to empathize with other persons, especially those whose circumstances may be different from their own.

• Value clarification enhances the ability of students to resolve problems as they arise.

• Value clarification enhances student's ability to assent and dissent as a member of a social group.

• Value clarification enhances the ability of students to engage in decision making.

• Value clarification enhances student's ability to hold and use consistent beliefs and disbeliefs.

The teacher should share his/her own values but should not impose them on students. Finally and most important, the teacher should never force any student to participate in values clarification activities.

SELF-TEST, CHAPTER 9

1. Which of the following is considered to be the major category of conflict with which students are confronted?

  a. boredom with school
  b. sexual and peer relationship problems
  c. value decisions
  d. emotional problems

2. Studies of human behavior maintain that most conflicts occur as a result of

  a. indecisiveness
  b. frustration
  c. our inability to make school progress
  d. being faced with a choice that involves the pairing of two or more goals.

3. An approach-approach conflict occurs when we are faced with a choice between

  a. two positive goals
  b. two negative goals
  c. conflicting emotional needs
  d. doing one thing and not doing another

4. Which situation describes an avoidance-avoidance conflict?

  a. two pleasant alternatives
  b. two unpleasant choices
  c. most moral decisions
  d. both positive and negative aspects of the same choice

5. Which conflict situation typically results in the vacillating circumstances of a stalemate?

    a. avoidance-avoidance
    b. approach-avoidance
    c. approach-approach
    d. moral-immoral-amoral

6. What is the basis of morality in Piaget's theory of moral development?

    a. organized behavior
    b. sensory perception
    c. cognitive reasoning
    d. emotional development

7. In Piaget's view of moral realism, children weigh an act according to

    a. intentions
    b. consequences
    c. unconscious motivations
    d. objective criteria of values

8. What is the basis of Piaget's concept of "morality of constraint?"

    a. fear of punishment
    b. sense of duty
    c. contingency rewards system
    d. an optimistic view of man

9. Who is the theorist that divides moral reasoning into preconventional, conventional, transitional, and postconventional stages?

    a. Piaget
    b. Kohlberg
    c. Bandura
    d. Belkin and Bloom

10. What principle of morality is expressed in Kohlberg's "Stage of Universal Ethical Principles?"

    a. respect for human beings as individual persons
    b. mutual sense of support
    c. morality of constraint
    d. morality acceding to individual wishes

11. In which way can a moral development theory be applied to school conflicts?

    a. to resolve conflict situations
    b. to improve learning skills
    c. to discipline
    d. to improve parental control

ANSWERS: 1. (c), 2. (d), 3. (a), 4. (b), 5. (a), 6. (d), 7. (b), 8. (a), 9. (b), 10. (a), 11. (a)

ADDITIONAL RESOURCES

Books and Publications

Brown, G. I. (1971). *Human teaching for human learning.* New York: Viking Press.

Greer, M., & Rubinstein, B. (1972). *Will the real teacher please stand up: A primer in humanistic education.* Pacific Palisades, CA: Good Year Publishing.

Postman, N., & Weingartner, C. (1969). *Teaching as a subversive activity.* New York: Dell Publishing.

Shaftel, F. R., & Shaftel, G. (1967). *Role-playing for social values: Decision-making in the social studies.* Engelwood Cliffs, NJ: Prentice Hall.

Simon, S. B., Hawley, R. C., & Britton, D. D. (1973). *Composition for personal growth: Value clarification through writing.* New York: Hart.

Simon, S. B., Howe, L. W., & Kirschenbaum, H. (1972). *Values clarification: A handbook of practical strategies.* New York: Hart.

REFERENCES

Albas, D., Albas, C., & McClusky, K. (1978). Anomie. Social class and drinking behavior of high school students. *Journal of Studies on Alcohol, 39*(5), 910-913.

Alexander, T. (1969). *Children and adolescents: A biocultural approach to psychological development.* New York: Atherton.

Bandura, A., & Mischel, W. (1965). Modification of self-imposed delay of reward through exposure to live and symbolic models. *Journal of Personality and Social Psychology, 2,* 698-705.

Bandura, A., Ross, D., & Ross, S. (1961). Transmission of aggression through imitation of aggressive models. *Journal of Abnormal and Social Psychology, 63,* 575-582.

Baron, R. A. (1974). Aggression as a function of victim's pain cues, level of prior anger arousal, and exposure to an aggressive model. *Journal of Personality and Social Psychology, 29,* 17-124.

Belkin, G. S. (1975). *Practical Counseling in the Schools.* Dubuque, IA: Wm. C. Brown.

Berelson, B. & Steiner, G. A. (1969). *Human behavior: An inventory of scientific findings.* New York: Harcourt Brace Jovanovich.

Beyer, B. K. (1979). Conducting moral discussions in the classroom. In G. S. Belkin (Ed.), *Perspectives in educational psychology.* Dubuque, IA: Wm. C. Brown.

Bloom, L. (1959). A reappraisal of Piaget's theory of moral judgment. *Journal of Genetic Psychology, 95,* 3-12.

Brown, W. A., Corriveau, D. P., & Monte, P. M. (1977). Anger arousal by a motion picture: A methodological note. *American Journal of Psychiatry, 134* (8), 930-931.

Buchanan, J. P. (1973). Quantitative methodology to examine the development of moral judgment. *Child Development, 44,* 186-189.

Castell, J. D. & Stahl, R. J. (1975). *Value Clarification in the Classroom.* Santa Monica, CA: Goodyear Publishing.

Dell, P. F., & Jurovic, G. J. (1978). Moral structure and moral content: Their relationship to personality. *Journal of Youth and Adolescence, 7* (1), 63-72.

Deutsch, M. (1973). *The Resolution of Conflict: Constructive and destructive processes.* New Haven, CT: Yale University Press.

Dollard, J., & Miller, N. E. (1950). *Personality and Psychotherapy.* New York: McGraw-Hill.

Durkin, D. (1960). The specificity of children's moral judgments. *Child Development, 32,* 551-560.

Egan, G. (1975). *The skilled helper.* Monterey, CA: Brooks/Cole.

Flavell, J. H. (1963). *The developmental psychology of Jean Piaget.* New York: D. Van Nostrand.

Graham, R. (1975). Moral education: A child's right to a just community. *Elementary School Guidance and Counseling, 9,* 299-208.

Hague, W. J. (1977). Counseling as a moral conflict: Making the disintegration positive. *Canadian Counselor, 12*(1), 41-46.

Hawley, R. C., & Hawley, I. L. (1975). *Human values in the classroom.* New York: Hart.

Hoover, T. O. (1977). Values clarification as an adjunct to psychotherapy. *Catalog of Selected Documents in Psychology,* 7, 110-111.

Jantz, R. K., & Fulda, T. A. (1975). The role of moral education in the public elementary school. *Social Education, 16,* 24-35.

Kay, W. (1975). *Moral education: A sociological study of the influence of society, home, and school.* Hamden, CT: Shoe String Press.

Kohlberg, L. (1968). Early education: A cognitive-developmental view. *Child Development, 39,* 1013-1062.

Kohlberg, L., Colby, A., Gibbs, J., Speicher-Dubin, B. S., & Power, C. (1978). *Assessing moral stages: A manual* (Part 1). Unpublished manuscript. Cambridge, MA: Center of Moral Education, Harvard University.

Kohlberg, L. & Hersh, R. H. (1977). Moral development: A review of the theory. *Theory into Practice, 16*(2), 53-59.

Kohlberg, L. & Kramer, R. B. (1969). Continuities and discontinuities in childhood and adult moral development. *Human Development, 12,* 93-120.

Lewin, K. (1936). *A dynamic theory of personality* (D. K. Adams & K. E. Zener, trans.). New York: McGraw-Hill.

Mancuso, J. C., Morrison, J. K., & Aldrich, C. C. (1978). Developmental changes in social-moral perception: Some factors affecting children's evaluations and predictions of the behavior of a transgressor. *Journal of Genetic Psychology, 132*(1), 121-136.

Maschette, D. (1977). Moral reasoning in the real world. *Theory into Practice, 16*(2), 124-128.

Maslow, A. H. (1970). *Motivation and Personality,* 2nd ed. New York: Harper & Row.

Mitchell, J. J. (1974). Moral dilemmas of early adolescence. *The School Counselor, 22,* 16-22.

Mitchell, J. J. Moral growth during adolescence. *Adolescence, 10*(38), 221-226.

Palomares, U. (1975). *A curriculum on conflict management.* La Mesa, CA: Human Development Training Institute.

Peters, H. J., Ed. (1962). *Counseling: Selected Readings.* Columbus, OH: Charles E. Merrill.

Peterson, J. A. (1970). *Counseling and values.* Scranton: International Textbook.

Piaget, J. (1932). *The moral judgment of the child.* London: Kegan Paul.

Piaget, J. & Inhelder, B. (1969). *Psychology of the child.* New York: Basic Books.

Pulaski, M. A. (1971). *Understanding Piaget.* New York: Harper & Row.

Raths, L., Harmin, J., & Simon, S. (1966). *Values and teaching: Working with values in the classroom.* Columbus, OH: Charles E. Merrill.

Sararwathi, T. S. & Verma, S. (1976). Social class differences in the development of moral judgment in girls of ages 10-12 years. *Indian Journal of Psychology, 51*(4), 325-332.

Sicinski, A. (1978). The concepts of "need" and "value" in light of the systems approach. *Social Science Information, 17* (1), 71-91.

Simon, S. B., Howe, L. W., & Kirschenbaum, H. (1972). *Values clarification: A handbook of practical strategies.* New York: Hart.

Smith, D. W. (1962). Value system and the therapeutic interview. In H. J. Peters (Ed.). *Counseling: Selected readings.* Columbus, OH: Charles E. Merrill.

Strickland, B. (1978). A rationale and model for changing values in helping relationships. In J. C. Hansen (Ed.), *Counseling process and procedures.* New York: Macmillan.

Swick, K. J., & Ross, C. (1979). Affective learning for the real world. In G. S. Belkin (Ed.), *Perspectives in educational psychology.* Dubuque, IA: Wm. C. Brown. (pp. 106-108).

Thomas, M. H., & Drabman, R. S. (1978). Effects of television violence on expectations of other's aggression. *Personality and social Psychology Bulletin, 4*(1), 73-76.

Trainer, F. E. (1977). A critical analysis of Kohlberg's contributions to the study of moral thought. *Journal for the Theory of Social Behavior, 7*(1).

Whiteman, J. L., Zucker, K. B., & Grimley, L. K. (1978). Moral judgment and the others-concept. *Psychological Reports, 42*(1), 283-289.

Chapter 10

EDUCATION FOR CULTURAL PLURALISM

The United States has been traditionally a gatherer of nationalities. Throughout history, people from a variety of countries came to America with aspirations and desires that could not be met in their homelands. One vision shared by most citizens of the United States is that the country's strength is maintained and even enhanced by the infusion of new people into its system. This vision assumes that immigrants assimilate into the American culture as quickly as possible. However, this vision, often called the melting pot, is being challenged in contemporary polity. The effects of this challenge are being felt in the educational community.

EXPECTED OUTCOMES

This chapter will focus on multicultural education. The historical antecedents of monoculturism, as well as contemporary concerns of multicultural education, will be discussed. By reading the material in the chapter you should be able to

1. distinguish the differences between compensatory education and multicultural education;

2. discuss the myth behind the melting pot theory;

3. list the advantages of education for cultural pluralism;

4. identify the main features of Mexican American culture; and

5. enumerate the main features of Asian American culture.

MYTH OF THE SUPERNATION

For nearly all of its history, the United States has been a multicultural entity espousing a monocultural identity. For a nation that has experienced continuing waves of immigration, the United States has been remarkably consistent in suppressing multicultural influences in its society. It has done this in a number of ways including social methods, such as segregation, and legal methods, such as the immigration quotas. Even in its earliest history, this nation consisted of people who spoke languages other than English and who came from a number of different countries. When the first census was taken in 1790, more than fifty percent of the people in the U.S. did not speak English (Benavidas, 1979). A lingering effect of earlier attitudes is that there appears to be an organizing concept accepted by many Americans that this country was to be a nation with an overwhelmingly European tradition and, perhaps, a sizeable black minority with a smattering of Asians and Latin Americans (Glazer, 1981).

Because most of the country's energies went into subduing an undeveloped land, early immigrants were viewed as a resource to aid in the process. Most of the first immigrants were European, thus they did not represent a radical departure in religion, customs, and values from the original settlers. However, this situation was to change, as the later immigrants came from southern and eastern Europe and Asia. Concern was voiced that these new people would change the face of America and in doing so would destroy the foundation of this country.

Results of these fears were discriminatory actions in social, economic, and political institutions. Blatant examples such as, "Irish need not apply"'' signs in front of industrial offices, poll taxes, and the changing immigration laws to favor northern European countries, were common (Hunter, 1974).

AMERICA AS A MELTING POT

Around the turn of the 20th century the idea of America as a nation of many people became prominent. Where previously the prevailing concept was that American traditions, culture, and value system should replicate those of northern European countries and England, the new organizational concept was that the new "American" was someone quite different from people of other countries and that these differences made us, if not superior, at least unique. Thus, the Super American was born as a product of a young country coming to grips with its tremendous potential. That this country was blessed with special consideration was internalized by many of its citizenry. One source of this country's strength was the renewal process of new immigrants taking their places in the American way of life. It was thought that immigrants merged with the existing population to forge some new entity, different yet stronger. This was called the Melting Pot theory of acculturation and assimilation. It was as though America was a huge crucible melting its different people into a new product. This melting process erased all vestiges of peoples' previous traditions, customs, and values. Thus, to hold onto foreign ways was seen as unAmerican. New immigrants were forced to assimilate into American culture as quickly as possible and were made to think that their native cultures were not acceptable in America.

A play that was very popular summed up the attitude that was prevalent at the time. *The Melting Pot* by Israel Zangwill (1914) opened in 1909. It popularized the concept of the Super American as a person incorporating the elements of many countries to make a super person (Benavidas, 1979). The play intimated that it was the American destiny guided by deity to become a super race. Looking back on the times, it may appear amusing because of the obvious racism in the concept. However, this concept became the guiding principle for the manner in which Americans viewed themselves.

Because the new immigrant had to give up old ways and customs and acquire new ones, there had to be a vehicle for this process. Education served that purpose. It was through the public schools that these new Americans and their children learned the new customs, but most importantly they learned English. The public school system in America was the major institution of assimilation in the years after the turn of the twentieth century.

In many respects, the schools accomplished a remarkable feat. They "Americanized" millions of immigrants. Some educational historians claim that this may be the American public education system's greatest achievement.

> Whatever their other failures, the big-city public schools of the age of immigration taught their charges English. Any child who had spent a few years in these schools could speak English. The curriculums were in many ways similar to those of the Mexican-American and Puerto Rican children for whom we are now told a different approach is necessary. They lived in dense ethnic communities, spoke their mother tongue at home, and played on the street with children of the community who used the same language. (Glazer, 1981, p. 389)

However successful education may have been in assimilating people into American culture, it did so at a heavy cost to students' native background. Often the student from a foreign country was ridiculed about dress, customs, and language that he/she used. These children were made to feel that their background and roots of identity were inferior to American ways. In many cases, students were punished by school personnel for maintaining vestiges of their native culture.

Additionally, the great melting pot did not melt everyone. It was more successful in the large urban centers of the northeast. In these areas, the major institutions of socialization, schools, churches, and industry, were highly developed and they were able to "Americanize" people more efficiently. In other areas with less developed socializing agencies, the assimilation process was less successful. Thus, in regions like the southwest, the Mexican-American population did not assimilate to the extent that others did. These areas had populations who, rather than assimilating into the culture of the society, became more of a conglomeration of separate communities each retaining its own identity.

The burden of socializing great numbers of ethnic groups into society was undertaken by the educational system. Schools were viewed as the major institution to incorporate American values and to teach their students to read and write English. In many respects, schools accomplished remarkable feats. They digested millions of youngsters from a variety of ethnic groups and developed them into "Americans."

However, the conditions that existed at the turn of the twentieth century were different from today's. Glazer (1981) stated that three sets of conditions make contemporary education unlike the conditions 85 years ago. The first is the general demise of the "Super American" system. The American economic system does not have an impact on world economy to the extent it did previously. The belief that America can do no wrong is no longer viable. In many respects, the United States has lost its innocence. As a result, Glazer claimed, learning the values and language of the American system is not as important to some as it once was.

The ever increasing role of the federal government in changing educational policy is the second set of different conditions. "Legislation has turned the modest support it gives to local school districts into a club to impose national requirements affecting the education of the handicapped, the integration of the sexes, the employment and distribution of teachers and administrators, the assignment of children by race and ethnic groups'' (Glazer, 1981, p. 387). Where legislation leaves off, court cases take over. Famous court cases cited earlier in this text have influenced policies on separation of races and language of instruction.

The third set of conditions takes place largely in the inner-city schools, but it also is evident in the wider community. This is the rapidly growing number of private institutions that are drawing off children from public schools. It appears that one of the reasons for the mushrooming growth of these schools is the loss of confidence that the public has in its schools to do the job of educating offspring effectively. Another reason is the ''white flight'' syndrome where parents are sending their children to private schools to avoid racial and ethnic mixing of students. Where the Catholic parochial school system dominated the private school arena, now Jewish schools, black schools, fundamentalist schools, and Christian schools have sizeable enrollments.

How these conditions influence the education of the new immigrants is unknown. The current wave of immigrants come from Asian countries and Latin American countries. Education was successful in acculturating the old wave immigrants. The extent to which education can shape these new immigrants into the fabric of American society may determine whether or not America can remain a viable community in the international forum.

DEFINITION OF MULTICULTURAL EDUCATION

Compensatory education programs that were devised to redress failures of the traditional educational system were doomed almost from the beginning. Programs were designed with the idea that people in certain ethnic and racial groups were deficient in some important qualities. Labels were thrown about which, when viewed with hindsight, appear inappropriate. Some members of ethnic groups were called culturally deprived, others were labeled disadvantaged. In any case, the assumption behind the programs was that students possessed insufficient quantities of certain features which prevented them from learning in schools. Thus, what was needed was to bring these children up to a standard set by a middle class-controlled public education system.

Beginning in the late sixties, some ethnic and racial groups rejected the concept of America as a monoculture. Organized groups began to pressure school systems to include ethnic and racial studies in their programs. It is not difficult to understand how members in these groups could not identify with George Washington and Thomas Jefferson as their founding fathers. A Puerto Rican child would have to strain his/her imagination to identify with Benjamin Franklin. Because little, if any, mention was made of minority group participation in the development of this country, then presumable present-day members of minority groups would have to conclude that their ancestors made no contribution to this country's development.

Perhaps the Melting Pot theory failed not so much because it was an invalid idea, rather it was the fact that education was seen as the main vehicle for assimilation. Social scientists have argued that other institutions may be more appropriate for this task. It would have been more productive if the process for the "melting" were also rooted in changes in political, social, and economic institutions.

The demise of compensatory education gave rise to multicultural education. The National Council for the Accreditation of Teacher Education (NCATE) has incorporated the concepts of multicultural education into its evaluation process. Beginning in 1979, all teacher education programs seeking accreditation or reaccreditation have to incorporate multicultural education in the training programs. NCATE defines multicultural education in its standards for curricula.

> Multicultural education is preparation for the social, political, and economic realities that individuals experience in culturally diverse and complex human encounters. These realities have both national and international dimensions. This preparation provides a process by which an individual develops competencies for perceiving, believing, evaluating, and behaving in differential cultural settings. Thus, multicultural education is viewed as an intervention and an on-going assessment process to help institutions and individuals become more responsive to the human condition, individual cultural integrity, and cultural pluralism in society. (*Multicultural Teacher Education,* 1980, p. 1)

Multicultural education is derived from the philosophy of cultural pluralism. By recognizing that our society has many ethnic/cultural groups we foster respect for diversity. On the other hand, the study of elements common to all groups is as important to multicultural education as the study of differences between groups (Baptiste, Baptiste, & Gollnick, 1980). The American Association of Colleges of Teacher Education stated:

Multicultural education is education which values cultural pluralism. Multicultural education rejects the view that schools should seek to melt away cultural differences or the view that schools should merely tolerate cultural pluralism. Instead, multicultural education affirms that schools should be oriented toward the cultural enrichment of all children and youth through programs rooted to the preservation and extension of cultural alternatives. Multicultural education recognizes cultural diversity as a fact of life in American society, and it affirms that this cultural diversity is a valuable resource that should be preserved and extended. It affirms that major education institutions should strive to preserve and enhance cultural pluralism. *(Multicultural Teacher Education,* 1980, p. iii)

While cultural pluralism is emphasized in multicultural education, it is necessary to distinguish between educationalists' and social scientists' meanings of cultural pluralism. Social scientists understand the term to mean separate ethnic/racial groups in a society that do not intermingle. Graphically, this concept can be shown in Figure 10.1.

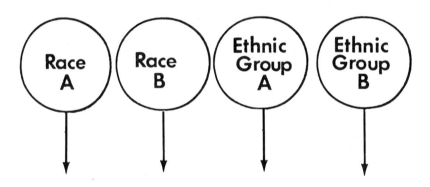

Figure 10.1. Social scientist concept of polarization of racial and ethnic groups.

The separation of the groups may be by political, geographical, social, or other means. South Africa is an example of a pluralistic society. Unquestionably, educators are not in favor of conditions that exist in that country. Cultural pluralism as used by educators may be represented in the following manner. In this representation each group interacts with other groups, but retains its own identity. Some consequences of the interaction of the groups are represented by the overlapping areas. To some extent each ethnic or racial group is affected by its interaction with other groups. Several assumptions are included in this definition of cultural pluralism and multicultural education. Six of these assumptions have been developed by the Commission on Multicultural Education under the auspices of the American Association of Colleges for Teacher Education.

1. Uniqueness of the American culture has been fashioned by contributions of many diverse cultural group into an interrelated whole.

2. Cultural diversity and interaction among different groups strengthen American society and ensures each citizen's inherent right to be an individual.

3. Total isolation or total assimilation of any cultural group changes the structure of the culture and weakens its basic intent of enhancing the maximum worth of every individual within that cultural group.

4. The education system provides a critical function of shaping attitudes and values necessary for the continuation of a democratic society.

5. Teachers must assume a leadership role in creating an environment supportive of multicultural teaching and learners.

6. To assume leadership roles, teachers must be trained in institutions where the environment has been supportive of multicultural teaching and learning (*Multicultural Teacher Education,* 1980, p. 2).

From these assumptions educators interpret the term pluralism to mean the condition where several cultural groups exist in a society on an equal basis, and though these groups retain their individual differences, a significant amount of interaction exists among them. Thus, this interaction serves as the common thread among the groups providing cohesion for the general society. Implicit in this statement is the concept that the interaction has an enhancing effect on members of individual cultural groups (Gutierrez, 1982). The understanding is that learning results from this as an essential product of the educational process. Indeed, the implications for education when an appreciation for cultural pluralism is identified as an important concept are strikingly different from implications for education when the melting pot theory operates.

In Figure 10.2 is illustrated the individuality of each cultural group with interactions possible. Thus, cultural pluralism can be appreciated with retention of cultural differences rather than contributions from each causing commonality among all—the melting pot theory.

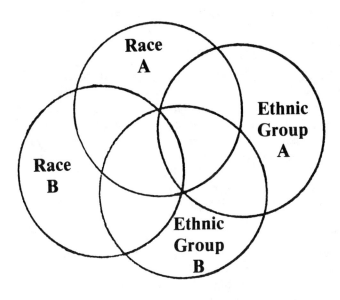

Figure 10.2. Group interaction in cultural pluralism.

TEACHER AS MEDIATOR OF CULTURE

If schools are viewed as institutions for cultural assimilation, then teachers are seen as the main agents for this change. Historically, it fell upon the shoulders of teachers to become the mediators of our culture to students who differed from the white/Protestant/English speaking population. This Americanization process has sometimes been called the "hidden" or "secondary" curriculum. The role of mediator of culture is one recognized as an integral part of teaching. It is unlikely that this role will diminish. In all probability, the mediator role for teachers will continue. What is likely to change are values and content of what will be transmitted. Where once an allegiance to a monocultural society with a homogenized system of values existed, now the possibility is strong that teachers will be asked to be the mediators for cultural pluralism. This shift is enormous for it presumes that teachers can meet "the challenge of reconciling the reality of American's cultural pluralism with its vision of an Anglo-Saxon homogeneity" (Grant, 1977).

Obviously, this new interpretation of what the teacher is transmitting as a mediator of the culture will require some substantial change in the teacher's behavior. Not all teachers are prepared adequately for this new interpretation. Similarly, not all pre-service teachers are equipped to handle this new challenge. Grant (1977) has suggested four means by which teachers can help prepare themselves for the role:

1. Teachers should be encouraged to analyze their attitudes about multicultural education.

This suggestion implies that teachers must gain a sense of self-awareness. Reviewing one's thoughts and values about multi-cultural education is an excellent method of developing a level of awareness. Asking certain questions of one's self help to facilitate the process. Typical questions might be: Am I intimidated when working with members from different cultural or racial groups? Do I sincerely believe that cultural and racial differences are not really deficiencies?

If a teacher finds after self-evaluation that he/she needs some improvement, there are some strategies that can be helpful. Small group discussions; reading textbooks and other literature about racial and cultural groups; viewing movies, plays, exhibits, displays, and so forth, featuring multicultural contributions; and individual counseling or therapy may help to develop the requisite attitudes for successful teaching in multicultural settings.

2. Teachers are encouraged to examine their behavior in monocultural and multicultural settings.

It is one thing to espouse a multicultural education philosophy and another to act appropriately. Thousands of subtle behaviors that a teacher exhibits during the course of the day reveal the validity of a person's views on multicultural education. For example, if a teacher "Americanizes" a foreign child's name, this act calls into question whether this teacher has genuinely internalized a multicultural philosophy.

Methods of evaluating whether a teacher's behavior is appropriate for multicultural education are enhanced by the increased use of videotaping. Reviewing tapes of one's actual teaching behavior may identify deficiencies. Alternative methods would be to invite teaching colleagues into the classroom as observers. Feedback through this procedure may help in identifying behaviors not compatible with multicultural education.

Certain teacher behaviors can add credibility to a person's commitment to multicultural education. Reading assignments, classroom displays, and teacher's willingness to engage in multicultural education issues, help to lend authenticity to the process.

3. Teachers are encouraged to develop communication skills that facilitate positive exchange between students of different backgrounds, cultures, and races.

The main vehicle for accomplishing this recommendation is the teacher. The teacher is the single most important element in developing classroom climate. Through the teacher's action, students appraise what can and cannot be voiced in class. Students become aware that certain topics receive special consideration by teachers. If a teacher models open and effective discussion on differences in race and culture, students will determine that the classroom is the appropriate forum for these kinds of discussions. Teacher as model has been discussed previously and its impact, again, is very influential in shaping student behavior.

4. Teacher advocates of multicultural education are to follow various legal conditions and educational policies regarding multicultural education.

These teachers also must become spokespersons for it. In order to become an active advocate, one must genuinely believe in the virtues of multicultural education and believe that American education will be better served under a multicultural philosophy.

Thus, teachers should be active in seeing that school staffing composition reflects that of the society in general. The key factor in this strategy is that students and faculty can acquire important information about cultural and racial variety by interacting with diverse groups.

Teachers should be active in advocating curricula that is unbiased in its treatment of racial and cultural groups, and curricula that present the contributions of minority groups in a fair manner. Instructional materials also should reflect this attitude.

Paradis (1981) wrote about competencies that describe a culturally effective counselor. By omitting the words counselor and client and substituting teacher and student, the competencies are useful for educators. Paradis claimed that the competencies should be a part of training programs.

1. The culturally skilled [teacher] is one who has moved from being culturally unaware to being aware and sensitive to his/her own cultural baggage.

2. A culturally skilled [teacher] is aware of his/her own values and biases and how they may affect minority [students].

3. The culturally skilled [teacher] will have a good understanding of the sociopolitical system's operation in the United States with respect to its treatment of minorities.

4. A culturally skilled [teacher] is one who is comfortable with differences that exist between the [teacher] and [student] in terms of race and beliefs.

5. The culturally skilled [teacher] is sensitive to circumstances (personal biases, stage of ethnic identity, sociopolitical influences, so forth) which may dictate referral of the minority [student] to a [teacher] of his/her own race/culture.

6. The culturally skilled [teacher] must possess specific knowledge and information about the particular group with whom he/she is working.

7. The culturally skilled [teacher] must have a clear idea and explicit knowledge and understanding of the genuine characteristics of [teaching].

8. The culturally skilled [teacher] must be able to generate a wide variety of verbal and nonverbal responses.

9. The culturally skilled [teacher] must be able to send and receive both verbal and nonverbal messages accurately and "appropriately." (APA Education and Training Committee of Division 17, 1980, pp. 11-14)

The concept of becoming an advocate for cultural pluralism is important because it casts the teacher in an active role. Whereas, in the melting pot phenomenon the expectation was that the student would change to conform to a set of prescribed behaviors. Currently, with an emphasis on cultural pluralism, not all the change is the student's responsibility. This is a substantially different role for both teachers and students. In multicultural education every person in the environment is changed as a result of the interaction of different sets of cultures. We can all profit from our interactions with individuals from different cultures. However, advantages are only forthcoming if there is parity in the value of different cultural groups. Different does not have to mean deficient.

Members of minority groups often feel powerless and isolated as a result of their status in society. Life chances are not distributed equally to all groups in our society. Minority groups have a disproportionately negative chance in life because of the unfair influences of economic, social, educational, and political institutions (Stadler & Rynearson, 1981). Problems that members of these groups encounter are numerous and they are complicated because often teachers are not aware of the impact that poverty and social inequality have on students. Teachers expect students from minority groups to come up with the same solutions as the more typical students. However, members from minority groups often perceive fewer options available to them in their environment. What may appear as an obvious solution to a traditional teacher may not be in the awareness realm of a member of a minority group culture. Often this causes conflict and misunderstanding between the two groups.

SYSTEMS STRATEGIES TO IMPROVE MULTICULTURAL PROGRAMS

It is very important while to develop multicultural programs through the individual teacher is very important, also important is that school systems share a commitment to culturally pluralistic education. Clearly teachers in systems that espouse the philosophy of multicultural education will find it easier to be an advocate. The support that is given at administrative and policy levels facilitates the teacher's actions. Conversely, the teacher who feels that he/she is just a voice crying in the wilderness may become discouraged.

In order for multicultural education to be implemented on a system-wide basis, certain strategies must be initiated. Valverde (1978) recommends six strategies. They are school district commitment, a multicultural philosophy, comprehensive planning, staffing diversity, differential staff development, and evaluation. These strategies imply that school systems recognize the growing diversity in our student population and that this trend will increase in the United States. It also recognizes that systems must take an initiative in adapting to the changing characteristics of student population. Further, systems should provide multicultural experiences to students and expose them to pluralism by having diversified faculties. Schooling for multicultural education cannot be done effectively without thorough and comprehensive planning involving as many components of the community as possible. Finally, careful and accurate evaluation of multicultural education is needed.

Valverde (1978) recommended *formative evaluation*. Formative evaluation is used to assess the process rather than the product of educational programs. Formative evaluation is often undertaken to gain feedback for program modification. It is like a continuous monitoring system where changes can be made at the time they are needed. *Summative evaluation* is a procedure for assessing the end product of the program. *Summative evaluation* is implemented only after multicultural programs have been firmly established and the "bugs" worked out.

BRIEF SKETCHES OF AMERICAN MINORITIES

The following section attempts to present cameos of several minority groups in the United States. There is a danger in attempting to provide information about groups of people in a few paragraphs. The main danger is the temptation to oversimplify the description and to assume that all members of a minority group act alike. This section is not without that danger. The reader is encouraged to read histories, bibliographies, and other books that do a more thorough work on portraying these special populations. Readers are especially encouraged to read original materials written by actual members of the minority groups.

Native Americans

Native Americans constitute a relatively small percentage of the American population (Lazarus, 1983). Approximately 900,000 native

Americans reside in the United States. Out of this number approximately ⅓ of these are school-age children. In addition, there are about 50 tribes that speak a variety of languages. To treat native Americans as a single group can be misleading. To try to understand their value system by conceptualizing all Indians as having the same beliefs is inaccurate. For example, reservation Indians differ from nonreservation Indians on many values and customs.

The history of the American Indians is tragic. The last two hundred years have witnessed the steady destruction and deterioration of the native American value system. This destruction has been so complete that in many ways native Americans are marginal inhabitants in a land they once freely traveled. The consequences of marginality have taken a tremendous toll on the Indian. The price of the Indian "adjustment" to American society has been paid in the social, economic, cultural, and personal aspect of native American life. In every major area of human activity, native Americans have experienced serious and impending consequences (Pedigo, 1983). There is more poverty, sickness, and death among Indians than non-Indians in American society. The nonreservation American Indians experience more substance abuse, unemployment, and suicides than any other minority. Clearly, the toll paid by native Americans is extremely high. Prospects of conditions improving are not great.

Many writers have suggested that the reason for the high toll can be traced to the way that the native American was uprooted from his/her culture (Rhodes, Marshall, Altneale, Echo Hawk, Bjorck, & Beiser, 1980; Redhorse, 1980; Pedigo, 1983). By being divorced from their cultural background, native Americans were asked to give up an ancient heritage and to accept an alienated way of life. The conflict that this caused resulted in behavior that some would describe as self-destructive.

One common thread running through most native American value systems is that it is paramount that the individual is one with self, family, tribe, and the universe. Unless the importance of the concept is appreciated by non-native Americans, it is doubtful that full understanding of Indian values can take place. In many respects, native Americans take a holistic view of living, that one's individual peace is secured by being harmonious with family, tribe, and nature.

Lazarus (1983) has synthesized research and has identified common values systems of native Americans. Some of these are reported here:

1. There is a universal respect for age in Indian communities. Older native Americans are integrated into the society and they have a useful and prominent role to play.

2. Cooperation and harmony with the environment is very important. Indians accept nature as it is and they are not compelled to change or conquer it.

3. The native American is concerned with the present context of time. To this person the here and now is important. Future planning is difficult.

4. Native Americans are judged by their respective contributions to the group. Generosity and sharing one's possessions are admired values. Prestige is awarded to those who share.

5. Group welfare is of prime importance. While competition is encouraged, it is directed toward self. Interpersonal competition is frowned upon as it possesses a threat to group harmony.

6. Children are prized. They are given nearly equal footing with adults.

7. Native American parents do not structure the activities of their children. The regimentation found in U.S. schools is foreign to native American children.

8. Loud reprimanding and physical punishment of native American children by adults is seldom practiced. It is considered rude to be loud.

9. Politeness is valued in relationship. Personal confrontation is avoided and it is usually met with social disapproval. (p. 84)

In many respects, native Americans are cut off from their historical roots. Their contribution to the American heritage is often seen as minor at best. The mass media have not always presented the native American in the best light, thus it is not difficult to understand how ambivalent the native American child must think about his/her cultural heritage. The more the native American student is exposed to typical U.S. education, the lower his/her self-esteem becomes (Lazarus, 1983).

Zintz (1963) has compared American culture with Pueblo cultures; the differences are striking. The comparison indicated widely divergent views on life and major values. Some of the comparisons are listed in Table 10.1.

Table 10.1

Comparison of American Western Culture and Pueblo Native
American Culture

Western Culture	Pueblo Culture
Aggression	Submissiveness
Striving for success	Follow the old customs
Competition	Cooperation
Conquer the environment	Harmony with nature
Plan for the future	Present-time thinking
Rational explanations of events	Magical explanations of phenomenon
Individuality	Anonymity
Clock watching	World without time
Win at all cost	Win once, but let others win
Work to get ahead	Work for present needs

Teachers need to understand the values of native American society.
During the acculturation process, educators should seek to regard native
American contributions and lifestyle with respect. Even though through
the acculturation process native American children may have to learn
new ways of behaving, they must be encouraged to cherish their traditional ways.

Teachers should be sensitive to the childrearing patterns of most
native American communities. There is a much told story of a young
Navaho boy being berated by a white American teacher because the
teacher thought that the boy was stealing money. During the teacher's
reprimands, the Navaho child looked away from the towering teacher.
This action served only to convince the teacher that she was correct in
assuming that the boy was a thief, because if the boy was not guilty he
would look at her right in the eyes. Apparently, the teacher was unaware
that in the Navaho system adults do not reprimand children by scolding
and that children do not look adults in the eyes when speaking. Thus, the
Navaho child was being asked by the white teacher to violate a social
custom. The white teacher judged the downcast eyes as the Germanic interpretation of guilt. The complete interaction was based on
misunderstanding. The result was probably mistrust on both sides and,
perhaps, alienation on the part of the Navaho student.

Latinos

For the purpose of this discussion, Latinos will refer to Mexican Americans and Puerto Ricans. Hispanics and Chicanos are other terms used interchangeably for individuals with Spanish surnames (Dawson, 1977). Generally, Puerto Ricans reside on the east coast and Mexican Americans live in the Southwest and Far West. Other groups with Spanish surnames will not be discussed in this section. Cubans, Jamaicans, Haitians, and Barbadians, though found in the U.S. in increasing number, are not numerous enough at this time to warrant treatment. However, special study by educators in areas of the country where these groups are concentrated is encouraged.

Mexican Americans

Mexican Americans comprise the second largest minority group in America (Muhs, Popp, & Patterson, 1979) and the fastest growing in terms of total numbers (Casas & Atkinson, 1981). The growth rate stems from the high American birth rate and the flood of legal and illegal immigrants from Mexico. All major indicators point to this trend as nonabating.

The estimate is that over 6 million Mexican Americans are living in the United States. The vast majority of them live in Arizona, California, Colorado, New Mexico, and Texas. However, recently some evidence is that this population is moving beyond the Southwest and far West areas.

Historically, Mexican Americans were found in rural settings. Their main means of survival was to seek out a living farming on marginal soil. As a result, in the past, Mexican Americans were poor, rural, and uneducated. Today this description is considered valid by many Americans. The description is incorrect in at least one respect. Most Mexican Americans live in urban settings. About 80% are found in urban areas working in nonfarm occupations. However, poverty still remains with Mexican Americans. Nearly 30% still live at the poverty level. A more accurate description about a Mexican American is ". . . typically a poor, urban dweller, with less formal education than other groups in our society, and performs jobs at the lower level of organizations" (Muhs et al., 1979, p. 21). There is always the hazard when constructing generalizations that within group differences are forgotten (Casas & Atkinson, 1981).

Aspects of Mexican American Cultures. Some controversy exists about the homogeneity of the Mexican American culture (Casa & Atkinson, 1981; Muhs et al., 1979; Peralosa, 1967.) Claims that the Mexican American culture is homogeneous must be taken with some caution. While it may be true that Mexican Americans are the least acculturated of the larger minorities, it is unwarranted to assume that the Mexican American culture is monolithic. It is also important to note that these aspects of the culture are shared in varying intensities by individual Mexican Americans. The prudent teacher does not automatically assume that all Mexican Americans subscribe equally to each of the cultural values.

The degree to which Mexican Americans share common values is related to a number of factors. Ramirez and Castaneda (1974) have identified some factors which help influence how closely attached Mexican Americans are to certain cultural values.

1. Time spent in American urban settings.

2. Distance that the main residence is from the Mexican border.

3. Degree of contact with Anglos.

4. Length of residence in the United States.

5. Economic and political status of the Mexican American community.

Acculturation by Mexican Americans appears to be related to their strength of the bond with a Mexican American community. One reason why the acculturation process was slow with Mexican Americans as compared to other ethnic or racial groups was that the Mexican Americans were a conquered group. Previously, they had a functioning society that had survived for centuries. This fact influenced their rate of adaptation because they resisted giving up their culture. Most of the other ethnic groups came to the United States on their own initiative. Thus, the motivation for acculturation was qualitatively different from Mexican Americans.

Family. To many writers in the field of Mexican American relations, the family constitutes the main social unit (Muhs et al., 1979; Padilla & Ruiz, 1973; Ramirez, 1967). In their view the family is a close-knit unit where loyalty to the family's welfare is utmost. The structure is generally a variation of the extended family that is characterized by a dominant father and a mother who is the family mediator (Ruiz & Padilla, 1979). Decisions are made based on the family's welfare.

Further, these writers tend to describe the family role as all inclusive. In many aspects, the Mexican American family provides for its own social security system. It becomes a protective unit from external forces. As such, the Mexican American family provides psychological security for its members.

However, other writers challenged this view of the Mexican American family. Casas and Atkinson (1981) made a case that past descriptions of family life may be overgeneralizations. The younger Mexican American men and women are beginning to disavow traditional roles based on gender in the family structure and they are beginning to share the views of the main society. It would appear to these authors that sex-role and family influences that once differed among ethnic groups are now quickly disappearing. As many intragroup differences as cultural group differences may exist.

Personalisms. Most Mexican Americans have a high degree of affiliation. Personal contact is extremely important to them. To many Mexican Americans, Anglos appear reserved and distant. Nonverbal behavior comparisons between these two groups vary considerably. Body language between Mexican Americans is different from Anglos. There are more touching, embracing, holding, and playful physical interactions between Mexican Americans. Anglos, on the other hand, seem to prefer an organized approach to interactions based on competition (Ruiz & Padilla, 1979) whereas cooperation is favored by Mexican Americans.

Much is written about fatalism and present time orientation in Mexican American culture that may be unfounded.

> Specifically, Latinos are presumably present time oriented, unduly emphasizing immediate gratification and displaying underdeveloped skills in future planning. This tendency to enjoy the moment and to defer unpleasant responsibilities to some vague, indeterminate point in the future, seems widely accepted despite a dearth supportive of supportive evidence. (Ruiz & Padilla, 1979, p. 174)

It may be that writers take literally the Spanish expressions used often by Mexican Americans. For example, *manana* ("tomorrow"), or *Lo que Dios desea* ("Whatever God wills"), may not translate exactly into English and the meanings may not be examples of present time orientation or fatalism.

Religion. The Roman Catholic religion has had a powerful impact on Mexican Americans. In many ways, the church reinforces ethnic and family values that are predominate in Mexican American values. Most Mexican Americans are Roman Catholic with estimates ranging up to 90%. This contrasts with the majority culture in the U.S. which is Protestant. While recognizing Casas and Atkinson's (1981) claim that increasingly Mexican Americans are turning to Protestantism, and more Mexican Americans are "likely to live outside of their religion than are other Catholics," the impact of the Catholic church cannot be discounted.

Summary. In summary, Mexican Americans, on the average, are urban dwellers (often living in *barrios*), employed in menial, low paying jobs, undereducated and living marginally in terms of finances. Thus, Mexican American students are apt to take into the classroom a cultural reference that is at variance with the majority culture.

When discussing the culture of minorities it is important not to fall into the culture blame trap. That is, to assign the cause of student failure to the student's minority culture. This approach assumes that the culture is somehow deficient and that it impedes the progress of students. A more appropriate method is to put the blame on the main culture's institutions. Educational practices have traditionally required minority students to forsake their traditions and take on values of the majority institutions. This process was exclusively one way. This was true even though educational systems "often contribute significantly to the barriers confronted by Mexican American students. The need to make basic, structural changes in these institutions, in order to better serve the needs of these Mexican Americans is totally ignored" (Casas & Atkinson, 1981, p. 475).

Implications For Educators. Based on what is known today, some implications for educators can be stated regarding Mexican Americans.

1. The practice of blaming the Mexican American culture for student failures should cease. Educational policies should be examined to identify where the institution is creating problems.

2. Refrain from explaining Mexican American's behavior in reference to Anglo-American norms. Remember that cultural diversity is an asset rather than a liability.

3. Treat Mexican Americans as persons with a valuable culture. For example, do not "Americanize" Mexican American names. Make every effort to pronounce and say names completely.

4. Utilize the strengths of the Mexican American culture. Involve the family and the community in the school. In teacher conferences, expect that mothers will often bring the children along. Receive the members of the family and provide for their welcome.

5. Make the cultural exchange between Anglo and Mexican American cultures a two-way process. Set a precedent in the classroom which indicates that there is much to learn from each culture.

Asian Americans

Discrimination against Asians has been as pronounced as any other racial group in the United States. However, to most Americans, especially younger ones, this fact is unknown (Sue, 1979). There have been lynchings, assaults, imprisonments, and legal discrimination practiced against Asian Americans during the last century and a half. However, since the end of World War II, discrimination against Asian Americans (Japanese and Chinese) has been reversed to such an extent that these groups are often conceptualized as model citizens. Being thought of as model citizens has some historical explanations and it also makes us unaware of some potential areas of concern in Asian Americans.

Recently, new Asian Americans have arrived on the American scene. Post-Vietnam War events have resulted in immigration of Cambodians, Vietnamese and others from Southeast Asia. These groups will not be discussed because of space constraints of the text. However, their impact has already been made in several communities and the reader is encouraged to explore the literature on these new groups.

Early American History of Asian Immigrants. The first Asians that came to the United States in large numbers were Chinese. In response to social strife and economic upheaval in their homeland, Chinese males immigrated to the U.S. by the thousands. Here they were welcomed as a source of cheap labor to build the western part of the transcontinental railroad. As long as the demand for cheap, reliable labor was high, open opposition to the Chinese was minimal. However, when economic conditions became depressed, the Chinese were seen as a threat. Many whites were disturbed because they saw the Chinese willing to take any job at a lower pay rate. Soon, derogatory terms were used and these terms were made "respectable" by being used in newspapers. "Pigtails," "yellow peril," and other labels were used to describe Chinese Americans. The popular conception was that the Chinese were a strange group, practiced a heathen religion, were dirty, and were not to be trusted. Public outcry against the Chinese resulted in laws that discriminated against them. In some states, Chinese could not marry, own land, or become citizens. In 1882, the U.S. government approved the Federal Exclusion Act which severely limited the number of Asians that could immigrate to the U.S. (Sue, 1979; Sue & Kitano, 1979).

The Japanese were brought into the United States as a replacement for the cheap labor that was once provided by Chinese. At first, the Japanese were more welcomed because they brought their families with them. Toward the last quarter of the nineteenth century, attitudes toward the Japanese hardened and soon the same labels were applied to them as were earlier applied to the Chinese. The yellow peril menace was raised again, as were concerns of being taken over by a foreign element. As with the Chinese, federal and state laws were passed to limit immigration and land ownership by Japanese.

Overt hostility toward Chinese and Japanese subsided through the first third of the twentieth century. Both groups assimilated into American society through hard work and frugality. It was not until World War II that discrimination became grossly overt. Internment camps for Japanese Americans were constructed. Thousands of Japanese were rounded up and placed in concentration camps because they were perceived as a source of internal threat to the United States. After the war, attitudes toward both Chinese and Japanese became more accepting. Sue and Kitano (1979, p. 73) traced the history of attitudes towards Asian Americans through time by the use of labels applied to the two groups. These labels are depicted in Table 10.2. It can be seen that most negative attitudes changed over time to more positive ones. However, as the following discussion on Asian American culture will point out, these attitudes are not without their drawbacks.

Asian American Culture and Its Implications. Before any discussion of cultural values, it must be recognized that Asian American cultural values are in a state of transition. Thus, the conclusions arrived at a few decades ago may not be as relevant today as they once were. However, while it is true that the Asian American cultural value system is not as strong today, it is safe to remark that this system still has impact on the behavior of most Asian Americans.

Table 10.2

Trends of Attitudes Toward Asian Americans

1850s	→ →	→ →	→ →	1970s
pigtail	foul smelling	sneaky	loyal	intelligent
strange	cheap men	criminals	assimilable	quiet
exotic	tricky		sly	hardworking
filthy				shy
immoral				
treacherous				

Asian Family Structure. No discussion of Asian American culture could be complete without mentioning the strong influence of the family. The Asian family is an ancient and complex organization that has survived for thousands of years. It has withstood social upheavals, wars, and economic chaos. Therefore, the family has come to be perceived as a protection from external forces. As such, much is asked of family members in return. Roles are rigidly defined and functions are adhered to unquestioningly. The family atmosphere can be described as formal, dignified, authoritarian, and aloof. A high premium is placed on obedience and acquiescence.

In all matters, the family comes first and individual members' desires are expected to be suppressed. Peace and harmony within the family are maintained at all costs. The fundamental guiding principle of the family is preserving face and enhancing the family's welfare. All else is secondary. Efforts are made and approved of in relationship to the overall welfare of the family. Sacrifices for the family are supposed to be made without question. The greatest act of ingratitude is bringing shame to the family. Family members' actions are evaluated in terms of how they enhance the family. Males especially are forced to produce scholastically and financially for the benefit of the family. Thus, many male Asians gravitate into highly technical fields such as engineering.

Because peace and family harmony are prominent values in Asian American culture, strong emotions are not encouraged. Disagreements and outbursts of anger are frowned upon. The prevailing custom is to hide one's emotion beneath the surface. This may account for the expression, "the inscrutable Chinese."

School failures, job dismissal, mental illness, and juvenile delinquency are viewed catastrophically by Asian American families. This may help to explain the high scholastic success rate and low juvenile delinquency rate of Asian Americans. The main means of Chinese success in our society is conformity to American values and high motivation.

However, there is a price to be paid for this. Sue and Kirk (1972) found, as a result of the cultural background of Chinese Americans, Chinese American students to be more pragmatic, conforming to authority, inhibited, and introverted than the general student body. These values may be in conflict with the larger society's values of extroversion and impulsiveness. It is likely that as Asians assimilate into the American culture, they experience problems balancing the two cultures. For some, the experience produces marginality, a label sociologists apply to people who live on the edge of two cultures but not fully accepted into either one. The propensity of Asian American families to control their children by shame and guilt produces high abasement scores in some Asian students (Sue & Kitano, 1979). That is, Asian American children are constantly chided about family obligations, the necessity of bringing respect and honor to the family name, and avoiding any actions that would bring dishonor to the family. Asian Americans are apt to feel guilty when events go astray on them, and they are prone to be afflicted with self-blame.

Chinese Youth Movement. Perhaps, as a reaction to the burden of conforming to American cultural values, and as a result of the impetus of the black movement, some Asian Americans are rejecting the process of assimilation and are espousing the worth of Asian values. These people see conforming to the main American value system as degrading, and they call those that do *bananas*; yellow on the outside and white on the inside. The price one pays for "bananaism" is high in terms of rejecting native cultural values. Wholesale assimilation is too much to ask for any group.

Effects of the movement may change some of the personality characteristics of Asian Americans. The tendency for abasement, guilt, and restrictive behavior may very well lessen in the near future for Asian Americans. However, at this point, it is too early to tell. What we do know is that psychological characteristics of Asian Americans are related to their unique background and their interaction with Western society.

Implications for Working With Asian Americans. Asian Americans students are apt to be quiet, obedient, and unassertive. Teachers should realize that these students may be more comfortable working in structured environments. While it may appear that they are withdrawn and shy, it is important to remember that Asian Americans tend to shun social contact outside of the family and racial group. American teachers tend to reward spontaneity and assertiveness in students. These are characteristics which have been repressed in Asian Americans. To expect them to project these characteristics is to place them in a bind. They should not be judged by Western norms.

Teachers may find that Asian American students are tense, apprehensive, and nontrusting in classroom interactions. Teachers can help by accepting the student as he/she is and building a relationship on trust. Because the tendency is for Asian Americans to deny their feelings, it may be difficult for Western teachers to know students' emotional states. Gentle, trusting interactions with these students may help open the doors to self-exploration.

It should be noted that most Asian Americans are highly motivated to learn and get ahead in school. While teachers may not approve entirely of the reasons for this, nevertheless, they may find working with Asian Americans can be delightful. One of the major tasks of the teacher is to help the Asian American student maintain a balance of his/her cultural heritage and to assimilate whatever parts of the main culture he/she desires.

SUMMARY

Clearly this country can never go back to the principle of uncritical acceptance of assimilation for its immigrants or its indigenous minorities (Larson, 1982). Education has yet to recognize that culturally different is not the same as culturally deficient. There is a moral imperative that we recognize and appreciate the legitimacy of alternative cultures. Equally as important, educators must stop "blaming the victim" for deficiencies and they must begin to help the minority person to come to grips with living with more than one culture.

To help students from minorities it is necessary to understand the process of acculturation a minority member goes through. Atkinson, Morten, and Sue (1979) have suggested that the person goes through five stages before developing a healthy minority identity. At the beginning, the first stage, the person is attracted to the dominant culture. This stage can be called the conformity stage. There are some serious implications for the individual who is in this stage. Often there is an element of self-hatred and hatred directed toward the minority's own race or ethnic group. In the second stage, the individual attempts to reconcile previous self-hate and rejection of the minority culture with an acceptance of self and ethnic or racial identity. Obviously, much confusion is experienced by the person at this stage. The third stage is marked with an outright rejection of the main culture values. In this stage, the individual adopts a minority identity with a deep mistrust of the dominant culture. The fourth stage witnesses a mellowing effect. The individual realizes that the rigidity of wholesale acceptance of one's culture with the wholesale rejection of the dominant culture is not effective. In the last stage, the individual integrates the minority culture with the dominant culture in an idiosyncratic fashion. The individual takes on a world view of events and sees the universality of all people. This stage is responsible for an integrated personality.

Teachers have a tremendous role to play in facilitating the process of positive minority cultural identification. The sensitive teacher is effective because he/she recognizes the tension between minority members and their reference groups, is aware of the stress between dominant and minority groups, and appreciates the ability in individuals to change, and seeks to change the environment when appropriate (Larson, 1982).

SELF-TEST, CHAPTER 10

1. The melting pot theory was

    a. accepted immediately from this country's beginning.
    b. very prevalent after World War II.
    c. popular at the turn of the twentieth century.
    d. never really accepted by most Americans.

2. Discrimination in our history was

    a. evident from our country's beginning.
    b. relatively subdued until the Civil War.
    c. never a serious problem.
    d. evident in certain pockets of the country.

3. The latter immigrants to the United States differs from earlier ones in

    a. religion.
    b. race.
    c. cultural values.
    d. all of the above.

4. Regarding the role of education in "Americanizing" immigrants, experts

    a. agree that the results have been disastrous.
    b. believe that more good than harm has been done.
    c. on balance there was more harm done.
    d. disagree on the value of education's role in the
    process.

5. Regarding the role of education in promoting cultural pluralism

    a. education's role will probably diminish.
    b. it will probably remain the same because of
    federal legislation.
    c. it will probably decrease as society becomes more
    technical.
    d. it will probably increase because of an increase
    sensitivity to the value of pluralism.

6. Teacher's role in promoting cultural pluralism is important because teachers are

   a. agents for transmitting the culture.
   b. supposed to be fair and equal.
   c. required by law to teach about cultural pluralism.
   d. influential to young minds.

7. Formative evaluation is

   a. taken at the very beginning of a project.
   b. useful for answering the question of how good a program is.
   c. helpful as feedback for program modification.
   d. a means for determining cost effectiveness of programs.

8. Native Americans in comparison to other minority groups

   a. have suffered the least from discrimination.
   b. have one of the highest suicide rates.
   c. have made an admirable adjustment to the dominant culture.
   d. assumed most of the white value system.

9. What phrase best describes the Mexican American?

   a. poor, urban, undereducated.
   b. rural, poor, illiterate.
   c. Catholic, rural, undereducated.
   d. undereducated, Catholic, migrant workers.

10. Asian Americans in regard to other minority groups

   a. have felt less discrimination.
   b. have been quieter about their plight in society.
   c. have been slow to accept American values.
   d. have been rejected by society throughout their history in the U.S.

ANSWERS: 1. (c), 2. (b), 3. (d), 4. (d), 5. (d), 6. (a), 7. (c), 8. (b), 9. (a), 10. (b)

11. Discuss the relationship between economic conditions and society's acceptance of immigrants. What evidence do you see today to indicate that this relationship exists in contemporary times?

12. Describe the development through the five stages that a minority group member goes through in reaching a reaching a cultural identity. Describe typical behaviors that a student would exhibit in each of the stages.

ADDITIONAL RESOURCES

Books & Publications

Multicultural Teacher Education: An Annotated Bibliography of Selected Resources. Commission on Multicultural Education, American Association of Colleges for Teacher Education, Washington, DC: 1980.

This source contains hundreds of annotated references on multicultural education. It is an excellent source for books, materials, and organizations.

Films (F) and Filmstrips (FS)

Multicultural Education: A Teaching Style, and Working in the Integrated Classroom. Media Five, 3211 Cahuenga Blvd., West Hollywood, CA 90068 (F)

Understanding Prejudice. Learning Tree Filmstrips, 7108 S. Alton Way, Englewood, CO 80155 (FS)

Prejudice Causes, Consequences, Cures. CRM McGraw-Hill Films, 110 Fifteenth St., Del Mar, CA 92014 (F)

Dream Speaker. Filmmakers Library, Inc., 133 E. 58th St., New York, NY 10022 (F)

Organizations

Clearinghouse on Rural Education and Small Schools, ERIC/CRESS, Box 3AP, New Mexico State University, Las Cruces, NM 88003

American Indian Studies Center, University of California, Campbell Hall, Room 3220, 405 Hilgard Ave., Los Angeles, CA 90024

African-American Institute, 833 United Nations Plaza, New York, NY 10017

Anti-Defamation League of B'nai B'rith, 325 Lexington Ave., New York, NY 10016

Asian Bilingual Curriculum, Development Center, Seton Hall University, 440 South Orange Ave., South Orange, NJ 07070

Chicano Studies Center, University of California at Los Angeles, Los Angeles, CA 90024

Immigration History Research Center, University of Minnesota, 826 Berry St., St. Paul, MN 55114

REFERENCES

APA Education and Training Committee of Division 17. (1980, September). *Cross-cultural counseling competencies, a position paper.* Paper presented at the meeting of the American Psychology Association, Montreal, Canada.

Atkinson, D. R., Morten, G., & Sue, D. W. (1979). *Counseling American minorities: A cross-cultural perspective.* Dubuque, IA: W. C. Brown.

Baptiste, H. D. Jr., Baptiste, M. L., & Gollnick, D. M. (1980). *Multicultural teacher education: Preparing educators to provide educational equity* (Vol. 1). Washington, DC: American Association of Colleges for Teacher Education.

Benavidas, A. H. (1979). Multicultural aspects of human relations. In H. Colangelo, C. Foxley, and D. Dustin (Eds.) *Multicultural nonsexist education: A human relations approach.* Dubuque, IA: Kendall/Hunt.

Casas, J. M., & Atkinson, D. R. (1981). The Mexican-American in higher education: An example of subtle stereotyping. *Personnel and Guidance Journal, 59,* 473-476.

Dawson, M. E. (1977). From compensatory to multicultural education. *Journal of Research and Development, 11,* 84-101.

Glazer, N. (1981). Ethnicity and education: Some hard questions. *Phi Delta Kappan, 62,* 386-389.

Grant, C. A. (1977). The teacher and multicultural education: Some personal reflections. In M. Gold, C. Grout, & S. Rivlin (Eds.) *In praise of diversity, a resource book for multicultural education.* Washington, DC: Association for Teacher Education.

Gutierrez, F. S. (1982). Working with minority counselor education students. *Counselor Education and Supervision, 21,* 218-226.

Hunter, W. A. (Ed.). (1974). *Multicultural education through competency based teacher education.* Washington, DC: American Association for Teacher Education.

Larson, P. C. (1982). Counseling special populations. *Professional Psychology, 13,* 843-858.

Lazarus, P. J. (1983). Counseling the native American child: A question of values. *Elementary School Guidance and Counseling, 17,* 83-88.

Muhs, W. F., Popp, G. E., & Patterson, H. F. (1979). The Mexican-American in higher education: Implication for education, *Personnel and Guidance Journal, 58,* 20-24.

Multicultural teacher education: Guidelines for implementation (Vol. I-IV). (1980). Washington, DC: American Association of Colleges for Teacher Education.

Padilla, A. M., & Ruiz, R. A. (1973). *Latino mental health: A review of literature.* Washington, DC: National Institute of Mental Health, U.S. Government Printing Office.

Paradis, F. E. (1981). Themes in training of culturally effective psychotherapists. *Counselor Education and Supervision, 21,* 136-152.

Pedigo, J. (1983). Finding the "meaning" of Native American substance abuse: Implications for community prevention. *Personnel and Guidance Journal, 62,* 273-277.

Peralosa, F. (1967). The changing Mexican-American in southern California. *Sociology and Social Research, 51,* 405-417.

Ramirez, M. (1967). Identification with Mexican family values and authoritarianism in Mexican-Americans. *Journal of Social Psychology, 73,* 3-11.

Ramirez, M., & Castaneda, A. (1974). *Cultural democracy, bicogenetive development, and education.* New York: Academic Press.

Redhorse, J. G. (1980). Family structure and value orientation in American Indians. *Social Casework, 61,* 462-467.

Rhoades, E. R., Marshall, M., Altneale, C., Echo Hawk, M., Bjorck, J., & Beiser, M. (1980). Mental health problems in American Indians seen in outpatient facilities of the Indian Health Service. *Public Health Reports, 95,* 329-335.

Ruiz, R. A., & Padilla, A. M. (1977). Counseling Latinos. *Personnel and Guidance Journal, 55,* 401-408.

Ruiz, R.A., & Padilla, A.M. (1979). Counseling Latinos. In D. Atkinson, G. Morten, & D. Sue (Eds.) *Counseling American minorities: A cross-cultural perspective. Dubuque, IA: Wm. C. Brown.*

Stadler, H. A., & Rynearson, D. (1981). Understanding clients and their environments: A simulation. *Counselor Education and Supervision, 21,* 153-162.

Sue, D. W. (1979). Ethnic identity: The impact of two cultures on the psychological development of Asians in America. In D. Atkinson, G. Morton, & D. Sue *Counseling American minorities: A cross-cultural perspective.* Dubuque, IA: Wm. C. Brown.

Sue, D. W., & Kirk, B. A. (1972). Psychological characteristics of Chinese-American students. *Journal of Counseling Psychology, 19,* 471-478.

Sue, D. W., & Kitano, H. L. (1979). Stereotypes as a measure of success. In D. Atkinson, G. Morton, & D. Sue, *Counseling American minorities: A cross-cultural perspective.* Dubuque, IA: Wm. C. Brown.

Valverde, L. A. (1978). Strategies for the advancement of cultural pluralism. *Phi Delta Kappan, 59.*

Zangwill, I. (1914). *The melting pot: A drama in four acts.* New York: Macmillan.

Zintz, M. V. (1963). *Education across cultures.* Dubuque, IA: William C. Brown.

Chapter 11

NONSEXIST EDUCATION

The major purpose of this chapter is to present information about sex bias in America and in U.S. public education, effects it has on men and women, possible school roles in the problem, and some concerns with certain actions that are recommended as strategies for remediation of sex bias.

EXPECTED OUTCOMES

By reading the chapter, the reader will be able to

1. discuss legal and educational bases for nonsexist education;

2. formulate a position regarding nonsexist education, including some precautions;

3. become aware of the covert and overt influences that methods, materials, and textbooks have on sex-role behavior; and

4. list at least seven activities that teachers can do to help overcome sexism in education.

accurately the fuller roles of women in contemporary America. The process of education should not portray women as subordinate, submissive, nor less important than men. While few educators would overly support such a negative role for women, education and teaching personnel have provided a somewhat subliminal message about female roles that is not very positive. The net effect on students over decades of schooling may be very profound, especially on women.

LEGAL BASIS FOR NONSEXIST EDUCATION

In 1972 the Federal government passed Public Law 92-318 more commonly known as Title IX. This was one of several educational amendments of 1972. Title IX became effective in 1975. Many people mistakenly believed that Title IX only applies to female participation in school sports. This arena of education has caught the public's attention, perhaps because of the media's treatment of several court cases involving women participation in sports activities. However, Title IX applies to all areas of the educational enterprise.

Essentially Title IX states that any educational program or activity which receives Federal monies must provide equal participation for students without regard to sex. Penalties for not adhering to the regulation may result in loss of Federal financial assistance. Some institutions, activities, and groups are excluded from the act. Beauty pageants, fraternities, sororities, YMCA, YWCA, Boy Scouts, Girl Scouts, Boys State, and so forth are not included under the provisions of Title IX. Private religious schools where compliance would be in conflict with their religious beliefs are also excluded. However, the American public school system, almost all of which receives some form of Federal assistance, must comply with regulations. The Project on Equal Education Rights (PEER) has provided a synopsis of Title IX provisions. Some of the summary follows to demonstrate the inclusive nature of Title IX.

Admissions

This regulation bars sex discrimination in admission (except to private, undergraduate institutions) to educational programs. Thus, women cannot be prohibited from admission because of marital status, pregnancy or related conditions, nor other criteria that are sex-related. Questions on marital status and sex that appear on application forms may be discriminatory if this information is used for selection procedures. The act encourages recipients of Federal assistance to recruit

At the end of the chapter, you will find a self-test and practice activities. Those materials can help you assess how much you have learned from the chapter, and they can help you apply the content of the chapter in a meaningful way.

THE CHALLENGE OF NONSEXIST EDUCATION

The challenge of nonsexist education rests on at least two points. Title IX provided a legal basis for this challenge. This Federal act makes it illegal for schools to engage in certain activities. The other point is from a professional stance. The major professional organization of teachers, National Education Association (NEA), passed a resolution supporting education free from sex bias and encouraging the elimination of sexism in schools. Other bases for nonsexist education come from a more philosophical stance. However, this stance is grounded in a particular view that holds certain values about the roles of men and women in American society. Basically, this position espouses the view that all people should become all that they are capable of becoming and any institution, law, or agency that thwarts fulfillment of this concept should be changed.

Often nonsexist education is associated with the feminist movement and positions and policies that feminists have taken. While the women's movement has been an enormous force in nonsexist education, equating nonsexist education with feminism is a mistake. The position authors of this book endorse is that males as well as females have been compromised to some degree by the educational system and the elimination of sexist education would have direct benefits to males as well as females.

Frequently, when controversial issues are discussed, certain terms become so value-laden that they cloud the real issue. In some cases, the mere mention of the term raises red flags. Nonsexist education may well be one of those issues. To speak of nonsexist education is not to address the issues of the women movement. The two must be separated completely. Recognizing that in some respects the women movement and nonsexist education may have many final goals that are similar does not necessarily mean nor imply support for the feminist position. Nonsexist education is a more narrowly defined concept referring to simply providing education to all students equally without regard to sex. Nonsexist education does not mean providing special emphasis on female roles, rather it means only to provide a more positive portrayal reflecting more members of each sex equally except in cases where past sex discrimination requires special efforts to recruit one sex over another.

Interactions With Students

While institutions may provide separate housing facilities based on sex, they must be comparable in number, quality, and cost to the student. Courses must be made available to both sexes equally (with the exception of sex education, some bodily contact sports, and choruses), and no person can be denied access to a course. Traditionally sex-segregated courses (vocational education, home economics, and typing) cannot now be organized by sex. Thus, if a female wants to take a course in electrical wiring, she has every right to do so.

An institution must provide athletic scholarships to each sex proportional to the enrollment in that school. Other scholarships and forms of financial aid may not discriminate on the basis of sex. Exceptions are single-sex scholarships provided by a will or trust. Similarly, an institution must provide equal athletic opportunity for both sexes. Guidelines for deciding whether athletic programs comply with Title IX regulations is that the sports program offered by the institution must adequately provide for the interests and abilities of both sexes. Included in these criteria is whether facilities and equipment are adequate for both sexes. The terms defining adequate are vague, thus violations under this category are probably numerous. One obvious result of Title IX has been the noticeable increase of women in secondary and post-secondary sports programs. No longer are girls relegated to cheerleading and pep squads. If they desire, females can participate in sports. The stigma attached to women in sports is slowly diminishing. A more healthy view is prevalent in society regarding women participating in sports.

The encouraging aspect of this phenomenon is that it condones females being active, taking the initiative, and being competitive. These characteristics were not encouraged in females as recently as a few decades ago. For youth recreational programs to have little league baseball for girls is not uncommon today. The trend of female participation in physical activities probably will continue. This is bound to have an effect on women in the future.

One regulation of Title IX that has changed customs in secondary schools is treatment of pregnant students. Previous to the 1960s, a pregnant student was more than likely encouraged to drop out of school. If she did not withdraw of her own will, steps were usually taken by the administration to remove her from school.

Currently, a school may not discriminate against any student in classes or extracurricular activity because of a student's actual or potential parental, family, or marital status. A student who is pregnant may choose an alternative instructional program. However, the alternative program must be comparable to the regular program.

One of the most controversial aspects of Title IX is the regulation regarding employment. This provision prohibits sexual discrimination in employment, recruiting, and hiring. Many women have challenged education institutions on their methods of awarding pay, promotion, and tenure decisions. In some cases, courts have awarded large sums of money to women who have been discriminated against in these areas. Administrators have to be accountable for their employing, terminating, and promotion policies. To terminate a women from her work simply because she is not the major wage earner in her family is no longer acceptable.

PROFESSIONAL BASIS FOR SEX-FREE EDUCATION

The National Education Association has been active in the campaign to provide nonsexist education to American students. The organization became so concerned about the program that it adopted a resolution and created a task force to investigate the dimensions of this concern.

The following resolution (NEA Resolution 78-55: Sexism in Education) has been adopted.

> The National Education Association believes that educational materials and processes should accurately portray the contribution of women both in the past and the present and that women must be involved in the selection of these materials and in preparing teachers for their use.

> The Association recognizes that many instructional materials portray women and men in sex-stereotyped roles. It urges educators to use those instructional materials that portray various careers and personal roles as acceptable and attainable for all individuals.

> The Association endorses the use of nonsexist language by all schools. It further believes that sexism and sex discrimination must be eliminated from the curriculum. (Martin, 1978, p. 61)

The position that NEA has taken leaves no doubt about the importance of nonsexist education in America. Clearly stated is the desired end that curriculum and teaching should be free of sex discrimination. This is the first step in a long process of making schools in America nonsexist. Title IX and professional endorsements of nonsexist education have produced remarkable changes in the last decade.

However, these changes have been made in the obvious and sometimes blatant examples of discrimination. The next phase is, perhaps, the most difficult one, that is, integrating a nonsexist conceptualization into the complete fabric of the educational enterprise so that it becomes a natural function. So often changes are made because people comply with the law. An obvious example is in the area of civil rights. Not until nonsexist education becomes a routine and acceptable concept will its goals be accomplished.

The manifestations of sexist education are both obvious and subtle. Anyone can recognize the damage done when a teacher tells a female student that she should become a nurse but not a physician because she is a girl. However, thousands of messages are sent that are not so obvious. For example how many girls run the audio-visual equipment in schools? Who does the heavy lifting in schools? Implications of these messages may not be in the awareness level of some teachers. Yet, these subtle messages played out thousands of times in front of boys and girls make an impact. Multiply this impact by what is seen and heard in the media over years, and what results is a very important and profound set of role expectancies for both men and women.

RECENT CHANGES IN
FAMILY PATTERNS AND ROLES

During the past two decades American society has witnessed a tremendous change in family patterns and roles. Most of these changes are focused on the roles women assume in society. Several factors contribute to these changes. Some factors serve as background and others are more central to the issue. This section of the chapter presents a brief resume of the forces that have contributed to the remarkable changes in contemporary American society.

World War II is one of the background forces that played an important, yet indirect role in changing family patterns in the U.S. Because of the demands that the war made on American industry, women were "drafted" into the production line. "Rosey the riveter" left her apron at home and picked up the tools of industry. Byproducts of her involvement in the world of work are still being felt today. She achieved a sense of financial independence, accomplishment, and identity rooted in an occupation. After the war a brief respite occurred. The American woman reestablished herself on the domestic scene, produced the baby boom, and moved into suburbia. However, she was changed profoundly by the experiences gained during her involvement in the world of work. However, a job was still thought of as being in addition to a homemaker and wife. In a sense, if a woman wanted a career she had to pursue it along with her role as wife and mother.

Another background factor was the women movement. Despite the controversial nature of this phenomenon, no doubt exists that the awareness level of the issues has been raised, and changes have occurred. The differences rest on the amount of change. The conservative movement of the 1980s threatens to stem the tide of change for women. However, little likelihood exists that positions will revert. In reality changes in roles will be slower, more pervasive, and more profound. The conservative movement may be less responsible for the slackened pace than the fact that the issues left are very difficult to resolve and that a period of adjustment and accommodation needs to take place.

More direct influences on changing patterns for women have been their increased longevity, having fewer children, and entry into the occupation work force after the birth of their children (Hoffman, 1977). The most noticeable feature of these influences is that they are interrelated. By artificially separating them for discussion, the global view may be lost. These influences were happening simultaneously and they continually interacted, and the confluence of these three acting together may have more impact than each acting separately.

Family Size

Women in American society are having fewer children. The number of children per family has been decreasing since the peak baby boom of the early 1950s. Today the average family unit has less than two children. For the first time in 50 years the birth rate has dropped below the low rate occurring during the great depression.

Not only are women choosing to have fewer babies, they are putting off having them until later in life. Coupled with this is the fact that the average age that men and women marry has been increasing steadily for the past two decades. Hence, women would have had considerable work experience before they have their first baby.

The extended period of time between marriage and the first child provides an opportunity for husband and wife to establish roles based more on companionship and common value sharing than on domestically defined roles. The possibility is increased greatly that each is treated equally in the marriage relationship when there are no children. The logistics of rearing children sometimes forces inequality. Even when children do arrive on the scene the husband today is more apt to participate in childrearing, and he will probably be more willing to take on some of the household chores.

The arrival of the first child does not necessarily mean that the wife ends her career. More women than ever are returning to work after giving birth to their children. Currently, more than 50% of married women who have children work. At least two reasons exist for this. Women want to continue with their careers at the same time as they are rearing children. In some cases this poses a dilemma for them. They are constantly struggling over how to satisfy the demands that each requires. Another reason is more purely stated as financial. Couples are committed to living on two incomes. The rising expense of home ownership and the seemingly unending inflation of the late 1970s and the early 1980s make single-income families almost an extinct breed. Couples have material expectations that necessitate a considerable outlay of money. In order to meet these demands, wives work. Though she may have worked in past decades, the difference now is that in many respects she *must* work. She no longer works for pocket money or to buy a specific additional item. Her income is seen as an essential part of the family budget.

As stated earlier, husbands, perhaps reluctantly, are sharing in childrearing responsibilities differently from that in the past by entering into the process more directly. Whereas before the father was seen as the provider and disciplinarian, today he is more concerned with the everyday activities of childrearing. This is not to suggest that he participates equally in the task, rather he takes on a greater share than he did previously. Roles, emotions, and values attached to them are changing. Some critics say they are changing too fast while others claim too slow. Those that say that roles have not kept pace with reality claim a cultural lag always exists between what society values in activities and what it does in reality. This point of view claims that women are penalized by restricting their roles and worth and that a discrepancy exists between what is said to be valued and behavior toward women.

Longevity

One of the most remarkable features of the twentieth century is the increased life span of people. The average life span is nearly doubled from what it was a hundred years ago. A woman born in the 1960s can expect to live for nearly 80 years. This fact combined with her shorter period of child-bearing years has produced an interesting dynamic. Where once women spent most of their adult years caring for and producing children, today a relatively short time is spent on these activities. Most women choose to limit their child-bearing years to about a decade. This means that more of her years can be devoted to other activities. In many instances, women choose to spend their time on career objectives.

Even when women are having babies, they may not opt to be the main caretakers. Child care centers and nursery schools have mushroomed in recent decades. This has enabled women to return to the workplace within a short period of time after childbirth.

Thus, women today can look forward to a longer involvement in career activities. By delaying the birth of their first child and by restricting births to about a decade, women, having experienced occupational rewards early in their lives, are increasingly finding their identity in work.

However, this process is not without its consequences. Traditional role expectations for women and career opportunities pose a dilemma. Competition also produces what has been called fear of success in women.

> Whereas men supposedly suffer from fear of failure in fulfilling their achievement needs, the hypothesis that women, particularly those of high ability, fear success because it conflicts with the traditional role and it introduces the risk of affiliation loss. In other words, if a woman is successful in the world of work, it may appreciably reduce her chances of being married. The subjective logic runs as follows: What man would want a woman who directly competes with him for the same (or even similar) accouterments of success? (Fitzgerald & Crites, 1980, p. 56)

Thus in many cases women often aspire to career choices that are below their capabilities and interests. This feature can be directly attributed to the socialization process in our culture.

Summary

The foregoing material presented the case that employment of women has increased dramatically while mothering functions have decreased over time. However, cultural patterns regarding sex-role behavior and expectancies do not yet reflect actual changes. Differences still exist between the sexes that are more cultural than biological. Family patterns have changed some. These changes can be expected to increase in the future especially as the cultural lag decreases. It is interesting to speculate what kinds of changes in sex roles will be forthcoming. Women may begin to assume behaviors more commonly labelled masculine (competitiveness, aggressiveness). Along with these behaviors, the American woman also is experiencing an increase in a number of health problems traditionally thought of as male. Some of these are alcoholism, heart diseases, and ulcers. The final results are not yet clear. However, the teacher's role in inculcating sex-role expectations can be influential.

SEXISM IN SCHOOLS

Schools have had a major role in maintaining traditional sex-role stereotypes. In this regard schools reflect values and norms of the general society. As major socializing agents, schools have accomplished some remarkable achievements in the past. Schools have educated people to a very high degree even though students come from diverse backgrounds.

However, charges have been leveled against schools for their role in perpetuating and in some cases encouraging sex-role stereotypes (Levy & Stacey, 1979; Marlowe, 1981; Sadker, 1975). Marlowe has documented evidence which indicated that school personnel act differently toward males and females and have been doing this for over 70 years. A discussion follows that will show how schools are sexist in the way they are organized, how teachers value students, the nature of sexism in textbooks used, and the impact schooling has had on boys and girls.

SCHOOLS AS AGENTS
FOR INSTITUTIONAL SEXISM

Sex-role stereotyping has an impact on both boys and girls. Often when discussing the effects of sex stereotyping, females and their concerns are highlighted. It would be an oversight if only females were discussed in relation to the effects of sex stereotyping. Behavior toward boys also limits their emotional development. In many respects the inexpressive male syndrome results from cultural practices and norms. Boys are encouraged to be "little soldiers" and not to cry when hurt. They are often admonished to act "like a man." Free expressions of feeling are not rewarded in males. Hence, that males generally are restricted in their emotional repertoire is no wonder. Communication problems between adult males and females often center on the different importance each sex places on the affective dimension of events. Women often report that males who are significant in their lives do not attend to feelings as much as they would like. This emotional stunting of males, in many respects, results from sex stereotyping.

ELEMENTARY SCHOOL ENVIRONMENT

In a large measure the elementary school environment is overwhelmingly feminine. This feature is not lost on boys. An elementary school age boy is apt to have all female teachers because 84% of elementary school teachers are female (Marlowe, 1981). Thus the norm for acceptable behavior in school is slanted toward "feminine" activities. Students are rewarded for being quiet, obedient, and respectful. Activities generally are slow-moving, involving small amounts of motor activity. All this puts boys at a disadvantage. These activities place the young boy in jeopardy because at home he is socialized to be active, outgoing, and aggressive.

Teachers, on the other hand, praise boys more, listen to, and teach boys more actively. Girls are rewarded for being docile, neat, and silent. Active participation, competitiveness, and independence are not seen by teachers as appropriate behaviors for girls. Thus while school environments may be feminine, boys are encouraged to break out of the mold while girls are encouraged to remain in the prescribed pattern of nonassertive behavior. Intellectual growth is enhanced by competitive, assertive, dominant, and independent behaviors. Eleanor Maccoby, a prominent child development specialist, claimed that these behaviors promote intellectual growth, while shy and dependent behaviors contribute to a decrease in intellectual growth. What may be happening is although the elementary school is overwhelming female, it still encourages boys to develop independence while girls are reinforced for passivity and dependence.

Boys do not escape easily from some of the consequences of being placed in the feminine elementary school environment. A majority of learning disabled students are boys. More boys have reading and behavioral problems than girls. While claiming that schools cause these problems would be extremely difficult, a certain relationship between the two does exist.

The school environment is constantly sending messages to students about sex roles. While most of the teachers are females, only 20% of the elementary schools have female principals. The situation in high school is not much better. Byrne, Hines, and McCleary (1978) have indicated that only 7% of secondary principals are females. This situation is not lost on students; men run the show. Decision making is a male activity as are leadership abilities. For women to be teachers is permissible, but to aspire to higher administrative levels is not particularly condoned.

Levy and Stacey (1979), perhaps in a somewhat strident manner, made a case for non-sexist education.

> Whether schools "make a difference" in dramatically changing the life chances of the poor, of minority groups, or of women, schools "do make a difference" in that they remain effective agents of social control, perpetuating the existing class, racial, and sexual divisions in our society. In documenting the ways in which schools maintain existing sex distinctions, we must remember the conflict between liberal ideology ("schools should treat all children alike") and the more conservative reality that schools in fact prepare youngsters for social stratification. (p. 210)

Because the awareness level has been raised about sex equality and certain legislation prohibits sex bias in school, to think that sexism does not exist in schools would be imprudent. Sex bias may now take a more subtle form. For example, Levy and Stacey (1979) and Wirtenberg, Klein Richardson, and Thomas (1981) commented on a popular reading series, *Alpha One*. Letters are assigned male and female characteristics. The 21 consonants are called boys and the five vowels are girls. However, each of the vowels has something wrong with it. Some material from *Alpha One* which illustrates the impact of subtle messages follows:

> Little Miss A (appearing before the boys). "Oh, no. It can't be true. Not Little Miss A sneezes 'ach-choo' all day.
>
> A girl, A girl. Oh go away: A girl's no good for work or play."

Little Miss A is characterized as so weak that she is hardly able to move or walk, thus the implications are clear. Boys are strong and valuable, girls are weak and need help. Research has indicated that where this material is used with children on a systematic basis, the exposed students had more stereotyped attitudes (Jenkins, 1977).

SEX STEREOTYPING IN TEXTBOOKS

Sex stereotyping in textbooks is evident in a number of ways; some are quite blatant while others are more subtle. Women and minority groups have not been well represented in typical curriculum materials. Examples of the material in *Alpha One* have been presented previously. The following discussion illustrates the manner in which sex stereotyping exists in texts. At one time textbook publishers printed special editions of textbooks for certain parts of the country. Previous to current equity laws racism, sexism, and propagandism were widespread in our history textbooks (Mitsakos, 1981).

Unequal Representation and
Stereotyped Portrayals

Repeated studies indicate that males are over-represented in stories appearing in readers. The ratios vary from males appearing 2 to 3 times more frequently than females depending on the types of stories included in the reader. Boys are portrayed as active, outgoing, taking the initiative, and able to solve problems while girls are characterized as dependent and in need of help. Sadker (1975) reproduced a line from a well-known reading series that illustrates the impact of sex typing in texts. "We are willing to share our great thoughts with mankind. However, you happen to be a girl" (p. 320). The message in this one line is so powerful that little more can be said. By repeating this type interaction with materials over a lifetime of schooling, the effect is dramatic.

> In short, although things are changing, especially in the area of children's literature, a female student desiring to read about another female who is intelligent, creative, powerful, interesting, or charismatic will have to wade through many books before meeting one. And it is hard to estimate the impact of this pervasive lack of inspiring models in school reading. (Sadker, 1975, p. 320)

Each textbook publisher has guidelines about avoiding sexist and racist material. The guidelines are often eloquent position statements. However, Britton and Lumpkin (1979) have documented a case that things have changed very little.

After the printed expressions of concern, publishers could have made a substantial attempt to eliminate the inequities—however, the evidence is to the contrary. Changes have been minimal; the "new" product appears to be teaching the same "hidden curriculum" as the preceding series. The great disparity remains between male/female representation as major characters in textbook series. (p. 294)

Teacher Education Texts

Textbooks used for teacher-training courses have not been exempt from scrutiny. They have come under criticisms as have those for public schools. Sadker, Sadker, and Hicks (1980) conducted a study of major textbooks used in teacher education courses. Their findings confirmed that bias exists in those texts as well. Over 95% of 24 textbooks dedicated less than 1% of page space to the topic of sexism.

As a result of omissions, inaccuracies, and imbalance, future teachers are given a lopsided introduction to the profession, a minimal view of sex equity as a contemporary issue, and no direction in how to counteract sexism in the classroom and the school. (Sadker et al., 1980, p. 55)

Professional education texts should take a leadership role in producing accurate and adequate information on sexism. To the extent that they do not, future teachers will have to provide their own resources to combat sexism. Past discriminations need to be addressed on a profession-wide basis, not left up to individual classroom teachers. To accept the current 1% solution is to ignore the issue.

POSSIBLE EFFECTS OF SEXIST EDUCATION

While attributing causal effects of sexist education is extremely difficult, a number of significant indices are suggested that schooling has profound differential effects on boys and girls. Some of these effects are listed.

- Girls are more prepared for schooling at entry level. They are more verbal, physically mature, and socially mature. However, by the time they reach secondary schools, the differences disappear and boys begin to achieve more.

- Boys feel positive about their maleness while girls are more ambivalent about their sex. Boys become more confident, more independent, and more self-reliant as they progress through school. Girls worry about acceptance and popularity.

- Girls are limited in their choices of possible occupations. Those that they choose are more often traditional (nurse, teacher, secretary, mother). Boys are able to identify more possible career choices.

- At late adolescence and onward girls begin to take on behaviors that typify the fear of success syndrome.

- Though women make better high school grades than boys, they feel less competent than boys.

- Significantly more high-achieving women than men *do not* enter college at all.

- More often than not girls underestimate their abilities while boys are apt to overestimate theirs.

The elimination of sex-role stereotyping is an attempt to improve upon the lives of 51% of our population. However, this will have benefits for both sexes. What this means is that boys and girls can share equally in the quest of full participation in the major activities of living: citizenry, working, and parenting. It may mean a new way of behaving for both sexes. To expect less is to achieve less. Schools need to eliminate the debilitating effects of myths about men, women, and families that in reality do not exist.

In the next section of this chapter materials and information are presented about how to combat sexism in the schools. No single method will always work and suggestions are not meant to be all inclusive—it is a beginning.

REDUCING SEXISM IN THE SCHOOLS

Overt sexism is illegal, however, to claim that the problem no longer exists is a naive position. Subtle forms of sexism remain in our schools.

Wirtenberg, Klein, Richardson, and Thomas (1981) listed eight strategies to help combat sexism in school and promote equity.

1. Secure help from members of groups concerned with sex equity and other colleagues who are sensitive to these issues.

2. Pay attention to potential bias in educational processes as well as outcomes.

3. Look for new and useful indicators of sex equity.

4. Insist that research and evaluation reports contain analyses by sex, by race or ethnicity, and by sex and race.

5. Remember to identify disparities even when the causal relationships are not clear and then try to examine the causes.

6. Look for instances of small but cumulative sex inequity.

7. Don't neglect the identification of sex differences just because they appear "normal" or natural and don't ignore behavior that fails to conform to stereotypes because it appears too unusual or "deviant."

8. Remember that subtle sex bias is more likely to be covered by the intent of the civil rights than by the explicit provisions of the regulations which accompany these laws (Wirtenberg et al., 1981, p. 310).

Sex equity can be promoted and sexism eliminated in a number of ways:

1. Promoting equitable treatment in traditionally sex-stereotyped courses,

2. Eliminating sex stereotyping in textbooks and instructional materials,

3. Eliminating bias in classroom interactions, and

4. Using nonsexist language in teaching (Wirtenberg et al, 1981, pp. 311-318).

5. Noting participation of males and females in courses and extracurricular activities and suggesting changes where there are imbalances.

6. Examining unequal treatment of boys and girls in punishments, rewards, and classroom assignments. Do only boys run the A-V equipment? Are girls assigned room cleaning duties?

7. Encouraging role models to help school children set nonsexist expectancies. For example are there male secretaries, female police officers and firefighters, female executives, etc.

8. Making a personal commitment to become involved in education equity (Martin, 1978).

Workshops provide valuable ways of developing awareness and knowledge of sex inequality. Using inservice education as a vehicle, workshops can help promote an awareness and commitment to the issue. Because of the sensitive nature of the topic, the workshop should be conducted from a professional point of view. Strident and obstreperous positions should not be a part of the program. Information can be presented in a factual way, leaving teachers to draw their own conclusions.

Olsen and Naughton (1979) have described elements of a workshop on combating sexism in schools. Their format consisted of several parts that mixed information sharing components with experiential activities. The format included:

1. activities to sensitize and bring into the open the issues in sexism;

2. presentation of models who were employed in nontraditional work, these individuals served as a panel;

3. films appropriate to the issue;

4. employing play-reader groups;

5. discussion of sex stereotyping;

6. presentation of statistical information about women's positions in occupations;

7. utilization and coordination of the school system's current resources;

8. self-evaluation of the existing practices that reflect sexism;

9. presentations by guest speakers; and

10. distribution of guidelines and resources on written and audiovisual material on sexism (p. 331).

Workshops can be an effective means for combating sexism in schools. Work, Wheeler, and Williams (1982) reported results from their workshops on nontraditional careers. The purpose of the workshops was to provide realistic and up-to-date information about nontraditional careers for women. The target audiences were teachers, counselors, and administrators. Presenters found that after being exposed to the workshop, teachers, counselors, and administrators provided more and better information to their students about a large number of careers. Especially noteworthy was the fact that nontraditional careers for women for example, engineering, and business, were being promoted.

SOME CAUTIONS ABOUT THE ISSUE

Criticisms about nonsexist education have been raised. Some criticisms rest on religious grounds while some others rely on reactionary positions. These positions will not be addressed. However, there have been a number of comments made that are based on psychological and developmental premises. These are more pertinent to educators and need to be discussed.

The central issue seems to be whether children should be exposed to gender related behavior in order to facilitate a secure identity in themselves. Some take the position that children should have clearly defined sex roles in order to facilitate a mature sense of identity (German, 1982). This position takes the stance that in order for individuals to explore nontraditional occupational careers they must first have a stable identity established in the childhood years. The best method of providing an established identity is to expose the individual to clearly defined behaviors based on sex differences, that is, to accept traditional ways of calculating gender identification. Only when this is firmly established should individuals be exposed to nontraditional roles. When this happens women will be able to explore and initiate a variety of roles available to them.

According to this view, when identity is not firmly established early in life, cognitive dissonance may occur when individuals are encouraged to explore nontraditional behavior. These people may feel confused about themselves, become unsure of what directions they should pursue, and be threatened by materials that encourage exploration into alternative behaviors.

Some problems occur with the bipolar approach to gender-role behavior. Bem (1977) maintained that rigid adherence to strict division of behavior by gender is in many respects dysfunctional. Research reports have indicated children who display exaggerated behavior that characterized their sex have lower IQ scores, poorer spatial ability, and less creativity than children with cross-sex behavior (Marlowe, 1981). Outcomes of basing appropriate behavior on male-female dichotomies are that in children certain behaviors have to be repressed and that the full range of behaviors are not open to 50% of the population.

The issue is also raised as to whether behavior appropriateness should be based on gender. This would presume that some behaviors are "healthy for one sex and less adaptive for the other. Rather, it is more probable that a trait or behavior is either healthy or unhealthy for a particular individual regardless of sex" (Marlowe, 1981, p. 212).

A resolution for this dilemma perhaps is to recognize that over adherence to sex role behavior is as unhealthy as inadequate sex identification. That is, the overly "feminine" girl and the overly "masculine" boy need as much help as the overly "feminine" boy and the overly "masculine" girl. Our schools and our society should allow the full range of behavior in individuals regardless of gender. Securing a gender identification is a major developmental task of the early school years.

SELF-TEST, CHAPTER 11

1. More academically bright girls than academically bright boys go on to college (True or False).

2. Nonsexist education is an education issue; there is no legal basis for this concept (True or False).

3. Adherence to extreme sex role behavior helps young children develop a sex identity (True or False).

4. Workshops on sexist education have been effective in changing attitudes and behaviors (True or False).

5. The view of this chapter is that human behavior should not be based on gender classifications (True or False).

ANSWERS: 1. (F), 2. (F), 3. (T), 4. (T), 5. (T)

Activity 11.1 Discuss the Elementary School Environment

Discuss the elementary school environment in terms of

    a. masculine or feminine milieu,
    b. textbook and materials related to sexism, and
    c. personnel related to sex composition.

Activity 11.2 Defend Exposing Young Children to Different Behaviors

Defend the view that very young children (less than seven years old) should be exposed to a variety of behaviors regardless of the gender label attached to them.

Activity 11.3 Develop a Workshop Outline on Sexism

Develop an outline for a workshop on sexism in the schools. The workshop is schedule for three hours and the audience consists of teachers.

11.4 Construct Lists of Feminine and Masculine Characteristics

Construct a list of adjectives describing feminine characteristics and one describing masculine characteristics.

Activity 11.5 Draw Conclusions from Comparing Lists of Feminine and Masculine Characteristics

Discuss the results of your lists compiled in Number 9 by comparing them. What conclusions can you draw?

Activity 11.6 Make a List of Sexist Words

Make a list that includes sexist words. For example—fireman, yeoman, chorus girl, and so on.

Activity 11.7 Examine a Reading Series for Elementary School

Examine a reading series for elementary schools. Evaluate the series on the following criteria:

a. Are males and females represented equally?
b. What roles do males have? Do females have?
c. In stories involving males and females which sex was the main character?
d. Were any sexist remarks made in the stories? (e.g., "This is not boys' work.")
e. Which sex was the main problem solver?

ADDITIONAL RESOURCES

Books and Publications

Adell, J., & Klein, H. D. (1976). *A guide to non-sexist children's books.* Chicago: Academy Press Limited.

Colangelo, N., Foxley, C. H., & Dustin, D. (1979). *Multicultural nonsexist education: A human relation approach.* Dubuque, IA: Kendall/Hunt.

German, S. C. (1982). Female role awareness programs and materials for adolescents: Is there cause for concern? *The School Counselor, 29,* 370-5.

Guttentag, M., & Bray, H. (1976). *Undoing sex stereotypes: Research and resources for educators.* New York: McGraw-Hill.

Marlowe, M. (1981). Boyhood sex-role development: Implications for counseling and school practices. *Personnel and Guidance Journal, 60,* 210-5.

Martin, L. A. (1978). How to reduce sex-role stereotyping. *Today's Education, 67,* 59-61.

Personnel and Guidance Journal (1981). Special issue on counseling males, *60,* 198-270.

Sadker, M. D., Sadker, D. M., Hicks, T. (1980). The one-percent solution? Sexism in teacher education. *Phi Delta Kappan, 63,* 550-3.

Films (F) and Filmstrips (FS)

How Many Eves? Walter Klein Company, Ltd., P. O. Box 220766, 6301 Carmel Road, Charlotte, NC 28222. (F)

Challenging Careers: New Opportunities for Women (Filmstrip). Guidance Associates, Communication Park, Box 3009, Mt. Kisco, NY 0549 (FS)

We are Women. Motivational Media, Los Angeles, CA. (F)

Title IX: The Regulation That Prohibits Sex Discrimination in Public Education (Slide/Tape). Don Cain, Marketing/Audio Visual Library Service, 3300 University Avenue, S.E., Minneapolis, MN 55414 (FS)

Sexism, Stereotyping and Hidden Values. Media Five Films, 3211 Cahuenga Boulevard, West, Hollywood, CA 90068 (F)

Organizations

Women's Educational Equity Act Program. Resources for Educational Equity 1981-1982 catalog, Education Development Center, Inc., 55 Chapel Street, Newton, MA 02160.

WEECN - Women's Educational Equity Communications Network. Far West Laboratory for Educational Research and Development, 1845 Folsom Street, San Francisco, CA 94103.

Organization for Equal Education of the Sexes, Inc. 744 Carroll Street, Brooklyn, NY 11215.

Project on Equal Education Rights (PEER). 1029 Vermont Avenue, NW, Suite 800, Washington, DC 20005.

Project on the Status and Education of Women. Association of American Colleges, 1818 R Street, NW, Washington, DC 20009.

Resource Center on Sex Roles in Education, The National Foundation of Education, 2101 16th Street, NW, Washington, DC 20036.

Awareness of Sexual Prejudice is the Responsibility of Educators (Project ASPIRE). Education Development Center, 39 Chapel Street, Newton, MA 02160.

REFERENCES

Bem, S. L. (1977). Beyond androgyny: Some presumptuous prescriptions for a liberated sexual identity. In C. G. Garney & S. L. MaMahon (Eds.), *Exploring contemporary male/female roles.* La Jolla, CA: University Associates.

Britton, G. E., & Lumpkin, M. C. (1979). For sale: Subliminal bias in textbooks. In N. Colangelo, D. Dustin, & C. H. Foxley (Eds.) *Multicultural nonsexist education a human relations approach.* Dubuque, IA: Kendall/Hunt Publishing Company, p. 294.

Byrne, D. R., Hines, S. A., & McCleary, L. E. (1978). *The senior high school principal: Vol I: The national survey.* Reston, VA: National Association of Secondary Principals.

Fitzgerald, L. F., & Crites, J. O. (1980). Toward a career psychology of women: What do we know? What do we need to know? *Journal of Counseling Psychology, 27,* 44-62.

German, S. C. (1982). Female role awareness programs and materials for adolescents: Is there cause for concern? *The School Counselor, 29,* 370-375.

Hoffman, L. W. (1977). Changes in family roles, socialization, and sex differences. *American Psychologist, 32,* 644-657.

Jenkins, S. (1977). Sexism in children's books and elementary class management. In A. P. Nilsen (Ed.) *Sexism and language.* Urbana, IL: National Council of Teachers of English.

Levy, B. & Stacey, J. (1979). Sexism in the elementary school: A backward and forward look. In N. Colangelo, D. Dustin, & C. H. Foxley (Eds.) *Multicultural nonsexist education a human relations approach.* Dubuque, IA: Kendall/Hunt, p. 210.

Marlowe, M. (1981). Boyhood sex-role development: Implications for counseling and school practices. *Personnel and Guidance Journal, 60,* 210-215.

Martin, L. A. (1978). How to reduce sex-role stereotyping. *Today's Education, 7,* 59-61.

Mitsakos, C. L. (1981). Textbooks need to change. *Educational Leadership, 38,* 331;350.

NEA Resolution 78-55: Sexism in Education. Washington, DC: National Education Association.

Olsen, D. M. & Naughton, J. (1979). Combating sexism in schools. In N. Colangelo, D. Dustin, & C. H. Foxley (Eds.) *Multicultural nonsexist education a human relations approach.* Dubuque, IA: Kendall/Hunt Publishing Company, 328-337.

Sadker, M. (1975). Sexism in schools. *Journal of Teacher Education, 26,* 317-322.

Sadker, M. D., Sadker, D. M., & Hicks, T. (1980). The one-percent solution! Sexism in teacher education texts. *The Phi Delta Kappen, 63,* 550-553.

Wirtenberg, J., Klein, S., Richardson, B., & Thomas, V. (1981). Sex equity in American education. *Educational Leadership, 38,* 311-319.

Work, C. E., Wheeler, J. H., & Willams, J. V. (1982). Guidance for non-traditional careers. *Personal and Guidance Journal, 60,* 553-556.

Chapter 12

PSYCHOLOGICAL EDUCATION

In this chapter information is presented about the relationship between cognitive, affective, and psychomotor learning. Although cognitive learning is the major focus of formal education, affective dimensions impact markedly on what is learned in school. Teachers realize on one level that cognitive and affective factors of learning are complementary and that an approach which integrates both aspects is most efficient. However, in practice teachers often concentrate only on the cognitive domain.

EXPECTED OUTCOMES

After reading this chapter, the reader will be able to

1. discuss the concepts behind developmental stages of child development;

2. give several implications for teachers drawn from basic principles of child development theory;

3. review roles of competition and cooperation in classrooms; and

4. list several teaching strategies for psychological education concepts.

FOUNDATIONS OF PSYCHOLOGICAL EDUCATION

A stated goal of nearly all educational systems is the positive character development of students. Knowledge is utilized best when tempered with a value base. Most of us may reject the idea that the end can justify the means and accept the idea that one's behaviors should be continually self-examined. In many respects the adage that a little knowledge can be dangerous without a value basis for behavior is appropriate.

This issue becomes confusing very quickly. Many national controversies focus on either the exploitation of knowledge and technology or the integration of knowledge and technology into the human system. Take for example the issue of nuclear energy. The arguments on either side are powerful. Another example is the use of natural resources. Most Americans probably are confused about these topics. This is not surprising. When it comes to common social values, Americans may be in less actual agreement than they espouse.

The situation is similar in schools. Educators claim that human rights, freedom, and dignity are paramount values and need to be developed in schools. However, observations of the typical classroom indicate a small range of behavior is exhibited toward students and that an even smaller range of student behavior is allowed or encouraged. Premiums are paid by teachers for obedient, passive, and controlled behavior. Rarely does the classroom actively promote diversity in thought, rather, acceptance of adult authority is prized. Thus, in many cases, a difference exists between what some educators value as important outcomes and what their actual behaviors portray. This paradox is not limited to typical educators. Sprinthall (1971) criticized Neill, a noted progressive educator, for the same thing.

Similarly, A. S. Neill opposes adult control and direction of children in his school, but then uses the old school tie and loyalty to the Summerhill community as a sanction for controlling behavior. Thus, he espouses freedom and individuality at one moment and then lectures an adolescent couple on the dangers of promiscuity, because such acts may endanger the future of the school . . . The pseudo-liberalism of proclaiming the sanctity of individual development and then appealing to the continuing existence of the school community as a sanction for preventing the adolescent couple from embarrassing that community is strikingly similar to many parents' lectures to their own adolescents. (Sprinthall, 1971, p. 43)

Perhaps the reason for the disparity between professed and actual values is because of assumptions that teachers hold about students. Apparently, most adults and many teachers believe that a "good" child is quiet, conforms in behavior to adult expectations, and unquestionably accepts adult authority. On the other hand, adults may view school as a place where creative thinking should take place. Obviously, the two positions are incompatible, and unless adults in general and educators specifically adopt new organizing concepts about children, disparity will continue to be practiced.

Throughout history adults have viewed child development in a number of ways. Some have had a profound effect on the way adults interact with children. In lay populations, one of the most persistent stances on child development is the homunculus view. This position envisions the growing child as a miniature adult. The child's dress is often adult clothing fitted to a child's body. Cultures that take this view of development rear children with the concept that each generation must be created in the image of the previous generation. Children must be molded, pulled, stretched, and reconstructed in the ways of adult behavior. Implications of this position are obvious. Children are seen as passive beings not able to do anything for themselves. Knowledge about life, values, customs, and behavior must be poured into the developing child. Indeed, the child is mindless and through society's religious, educational, and other social institutions the child is civilized.

Though most professional educators reject the homunculus view of development, parents often operate on its assumptions about children. While educators are aware of different developmental theories of human development, their manner of behavior in the classroom suggests that in practice a large number of teachers act toward children as though they espoused the homunculus view.

A more pleasing view of child development is the naturalistic view. Ideas about children in this position are romantic in the sense that children are seen as gently unfolding organisms. Rousseau, the main proponent of this theory, speculated that adults should get out of the children's way as they develop. The laissez-faire approach assumes that the child will develop his/her potential if left alone.

Obviously, the previous views are not suitable for psychological education. Whether one thinks of children as entering the world in a

tabula rasa condition, thus needing to be molded, or as having all re-
quisites of development innately, thus needing to be left alone, neither
view provides an adequate basis for educators. What is needed is an
organizational concept about children that will blend into an existing
theory of development.

Sprinthall (1971) provided an organizational concept that is suitable
for teachers interested in psychological education. In his position he
described human behavior as being motivated by a drive for competence;
he viewed human development within a developmental framework.

> If the child is not an empty organism, which he/she is not, and if development
> does not unfold automatically, which it does not then we may decide that an im-
> portant educational function may be to guide and nurture that personal growth
> to foster efficacy and mastery. (Sprinthall, 1971, pp. 29-30)

Sprinthall claimed that the human organism strives for competence,
autonomy, and mastery. This potential in individuals suggests that personal development is not fixed nor is it ensured. Thus, if the environment
does not adequately provide necessary conditions for the drive toward
mastery, no assurance is given that it will take place. The assumption
cannot automatically be made that potential will develop in children. In
fact, the individual who has no opportunity to develop his/her mastery
potential may have it stunted.

Education is involved profoundly with the psychological development of students. This development generally focuses on the questions of
values and value development. Whether or not recognized explicitly,
education influences how students develop self-esteem, ego strength, and
personal autonomy (Sprinthall, 1980). To leave this development to
chance invites the potential for inadequate growth in students. The student's drive toward competency can be capitalized on by promoting the
psychological health of students.

In addition to accepting the drive toward competency as motivation
for persons, accepting psychological growth as developmental is important. Developmental growth means that each new stage presents a different manner by which human behavior is organized and exhibited by
the person. Thus, behavior of a three-year-old is qualitatively different
to a given event than behavior of a 12-year-old. For example, obedience
for infants is based on punishment where might makes right. For later
adolescence, obedience may be based on a set of universal principles that
guides one's behavior. A response of a student must be evaluated in the

context of the developmental stage of the student. Educators can aid students by knowing what is typical behavior for each stage as students progress through the stages of development.

Upon birth the child goes from random to behavior control led by words and punishments. As a child develops, right from wrong is learned in terms of negative consequences. Thus, the world is divided into two camps, good and bad. Rules are rigid, unchanging principles devised by adults. Later on, at the age of 10 or 11 the child will begin to see that rules are made by social agreements and as such are capable of being changed. While children are able to cooperate with rules of behavior at this stage, they begin to realize that rules can be negotiated.

The concept of justice is developed in much the same way for children. Children's first concept of justice is based on the notion that justice is inherent in the order of things and is fixed and unchanging. Later as they mature, children develop a sense of justice that is more sophisticated. They begin to realize that extenuating circumstances are involved in some "bad" acts and that punishments may vary for the same act. Principles of equality and fairness begin to weigh in their thinking.

The foregoing has attempted to lay a foundation for psychological education by providing an organizing conceptual framework for educators. That framework states that the overriding motivation or drive in individuals is their striving to master their environment. While this is a given feature of individuals, no guarantee exists that mastery of environment will happen automatically. In conjunction with this idea is the concept that children's cognitive, affective, and physical growth is developmental and consists of stages that once accomplished are irreversible. However, development in these stages is not automatic either.

The concept of psychological education is not a new one. Plato recognized that good character formation was the basis for all learning. The mind-body schism is a recent one. However, most educators realize that learning does not take place in a vacuum and that characteristics of the learner influence how much and how well learning will take place. Affective and cognitive behavior are integrally linked. To focus on one at the expense of the other can be harmful. This is especially noteworthy for younger students whose affective needs often take preference over other more cognitive-oriented needs.

Recent critics of education sometimes disparage affective education as "frivolous." In times of diminishing resources allocations of money, materials, and personnel resources are thought to be utilized best by channelling them to basic education. Anything else in the curriculum is regarded as superfluous (Combs, 1982).

The mistake in this view is not recognizing that learning by students comprises the totality of cognitive, psychomotor, and affective domains. Teachers are well aware that unmotivated students, for whatever reasons, are difficult to teach and that learning is limited when motivation is not present. Motivation is basically concerned with the affective or psychological characteristics of the student. In order for effective learning to take place, all behavior domains of the student must be mobilized. The research evidence in some studies indicate that affective education has raised reading scores, improved comprehension, and made students feel more positive about learning (Newburg & Loue, 1982).

DEVELOPING A POSITIVE ATMOSPHERE
FOR PSYCHOLOGICAL EDUCATION

Much of American education has slighted the psychological growth and development of students. Many educators believe that growth and development unfold automatically in children. However, self-esteem, personal autonomy, and ego strength develop adequately or inadequately depending on the environmental constraints placed on the individual. To conclude that educators can do little to facilitate the maximum development of these variables would be inappropriate.

Generally, it has been assumed that healthy self-concepts, positive psychological growth, and pro-active egos would result in a by-product of carefully monitored academic learning, usually in the five "sacred" disciplines. Recent studies have shown that schools are engaged in psychological education and are teaching for personal learning, but the resulting psychological learning is negative . . . The studies . . . show that the longer the pupil remains in school, the more his intrinsic interest in learning declines. Negative self-concepts increase with time in urban ghetto schools. Personal efficacy declines. Prejudice thinking increases. The litany mounts, detailing educationally noxious results. (Sprinthall, 1973, p. 361)

Sprinthall claimed that schools impact on the psychological growth of students whether they accept it or not and that this impact is often negative. Sprinthall argued forcefully for deliberate psychological education rather than hoping that good citizenship and healthy personalities would result as a by-product of academic learning.

A number of deliberate psychological education programs have been implemented in schools within the past two decades. They have been applied to elementary, secondary, and university settings. Some programs are highly structured, integrating cognitive curricula with affective curricula, while others are attached to existing school programs. This chapter does not focus on these programs, rather it elaborates on what the teacher can do to foster psychological education in typical classroom interactions.

Through classroom interactions positive self-concepts, respect for self and others, the dignity and value of work, independence, and autonomy can be enhanced in students. The quality of the student-teacher interaction determines how effectively these characteristics are developed.

Consequences of Competition

Teachers unknowingly create a classroom atmosphere that may produce some of the negative psychological characteristics discussed earlier. This may happen even though the teacher strives to create a positive atmosphere. For example, many teachers develop a win-lose classroom environment. This type of environment pays a premium for competition among students. Thus, a considerable number of children inevitably lose each school day. The daily frustration of losing for 12 years can add up to tremendous feelings of failure. Students who continually experience failure will avoid failure in the future. These students are apt to take risks less often and spend a considerable portion of their energy protecting themselves from risk-taking situations. A result of this behavior in some students may be that they forsake opportunities for potential growth by choosing the "safe" course.

Practices of teachers can promote competition that may contribute to win-lose situations. For example, when the teacher asks another student to give the correct answer to the question that Johnnie was not able to give, this teacher creates a situation where one student "wins" at the expense of another. The potential exists for students to view peers as obstacles. Some may harbor feelings of hostility and anger toward others as they compete for rank in class.

For the teacher who is truly interested in intellectual functioning, one of the saddest probable consequences of the continual use of competitive goal structures is that intrinsic motivation for learning and thinking will become subverted. A highly competitive person does not learn for intrinsic reasons: learning is a mean to an end, the end being "winning." Intellectual pursuit for itself becomes unheard of; knowledge that does not help one "win" becomes a waste of time. (Johnson & Johnson, 1975, p. 43)

Some of the results of competition on students reflect the negative and sometimes antisocial aspects of competition. Johnson and Johnson (1975) listed some of the negative effects of competition:

1. Students become dissatisfied if they are not winning.

2. Students dislike behaviors or events that enhance other students' chances of winning.

3. Students dislike students who are successful.

4. Competition encourages misleading or distrustful communication among students.

5. Students often misperceive other students' intentions.

6. In competitive situations differences in students' background and values are accented thereby increasing the probability of prejudice and discrimination toward minority groups.

7. Anxiety is higher and more debilitating in competitive situations.

Many individuals, including teachers, defend the use of competition for several reasons. Proponents claim that society is highly competitive and in order to survive "dog-eat-dog" nature, children must know how to compete. However, if society is examined thoroughly this myth does not stand. In order for groups of people to function effectively, cooperation and agreement need to exist at high levels. Society agrees upon commonly accepted norms of behavior, for example, to stop at red traffic lights. Individuals who do not cooperate in carrying out social contracts are punished often.

Often the use of competitive athletics is used to convince people that competition builds character. To this point Johnson and Johnson (1975) concluded:

> There is evidence that athletic competition limits growth in certain areas. It is possible, they say, that competition doesn't even require much more than a minimally integrated personality. Most athletes have a low interest in receiving support and concern from others, a low need to take care of others, and a low need for affiliation with others. Research indicates that the personality of the ideal athlete is not a result of any molding process of participating in competition, but rather comes out of the ruthless selection process that occurs at all levels of supports. (p. 47)

Learning how to lose is another important life skill. What a student does with a loss is an important indicator of maturity and self-concept. Some students generalize a loss in one part of their lives to all the other parts. A loss in a particular event is thought to be evidence of poor performance in all other aspects of life. Thus, for a young boy, being a poor baseball player may mean being a poor performer in all events. This tendency to overgeneralize sometimes makes children reluctant to engage in risk-taking behavior or to compete with other children.

A more effective approach to losing is to be able to analyze the loss in terms of improving future behavior. Students who are able to take their losses in the appropriate manner can utilize the loss to find ways to improve their behavior. This entails a realistic evaluation of their roles in the loss. The students who is able to assess his/her performance realistically learns more from experiences. Frequently, students will take on excessive blame for a loss, such as not trying hard enough when in fact a reasonable effort was given; or they project blame outside of their locus of control, such as it was "bad luck" that caused the failure. In either case, very little is accomplished toward improving performance in the future. The student who realizes that he/she cannot always succeed and that losses in one area do not diminish a person's total worth is more able to view wins and losses realistically and in the process profit from these experiences.

Teachers can facilitate the learning process that may come from losses by providing examples in the classroom. At times the teacher's efforts in the classroom may not be successful. Perhaps, a lesson was not given as well as was expected, and the teacher realized the students did not accomplish as much as was projected. The teacher who can admit this fact to the class and then proceed to evaluate, with the class the probable reasons for the poor lesson models appropriate skills. This type of teacher sends a message to students. The message is that at times lessons will not go as well as anticipated. This is to be expected. Also, a number of explanations may be possible for poor performance, some of which the teacher may have to "own" and some of which may have been out of the control of the teacher. What is important is that performance is viewed with the objective of improving future behavior.

GENERAL STRATEGIES FOR TEACHING
PSYCHOLOGICAL EDUCATION

Teaching for psychological education can be considerably more challenging than teaching for cognitive education. In psychological education teachers help to develop positive self-image, autonomy, moral reasoning, and self-direction in students. Unlike the multiplication tables or other aspects of the cognitive curriculum, the affective curriculum is less well-defined.

No scope or sequence is established in the curriculum for developing positive self-concepts which presents some problems to teachers. The study of methods of teaching psychological education is difficult; and because it is a relatively recent area for study, not much research has been completed. For these reasons, the area is open-ended in the sense that no complete and authoritarian answers exist about how best to teach for psychological education. Several programs in psychological education have been developed for elementary, secondary, and postsecondary settings. These programs differ in their approach and content. No attempt will be made here to evaluate these programs. Instead, suggestions will be made for classroom teachers that are applicable for the general approach of teaching psychological education. Most of these suggestions can be utilized with specialized programs and materials.

Goals for Students

Tasks for students in psychological education regardless of specific programs are included in the following discussion.

Students Will Accomplish a Degree of Emotional Security. Students should develop some control over their environment regarding potential sources of harm. This includes psychological as well as physical aspects of the environment.

Students Will Achieve a Sense of Belonging Through Acceptance of Self and Others. Schools in general and classrooms in particular can be helpful in developing a sense of shared togetherness in students. This is particularly important for those students who may not be able to develop belonging in their homes with their immediate families. Classrooms that utilize shared responsibilities and operate on a whole classroom identity can be influential in the process of developing a sense of belonging in students.

Students Will Develop Constructive Skills for Dealing with Frustrations. Individuals confront frustrations in their daily interactions. Learning appropriate methods of resolving these frustrations is a fundamental learning task of psychological education. Inappropriate methods of relieving frustrations are sexual exploitation, substance abuse, violence, and aggression. More appropriate strategies are cooperation, conflict resolution, and constructive problem solving.

Students Will Develop Ability to Evaluate Long- and Short-term Consequences of Methods of Meeting Needs. A process of maturation involves increasing responsibility for personal decision making. Some decisions that students make have profound influences on their future lives. Career and academic choices are such examples.

Students Will Understand the Basic Dynamics of Human Behavior. Students should understand and appreciate that all humans are faced with psychological, physical, and social needs. Human behavior can be viewed as an individual's actions towards satisfying these needs.

Students Will Learn Basic Skills Needed to Have Satisfying Interpersonal Relationships. These skills if not developed can have serious implications in lives of students. Children who have not developed these skills adequately often have problems in social, personal, and vocational aspects of their lives.

General Strategies for Teachers

The goals and tasks for psychological education are more difficult to delineate than those typical of the cognitive domain. The existence of few rights and wrongs makes teaching effectively even more difficult. However, some general strategies for teaching psychological education do exist and will aid teachers in initiating psychological education.

Classroom Environment Should Be Nonjudgmental. The teacher holds the key to the kind of classroom environment that exists in a school. The ideal atmosphere for psychological education is one that is nonjudgmental. In this type of classroom students "putting down" other students is noticeably lacking. Students respect the right of other students to hold opinions different from their own.

Teachers who maintain nonjudgmental classroom atmospheres establish clear ground rules for behavior regarding the rights of others in the classrooms. When incidents occur in the class where one student puts down another, the teacher seizes the opportunity to generalize the consequences of such acts without necessarily punishing the student who demonstrated disrespectful behavior. The student does not necessarily need to think that he/she is being punished for the behavior; however, the student should realize consequences do exist in the kind of language used toward others.

One way of dealing with this is to use the incident as an example for studying being disrespectful of one another. The teacher can ask the student what kinds of feelings are generated in a person when he/she is put down. A list of words describing feelings can be written on the chalkboard. The teacher can also ask the class to discuss different ways of behaving that may be less destructive.

Similarly, the class can investigate the role of the put down person in the incident. His/her behavior may have had an instrumental role in producing the put down.

Teachers need to be careful that they do not encourage inappropriate behavior between students. Regardless of how obnoxious a student's actions may be, disrespectful behavior by either the teacher or the student's peers does not solve the concern. Instead, it may encourage students to act in inappropriate ways in dealing with peers.

Awareness of Feelings Involved in Actions Should be Encouraged. Much of the content of the school's curriculum has an emotional component. Students also will have feelings about what they are studying. Students should be encouraged to express their feelings about what they are investigating. Ideals and behavior under discussion can be examined in terms of what effects they have on behavior. Students need to understand that on any one given issue a variety of feelings may exist, and that people who hold different views are not necessarily wrong in their thinking. The fundamental concept underlying the basic framework of the class's behavior is that each person has a right to the way he/she feels, but that each person must bear the ultimate responsibility for the feeling.

One responsibility is to acknowledge one's own feelings and to respect the right of others to hold differing views. Additionally, the differing views may be argued or debated, but they are not to be disparaged. The teacher can model how this process takes place. The teacher and his/her students quite likely will differ on a number of issues. The teacher can model respect for differing opinions by stating his/her feelings on issues under discussion when appropriate. When differences do occur, the teacher can acknowledge the difference in a nonjudgmental way. In this manner the teacher is making a statement to the effect that he/she accepts the student regardless of particular values held; and though the teacher may question the value, he/she understands that the student is entitled to it.

Listening for Understanding. Listening for the purpose of understanding what students are really saying is a difficult task. Many behaviors work against active listening. Sometimes teachers are so concerned with what they want to say that they do not really listen to the student. An example of this is when a teacher begins a response before the student has finished talking. The teacher cannot possibly demonstrate genuine listening then this happens.

When one disagrees with another it makes listening difficult. The disagreement may be felt so strongly that it interferes with authentic listening. Another factor which interferes with listening is lack of concentration. Teachers sometimes have so many things on their minds that they find concentrating on what students are saying is not easy. However, a teacher who puts these factors aside and concentrates on listening to students demonstrates an effective model for interpersonal classroom communication.

Dealing in the Present Context of Time. When classroom discussion is focused on general issues, students often present issues specific to themselves. Some teachers avoid dealing with these issues. Acknowledging that specific concerns may sidetrack the class, the sensitive teacher is able to discern when the issue is very important to the student and when to decide to focus on the student's particular issue.

Conversely, the discerning teacher knows when to take a general issue and relate it to specific concerns of students. This practice makes real the concern under study. Whenever students can relate what they are studying to their own lives, it makes the curriculum come alive. Learning is automatically transferred outside of the classroom which can be greatly beneficial to the class because it can contribute immensely to classroom motivation. The classroom becomes a dynamic and stimulating place.

Undertaking Controversial Issues. Students vary in their ability to handle controversial issues. Some students are willing to take risks in confronting these issues while others prefer not being exposed to them. The teacher constantly monitors the classroom to determine what issues can be dealt with and how deeply they can be exposed. Going beyond the capacity of students can be threatening because of the risk of introducing anxiety which in turn creates a defensive atmosphere in the classroom.

Teachers need to be in touch with their own abilities to handle controversial issues. An open and honest approach is recommended. At times acknowledging discomfort with certain topics is necessary. Other times teachers may need to admit that their information is not adequate to handle the topic effectively.

Evaluating Classroom Discussion. In dealing with issues in psychological education an evaluation or debriefing session must follow the activity. This time should not be devoted to deciding wrong or right, or which position won, rather this time should be spent on summarizing main points. This is an appropriate time to ascertain whether unresolved feelings are left over. The teacher and the class can explore the process that took place during discussions. The evaluation activity puts a tangible closure to the activity. This is especially important when discussing controversial issues.

SPECIFIC STRATEGIES FOR PSYCHOLOGICAL EDUCATION

Most people have a need to feel wanted, to be of value to others. This need is included in the general need for self-esteem. Self-esteem is a complex term. Basically, it means the appraisal a person makes of him/herself and the value that he/she has to others. Thus, it can be seen as a need for self-respect and respect from others as determined by the person's *real* abilities and potential for growth.

The interplay between what a person thinks of him/herself and what others think is closely related. As the person develops, what other persons think of him/her is extremely influential in what the person thinks of self. Esteem is conceptualized graphically in Figure 12.1.

The components listed in Figure 12.1 are central features in psychological education. Children need to understand that some of their behavior is determined by these needs. They also need to realize that this is typical of all humans. Students also need to recognize that people exhibit constructive or destructive behavior in carrying out their needs.

In the the following descriptions constructive and destructive behavior is demonstrated in persons as they strive to attain self-esteem.

> Robert: *He attempts to make friends by actively participating in after-school activities. He is the editor of the school newspaper and a member of the cross-country team.*
>
> Cindy: *She makes friends by flirting with boys. She wears provocative clothing and tends to be loud and brassy.*

ESTEEM
(the need to be valued or prized)

Self-esteem	Respect
confidence	status
adequacy	attention
independence	recognition
freedom	acceptance

Figure 12.1. Central features in psychological education conceptualizing esteem.

These descriptions may suffer from being drawn too stereotypically. However, they demonstrate the need for self-esteem in relationship to a person's behavior. The classroom can be a laboratory for examining behavior in the context of basic needs. Constructive as well as destructive examples should be used. Too often teachers concentrate on negative examples without providing models for positive behaviors.

Here again, as with all aspects of psychological education, the teacher has a central role in modeling. Teachers will sometimes exhibit behavior that is not as positive as it should be. If the teacher can use the incident as an opportunity for learning, it will demonstrate to students how the process of psychological growth takes place.

In classroom discussion of the teacher's inappropriate behavior, four questions can be asked of students:

1. What do you think my (teacher) needs were at the time I exhibited the behavior?

2. In what ways did these needs affect my behavior and the behavior of the others involved?

3. Could the needs of each of us have been satisfied in other ways?

4. What are some of the short- and long-term effects of different alternatives?

One aspect of self-esteem is rating and acceptance of self. In some cases students have unrealistic ideals of themselves. Student evaluations of themselves may be over inflated or underestimated. In either instance, students are apt to act less constructively toward themselves and others. Thus, students need to develop accurate self-evaluation. Classroom activities can help students develop accurate assessment of themselves. Devising personal inventories is an easy method for this task. The inventory in Table 12.1 demonstrates one of many types of classroom activities.

The "I am" activity also can be helpful in self-assessment. This activity provides an opportunity for the student to check his/her self-assessment against what peers think. Students are asked to write a 50-word description of themselves without including their identification.

Table 12.1

My Personal Inventory

My Strong Points	How I Can Use My Strong Points	How These Things Help Me Later

My Greatest Needs	What I do to Meet These Needs	Consequences of My Behavior

The teacher stresses that the description should rely on "personality" aspects of the individual, rather than physical indicators. The teacher then reads the description and the class tries to determine who it is. Discussion about anyone's description is reserved until all the descriptions have been read. Classroom discussions can revolve around what descriptions were recognized more easily. In this activity students can assess how others react to how they see themselves.

SUMMARY

The central concept in this discussion has been that individuals are motivated toward positive mastery over their environment. Additionally, in their struggle their behavior is guided by a developmental sequence. The implication drawn from this organizing concept is that while all students strive for competence, their behavior will be qualitatively different depending on their position in the developmental stages of behavior.

The importance to psychological dimensions of learning was stressed. Any learning activity has three components associated with it: physical, cognitive, and affective. Unfortunately, most educators leave the psychological component to develop by chance. Teachers need to deliberately integrate psychological education concepts into their classrooms.

The classroom atmosphere is the greatest determiner of how well certain psychological needs develop in students. A cooperative classroom that recognizes and emphasizes needs of all students to be accepted provides requisite conditions for psychological growth.

Students recognize through psychological education that they may employ constructive or destructive behavior in the process of meeting their needs. Further, by using the classroom as a laboratory, students learn alternative problem-solving strategies.

SELF-TEST, CHAPTER 12

1. The view espoused in this chapter is that the main motivating force for humans is a drive for pleasure. (T or F)

2. The developmental theory of children states that most children skip at least one stage in their development. (T or F)

3. The homunculus theory of child development perceives children as miniature adults. (T or F)

4. Generally not enough attention is devoted to the affective aspects of learning in classrooms. (T or F)

5. Competition is very important in learning, schools should encourage more of it in classrooms. (T or F)

6. In reality our society is primarily based on cooperation. (T or F)

7. Children have an innate sense of right and wrong. (T or F)

8. At age 16, children insist on very rigid interpretation of events when they judge them right or wrong. (T or F)

9. The use of intense competition in sports has produced productive characteristics in outstanding athletes. (T or F)

10. The main drive motivating humans is their striving for mastery over their environment. (T or F)

11. Describe three different approaches to the study of child development.

12. List and describe briefly four general strategies for teaching psychological education concepts.

ANSWERS: 1. (F), 2. (F), 3. (T), 4. (T), 5. (F), 6. (T), 7. (F), 8. (F), 9. (F), 10. (T)

Activity 12.1 Develop a Brochure to Advertise Yourself

Make up a brochure advertising yourself as you would if it were to appear in a newspaper.

Activity 12.2 Examine Characteristics of Self

Activity 12.2 Check sheet for examining characteristics of self. (Check one of the five frequency columns for each statement.)

STATEMENT	NOT AT ALL	NOT VERY MUCH	SOMETIMES	MOST OF TIMES	ALWAYS
I would like to be friendly	———	———	———	———	———
I would like to be popular	———	———	———	———	———
I would like to be likeable	———	———	———	———	———
I would like to be bashful	———	———	———	———	———
I would like to be pretty/ handsome	———	———	———	———	———
I would like to be clean	———	———	———	———	———
I would like to be helpful	———	———	———	———	———
I would like to be honest	———	———	———	———	———
I would like to be happy	———	———	———	———	———

ADDITIONAL RESOURCES

Books and Publications

Kolhberg, L. (1966). Moral judgment in the schools: A developmental view. *School Review, 74,* 1-30.

Metcalf, L. E. (Ed.). (1971). *Values education: Rationale, strategies, and procedures.* Washington, DC: The National Council for the Social Studies (Forty-first Yearbook).

Rabin, L. J. (Ed.). (1973). *Facts and feelings in the classroom.* New York: Walker & Co.

Films and Filmstrips

Moral Judgment and Reasoning CRM/McGraw-Hill Films, 110 Fifteen Street, Delmart, CA 92014

Nicky: One of My Best Friends CRM/McGraw-Hill Films, 110 Fifteen Street, Delmart, CA 92014

Personality: Adolescents CRM/McGraw-Hill Films, 110 Fifteen Street, Delmart, CA 92014

More Than Hugs and Kisses Filmmakers Library, Inc., 133 East 58th Street, New York, New York 10022

REFERENCES

Combs, A. W. (1981). Affective education or none at all. *Educational Leadership, 39,* 495-597.

Johnson, D. W., & Johnson, R. (1975). *Learning together and alone: Cooperation, competition, and individualization.* Englewood Cliffs, NJ: Prentice-Hall.

Newburg, N. A., & Loue, W. E. (1982). Affective education addresses the basics. *Educational Leadership, 39,* 498-500.

Sprinthall, N. A. (1971). *Guidance for human growth.* New York: Van Nostrand Reinhold Company.

Sprinthall, N. A. (1973). A curriculum for secondary schools: Counselor as teachers for psychological growth. *The School Counselor, 20,* 361-369.

Sprinthall, N. A. (1980). Guidance and new education for schools. *Personnel and Guidance Journal, 58,* 485-489.

Chapter 13

ALL CHILDREN EDUCATION

Today more than any other time in American educational history classrooms contain a representative slice of society's population. This situation has not always been the case. Children have been educated for different purposes at various times throughout our country's development. Some children have been excluded from schooling while others have been encouraged to continue. Much of the cause for this can be attributed to the political, economic, and social context of the periods involved.

Today's heterogeneous classrooms are the results of legal, social, and political realities of the second half of the twentieth century. These new realities have created a set of circumstances that would have surprised the classroom teacher of 100 years ago.

The purpose of this chapter is to acquaint readers with some of the new legislation that has impacted on every classroom in American public education. In addition to providing a brief background to the current situation, suggestions are listed that can be helpful in dealing with the new composition of students in the classroom.

EXPECTED OUTCOMES

By reading the material in the book, the reader will be able to

1. discuss the recent legal history affecting special education students;

2. list major components of an Individualized Education Program (IEP);

3. discuss the pros and cons of mainstreaming; and

4. list at least seven characteristics of schools that have met with success in mainstreaming.

LEGAL BASIS FOR ALL CHILDREN EDUCATION

Just as legal bases exist for nonracist and nonsexist education, a legal basis exists for the education of handicapped and/or special education students. The Brown court case, which mandated desegregated schooling, is one of the most influential court cases in U.S. education. Public Law 94-142 mandated regulations and provisions for the handicapped student. Passed in 1975 and effective in 1978, the law promises to be another milestone in American education. P.L. 94-142 and Section 504 of the Rehabilitation Act of 1973 have already made a noticeable impact on teachers and the public. The full ramifications are not yet known because aspects of P.L. 94-142 continue to be decided in the courts. What is known is that American education will never be the same as it was before 1975 and that every teacher is affected by the provisions and regulations in the law.

OVERVIEW OF P.L. 94-142

Educational rights of the handicapped student evolved over a decade between 1963 and 1974 and culminated in P.L. 94-142. The Division of Handicapped Children and Youth, housed in the U.S. Office of Education, and the Elementary and Secondary Act of 1965 provided the impetus for legislation aimed at providing free and appropriate education to handicapped children. Parents of handicapped children became assertive in requesting more services from school systems. Parents took their demands to court, and in many cases courts decided in favor of parents. During the same time period questions were being raised about the use of tests and the labeling effect they have on children. Parents were discovering that to amend a label once it was applied by school personnel was difficult. Parents found that their children were sentenced without any relief to certain programs and their associated prejudices.

Special education classes and services were often relegated to school basements or located away from the central population of students. Typical school children were segregated from special education students, and the attitudes developed toward the handicapped often were negative. Opportunities for handicapped and nonhandicapped children to interact freely were limited severely. This condition often promoted adverse opinions about the special education student.

P.L. 94-142 was a response to many issues raised by parents and concerned educators. The questions of due process of handicapped students' rights and appropriate educational services became the cornerstones for constructing the contents of the law. The law itself was an attempt to ensure a mechanism to provide educational services to handicapped students who were receiving inadequate services or no services at all in order to guarantee that these students' needs were being met. The law is both very specific and vague. For example, it defines the age level of affected students as between three and 21 but the phrase "appropriate education" is not defined clearly. Thus, certain aspects of the law are continually under scrutiny. Many vague areas will have to be settled by the courts.

As recently as the summer of 1982, the Supreme Court decided a case that reflects on the meaning of free, appropriate education for handicapped students. In this case the parents of a deaf child petitioned the school system to provide a sign-language interpreter to the student's class. The school system was providing special services to the child including tutoring and a hearing aid. The child's progress in school was above average. The Supreme Court decided in a 6-3 decision that the school was providing an appropriate education for the handicapped student. Perhaps, more importantly, the court opined that school systems are not required to guarantee a particular level of education for students.

In this case the court's opinion was that schools do not have to provide maximum levels of instruction for students. Thus, providing education so that each child achieves what he/she is capable of becoming is a philosophical position and is not an entitlement for students. It is anticipated that other court cases will result in a clearer definition of "an appropriate" education.

P.L. 94-142 is a wide-ranging piece of legislation that contains several components. Some of the components that will be discussed in this chapter are

1. least restrictive environment,

2. Individual Education Program (IEP),

3. handicapped children,

4. due process procedures, and

5. confidentiality.

Least Restrictive Environment (LRE)

Although mainstreaming is never mentioned in P. L. 94-142, it has come to be phrase of choice when aspects of least restrictive environment are discused. This may be because mainstreaming is such a self-descriptive word and because it is meaningful to many educators. The two terms least restrictive environment and mainstreaming are *not* synonymous. Confusion arises when they are equated and implemented into school policy.

Mainstreaming is the wholesale integration of special education students into regular classrooms. Ideally, mainstreaming provides classrooms that typify the general school population. Least restrictive environment (LRE) is placing special education students into regular classroom settings whenever possible with exceptions being made only when the handicap is so severe that it precludes entry into regular classroom. The law itself states that educators need to establish

> procedures to assure that to the maximum extent appropriate, handicapped children, including children in public or private institutions or other care facilities, are educated with children who are not handicapped, and that special education classes, separate schooling, or other removal of handicapped children from the regular education environment occurs only when the nature or severity of the handicap is such that education in regular classes with the case of supplementary aids and services cannot be achieved satisfactorily. [P.L. 94-142, Section 612 (5)(B)]

The Law further states that

> to the maximum extent practicable and consitent with the provisions of section 612 (5)(B), the provision of special services [are] to enable such children to participate in regular classroom programs. [P.L. 94-142, Section 614 (1)(C)]

Obviously the placement of all handicapped children into regular classrooms is not mandated by P.L. 94-142. The intent of this component of the law is to reduce labeling and stigmatization by integrating special and regular education students. The purpose of the law was to obviate the findings that "one million of the handicapped children in the United States are excluded entirely from the public school system and will not go through the educational process with their peers" [P.L. 94-142, section 601 (3)(a)].

Safeguards for LRE are contained in the Individual Educational Program (IEP) which must specify the possible extent of the student's participation in regular educational programs. Aspects of the IEP are detailed specifically in the law, and they will be discussed later in the chapter.

LRE can be integrated into a conceptualization of the educational process. Special support services to a child can be placed on a continuum of little to very much. Children placement on this continuum is done with the idea that an effort will be made to move the student toward the "little special support" end of the continuum. Glick and Schubert (1981) provided a model that graphically displays the concept. Their model is presented in Figure 13.1.

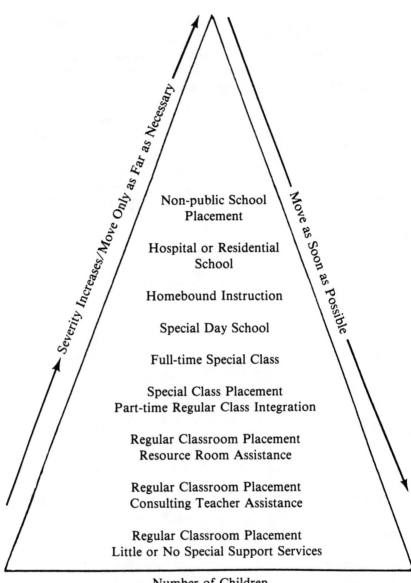

Figure 13.1. Sample continuum of special support services provided to establish LRE for handicapped student. Adapted from H. M. Glick and M. Schubert (1981) Mainstreaming: An unmandated challenge. *Educational Leadership, 39,* p. 327.

In Figure 13.1 each level of severity consists of different amounts of special support services needed. The child is placed at a level after a comprehensive evaluation. He/she is moved down through the levels as soon as possible based on the goals and objectives of his/her IEP. Ideally, when possible all children will be placed eventually in regular classrooms.

The intent of P.L. 94-142 was to help negate some of the negative results of special education, especially the ubiquitous labeling process that produces lower expectations in people, and to provide a more ''real'' world for all children. The idea behind this concept is that if all children can function adequately in the classroom, then they can function adequately in society when finished with schooling.

A number of concerns have been raised by educators regarding LRE. After the enactment of P.L. 94-142 teachers were faced suddenly with having to provide instruction to special education children. The spectre of interacting with children with a variety of disabilities created fears and uncertainty in many teachers. Teachers felt that they were not prepared adequately to meet this challenge. Other teachers were confused about how to arrange and present information to their new students. For years, teachers screened students into special education classes when they suspected some form of a handicap. Teachers are confronted with the same students in their own classrooms that they would have screened out earlier.

Teachers and administrators complain about the amount of paperwork involved with mainstreaming handicapped children. The regulations are very specific about reports and evaluations. In some cases IEPs are dozens of pages. The demands of due process further contribute to the time and paperwork involved in fulfilling the mandate of 94-142. Parents of nonhandicapped children sometimes resent the apparent extra resources and money channeled to the education of handicapped students. This is particularly noticeable in current times of diminishing resources for public education.

As time passes teachers and the public will become accustomed to working with P.L. 94-142, and LRE as a concept will be accepted fully into the fabric of American education. The transition will not always be easy; however, similar to school desegregation, LRE will take place and it will have an impact on students.

Individualized Education Programs (IEP)

The foundation of P.L. 94-142 is the IEP. Its intent is to move away from classical diagnosis and its incumbent labels into a more prescriptive and behavioral approach. The term individualized education program means

> a written statement for each handicapped child developed in any meeting by a representative of the local educational agency or an intermediate educational unit who shall be qualified to provide, or supervise the provisions of, specially designed instruction to meet the unique needs of handicapped children, the teacher, the parents or guardian of such child, and whenever appropriate, such child, while statement shall include (a) a statement of the present levels of educational performance of such child, (b) a statement of annual goals, including short-term instructional objectives, (c) a statement of specific educational services to be provided to such child, and the extent to which such child will be able to participate in regular educational programs, (d) the projected date for initiation and anticipated duration of such services, and (e) appropriate objective criteria and evaluation procedures and schedules for determining, on at least an annual basis, whether instructional objectives are being met. [P.L. 94-142, Section 602 (19)(a)]

Without doubt IEPs are comprehensive in scope, and to some, overwhelming in detail. However, the intent of an IEP is to provide the handicapped child with a dynamic plan of action to implement an appropriate education for him/her. The plan must contain at least five provisions, and when combined with due process procedures to be discussed later, it appears inordinately time consuming and fraught with paperwork. The inherent monitoring process alone requires hours of teacher time for each child. The purpose for the close inspection is to prevent some of the past abuses of handicapped children and to bring special education students as quickly as possible into the regular education program. The emphasis on stating behavioral goals and expectant timetables is to prevent children from being tucked away in special education classes. The law takes seriously the concept of free, appropriate education.

Some educators envision that all children should be provided with IEPs. That is, the precedent is set whereby individualized instruction eventually may become a reality for each child in school regardless of the presence or absence of a handicapping condition. With the advent of computer technology and the recent programs made for data reduction and word processing equipment, easing the burden of paperwork and monitoring for teachers, administrators, and pupil personnel services may be possible. Microcomputers will aid in this process. New equipment eventually can be utilized beyond its record keeping abilities and into more instruction-related roles.

Teachers need special resources in order to cope with the details of IEPs. In this regard many special education teachers are trained to develop IEPs, however breakdowns can occur in translating the contents of IEPs into instructional procedures. Cooperation between teachers, special education teachers, counselors, and administrators is absolutely essential if the plan is going to work. The classroom teacher must look toward these individuals as resources and demand their assistance in implementing IEPs.

Handicapped Children

Handicapped children are defined as any children who are handicapped and in need of special education and related services. Special education is specially designed instruction to meet the unique needs of a handicapped child. This may include classroom instruction, home instruction, instruction in institutions or hospitals, physical education instruction, and vocational education instruction. Related services are defined broadly as to include transportation, psychological services, speech pathology, cardiology, physical and occupational therapy, counseling services, school social work services, and parental counseling and training. The important aspects of this definition are that the child must be handicapped and in need of special education and related services. Thus, some handicapped children may not fall under the provisions of the law.

Handicapped children generally include
1. mentally retarded,
2. hearing impaired,
3. deaf,
4. speech impaired,
5. visually handicapped,
6. blind,
7. seriously emotionally disturbed,
8. orthopedically and other health impaired,
9. blind-deaf, and
10. specific learning disabilities.

Most of the categories are self-explanatory. However, identifying the seriously emotionally disturbed child may present some difficulty. Characteristics which help in defining this child are
1. symptoms have been exhibited over a long period of time,
2. behavior affects educational performance,
3. learning difficulties cannot be caused by mental deficiency,

sensory or health impairments,

4. poor interpersonal relationships with peers and teachers,
5. inappropriate affect,
6. pervasive unhappiness/depression, and
7. development of phobic-type behavior toward school.

Regular classroom teachers may worry excessively over the prospect of having severely emotionally disturbed children in their classrooms. These worries may be unfounded because "appropriate and free" education does not necessarily mean instruction in a regular classroom. Sometimes administrators become oversensitive in placing handicapped children into regular classrooms and assume that all handicapped children must be placed in regular classrooms. As shown in Figure 13.1, placement of the handicapped can be in any one of nine possible alternatives. Granted that making an exact placement of each handicapped student is difficult, to expect that all handicapped children's needs are served best in regular classrooms is unreasonable.

Due Process Procedures

Due process procedures are established by the stated purpose of the Act:

> It is the purpose of this Act to assure that all handicapped children have available to them, within the time periods specified in section 612 (2)(B), a free, appropriate public education and related services designed to meet their unique needs, to assure the rights of handicapped children and their parents or guardians are protected, to assist States and localities to provide for the education of all handicapped children, and to assess and assure the effectiveness of efforts to educate handicapped children.

This portion of the law is specific. It regulates by legislation procedures to ensure that handicapped children and their parents' rights are protected. The act backs up its statement "to assure that the rights of handicapped children and their parents are protected [P.L. 94-142, 601(B)]" by stating

> any State educational agency, any local educational agency and intermediate unit which receives assistance under this part shall establish and maintain procedures in accordance with subsection (b) through (e) of this section to assure that handicapped children and their parents or guardians are guaranteed procedural safeguards with respect to the provisions of free appropriate public education by such agencies and units. [P.L. 94-142, section 615(a)]

Safeguards cover both evaluation process and components of the individualized education program. The following list summarizes the procedural safeguards of the law.

1. Parents (or guardians) must be informed in their native language that their children are going to be evaluated for degree of handicap.

2. Parents must agree in writing to the evaluation, and they must understand that giving their permission is voluntary.

3. Parents should be provided the opportunity to inspect all education reports with regard to evaluations and IEPs.

4. Evaluations must be valid and conducted by several people in different areas of educational expertise.

5. Parents have the right to have independent evaluations conducted by qualified examiners.

6. Prior written notice must be given to parents of any proposed changes in identification, evaluation, and educational placement. The statement must include at least:
   a. explanation of procedural safeguards,

   b. a description of the action proposed or refused by the school,

   c. a description of the assessment procedures used, and

   d. a description of other relevant variables affecting the action plan.

7. Consent must be given previous to conducting an evaluation or placing a student in a special educational program.

8. Parents of handicapped children have the right to a hearing on any of the above conditions and they may be accompanied by counsel and experts.

9. Parents of handicapped children have the right to appeal any hearing decisions.

While the intent of the law is to bring parents into the decision-making process in developing education programs for their handicapped children and to keep parents informed of their children's treatment, the due process procedures have a tendency to cast the parents and the schools in adversarial roles. Unfortunately this has negative consequences. School personnel often view record keeping, notification of parents, and permission gathering aspects of the procedures as inordinately time consuming. Without question the documentation that P.L. 94-142 requires is considerable. However, to consider this aspect of the law as grounds to abrogate the law's intent would be a mistake. After all, neglect, abuse, and inadequate education of handicapped children created the impetus for the law. School systems and their personnel are forced to live with these restrictions. To devise ways and methods to uphold the due process aspects of the law on the one hand and to provide a free appropriate education to handicapped children on the other is the responsibility of the school system. The handicapped child and his/her welfare must not become lost in the apparent maze of requirements contained in the law.

Confidentiality

According to the Family Educational Rights and Privacy Act of 1973, certain guarantees are afforded parents and students. P.L. 94-142 adheres to these restrictions. This law is often called the Buckley Amendment, because Senator William Buckley sponsored the section of the law. According to the law, parents or guardians are entitled to

> inspect and review any and all official record files and data directly related to their children. . . . Specifically including but not necessarily limited to identifying data, academic work completed, level of achievement (grades, standardized achievement scores), attendance data, scores on standardized intelligence, aptitude and psychological tests, interest inventory results, health data, family background information, teacher or counselor ratings and observation, and verified reports of serious recurrent behavior patterns. (P.L. 93-380)

The Buckley Amendment stated these parental rights are valid until the student reaches 18. However, with handicapped children, depending on the severity of handicap, parents may maintain these rights indefinitely. In most cases the rights are transferred to the student upon becoming 18 years of age.

Parents have the right to inspect their children's school records along with explanations and interpretations of information. Parents may have representatives with them when they inspect and review information collected about their children.

If parents think that information about their children is inaccurate, misleading, or an invasion of their privacy, they have a right to request that the information be changed. The school (or agency) may or may not change or amend the information depending on how data are interpreted. However, if the school unit disagrees with the parent, it must provide a hearing on the matter. At this hearing a decision is rendered regarding whether or not the information is to be amended.

Initially, equity in educating the handicapped may appear to have reached a point where some educators claim that the handicapped are receiving more than their equal share. In this period of diminishing resources, extra scrutiny is given to how much is spent. However, many of the aspects of recent legislation apply to all children regardless of handicap. Regulations of the Buckley Amendment are applied to all children. Certain components of P.L. 94-142 may become integrated into regular teaching procedures. IEPs, so essential to P.L. 94-142, are rooted in the concept that each student is an individual learner. This is an old educational concept that has many supporters. Possibly in the future all children, regardless of whether or not they are handicapped, will have a version of the IEP which apparently is a pedological methodology whose time has come.

COMPONENTS OF SUCCESSFUL PROGRAMS

Some school units will adapt to the regulations of new laws better than others. Even though the law states very specifically that school personnel will receive training in working with the handicapped, the quantity and quality of the training may be questioned. The law states that

the development and implementation of a comprehensive system of personnel development which shall include the in-service training of general and special educational instructional and support personnel necessary to carry out the purposes of this Act are appropriately and adequately prepared and trained, and effective procedures for acquiring and disseminating to teachers and administrators of programs for handicapped children significant information derived from educational research, demonstration, and similar projects. [P.L. 94-142, section 613 (a)(3)]

States are responsible for implementing a plan for accomplishing teacher in-service training goals stated in the law. The intent was to provide teachers with the necessary skills and materials needed to carry out a free, appropriate education of handicapped children. Glick and Schubert (1981) wrote that while teachers in general support the concept of mainstreaming, they feel that they are not provided with enough help and resources to implement mainstreaming effectively. In many respects teachers think that they have been deserted and that they have the burden all to themselves.

Some schools manage the implementation of P.L. 94-142 better than others. Schools that have been successful at implementing mainstreaming share certain characteristics. A team visited successful programs and concluded that good programs had

> Effective communication network between regular and special education staff. Considerable evidence supported the fact that sharing successes and failures was frequent.

> Communication that was less structured and formalized between staff and that was integrated within school activities (lunch, before school, and so forth) was more effective than formalized meetings.

> Full support of the administration. This was recognized by the teachers and not merely lip service.

> Freedom to change schedules. The overriding concern was getting help for the student, and teachers were flexible in arranging class times.

> Appropriate and positive expectations of regular classroom teachers toward handicapped children. Seemingly when teachers expected these children to learn, they did.

> A history of dealing with handicapped students. Successful programs had an average of nearly seven years of experience in mainstreaming before the mandates of 94-142.

> A method of sharing responsibilities of special education and that of regular classroom by teachers. Duties, committee work, and physical location of special education teachers did not differ from regular classroom teachers.

> Special education teachers who believed that mainstreaming would work. These workers were invested in the process of making 94-142 work for the nonhandicapped as well as the handicapped student.

> Regular students who accepted handicapped students. Regular students previously interacted with handicapped students in successful program. (Glick & Schubert, 1981, pp.328-329)

To separate cause and effect in these programs is extremely difficult. That is, did the fact that there was a successful implementation of the mandate create the positive attitudes, or did the positive attitudes create the successful implementation? Nevertheless, certain characteristics are helpful in making programs successful. Administrative support is essential. Also, an open communication system between special education teachers, regular classroom teachers, and administrators increases effectiveness. Good dialogue among these elements is essential. Where information is shared and interaction is systematic, an effective educational program results.

Many regular classroom teachers have little experience and knowledge of special education students. To have these teachers visit special education classes to view the interaction may be helpful. Some concerns that regular classroom teachers have may be a result of ignorance. Interacting with handicapped students may help to dissipate some of the fear and concern.

Simulation activities in inservice training help teachers familiarize themselves with the handicapped. Using a cane or a wheelchair by an able-bodied person develops an appreciation for the handicapping condition.

Without question, regular classroom teachers are going to have to have support in order to implement the mandate of P.L. 94-142. Principals, special education teachers, counselors, and other school personnel need to provide support in terms of information, materials, and reassurance. Principals can check with regular classroom teachers systematically to provide what material and human resources are needed. Special education teachers can consult with teachers to develop specialized programs and teaching strategies for handicapped students.

If the regular classroom teacher knows that support and assistance are available, and he/she is confident that support will be forthcoming upon request, this support makes the task of mainstreaming less difficult. The law does not provide the positive attitudes that are necessary in order for mainstreaming to work. Positive attitudes are accomplished by providing an open forum for communication, a dialogue among all school personnel, and a commitment to the concept that each child is entitled to a free, appropriate education.

TEACHER TRAINING INSTITUTIONS

Inservice training, no matter how well it is implemented cannot succeed without adequate preservice instruction of undergraduate students. Most states require some course work in exceptionality. This may be a response by institutions to the mandate for training contained in P.L. 94-142. However, a piecemeal approach is rarely as effective as an integrative one. The American Association of Colleges for Teacher Education (AACTE) has produced a position statement on this issue. The statement recommends a broad-based view that incorporates several other current concerns with quality education. These concerns include, among others, multicultural education, nonsexist education, and individualization of instruction. The AACTE's position could be subsumed under the comprehensive definition of human relations training developed in this text.

Teacher education curricula have the tendency to have students exposed to a collection of courses. While these courses individually may be invaluable, the student is left to integrate the content into a meaningful whole. Inherently, this is a very difficult skill to master. Integration of information is a high-order skill that makes difficult demands on students. In addition, because preservice students are not likely to have much experience with exceptional students integrating the information becomes that much more difficult.

A workable approach to teacher education is to develop the concept that skills needed to teach effectively are appropriate regardless of students' exceptionality. Creating separations between special education and regular education may promote an artificial dichotomy. Given that a body of specialized information is needed when dealing with exceptional children, a sound teacher education program provides most of the competencies needed to interact with most students. The following quote summarizes this point of view:

> The broad prospective—the generic view—is not contrived, it is inescapable. One is reminded of John Dewey's response to the criticism that he was suggesting that teachers should "make learning interesting." Dewey said, in effect, that making learning interesting was unnecessary, that learning *was* interesting and he couldn't understand why teachers tried so hard to make it dull! The parallel response to critics who charge mainstreaming change agents with making teacher training generic is that much of teacher training *is* generic . . ., it must be, since the American educational system is inclusive. It is hard to understand why we view a response so long overdue as an "innovation." (Morsink, 1980, p. 11)

GENERAL SUGGESTIONS FOR WORKING WITH HANDICAPPED CHILDREN

Developing a list of suggestions appropriate to all handicap students would be difficult. One danger is that in being too general, suggestions lose specificity and usefulness. Thus, the following list probably applies to any classroom regardless of whether or not it contains handicapped children.

1. Interpersonal relationships should be genuine. Empathy, genuineness, and self-disclosure are important qualities when communicating with handicapped children. Above all, handicapped children need to interact with teachers who will be honest with them regarding their disability.

2. Classroom instruction should be clear and concise. Little room for misunderstanding directions should exist. Concreteness helps in communicating clear instructions. While the teacher is giving clear instructions he/she must not appear to be talking down to handicapped students. Regular students will be looking to the teacher for ways of interacting with handicapped students. Patronizing communication rarely facilitates independent functioning.

3. The teacher can make sure that handicapped students are off to a good start by monitoring them as they begin new assignments. Reviewing with students their understanding of the assignments before they plunge into work is also helpful.

4. Classroom routines need to be consistent. Consistent routine provides a sense of security to students. This is especially important for special education students who have learning disabilities. Too many distractions and inconsistent classroom procedures are difficult to handle for these students. Discipline should be firm, but applied fairly. Limits of behavior should be established and known to the special education student. The teacher cannot assume that the special education student knows what constitutes appropriate classroom conduct. For this reason the teacher should make exceptions rarely.

5. Traditional suggestions for classroom management are practiced. When a classroom contains special education students, rewarding children for their appropriate and positive behavior becomes even more important. The special education student may have a long history of failures with school tasks. To envision the effects that constant failure has on these students is not difficult. Successful experiences should be built into the school program for handicapped pupils.

The intent of P.L. 94-142 was to address some of the inadequacies of educational programs for special education. Framers of the law concluded that in many cases special education student needs were not being met. In addition, they took issue with the concept of providing all special educational services outside the regular classroom setting. In the framers' opinion isolating special education students from regular classroom students was neither appropriate nor educationally sound.

Voices have been raised about regulations contained within the law. Some critics think that special education students are receiving more than equal treatment. Others resent spending extra money in times when financial resources are stretched to their limits. Certain aspects of the law are vague and litigations are continually taking place. A recent court case in the summer of 1982 stated that educational systems do not have to provide maximum educational opportunities for handicapped students.

However, the real importance of the law may lie more in its intent and spirit rather than its regulation. The concept of treating each student as an individual in his/her educational program has tremendous implications for all students. Someday all students may have IEPs written for them. The idea that evaluation is prescriptive rather than descriptive is a step away from the negative effects of labeling. If school related services personnel, counselors, social workers, psychologists, nurses, and so forth can be trained to evaluate prescriptively, their evaluations will have more utility for classroom teachers. Prescriptive evaluations are defined as assessments that are behavioral and objective which minimize psychological or medical labels. Descriptive evaluations emphasize tasks that students can do currently and projects tasks that students should be able to accomplish in a reasonable amount of time.

Finally, the concept that isolating special education students from regular students is inherently undemocratic. Classrooms can be thought of as microcosms of the larger society. To think that handicapped people do not exist in society or that they are shunted away is unrealistic. As physical barriers are removed and technological innovations are implemented, handicapped individuals will become even more visible in society. The classroom should be a place where the handicapped and nonhandicapped can interact. The perspective that only the handicapped benefits from this interaction is naive. All students can benefit and learn from each other—in the final analysis that is what human relations is all about.

SELF-TEST, CHAPTER 13

1. By 1985, full compliance with P.L. 94-142 was to take place. (T or F)

2. IEP procedures do not have any application to regular students. (T or F)

3. P.L. 94-142 reads that schools must provide educational programs that will maximize each handicapped child's potential. (T or F)

4. The concept of mainstreaming is in actuality an interpretation of the regulations of P.L. 94-142. (T or F)

5. In real terms, P.L. 94-142 has not increased in the amount of paperwork required by school systems. (T or F)

6. P.L. 94-142 endorses the concept that student evaluation for handicaps should not rely on one source. (T or F)

7. While teachers are ready to accept the concept of mainstreaming, they feel unprepared to deal with handicapped children. (T or F)

8. The concept of mainstreaming handicapped students into regular classrooms does not fit well with our democratic system. (T or F)

9. For the most part, the due process procedures of P.L. 94-142 are identified clearly. (T or F)

10. In all probability, the effects of P.L. 94-142 will alter the role of special education teachers. (T or F)

11. Discuss the implications of least restrictive environment by using the figure found in this chapter.

12. What have been the main concerns of the public and teachers over P.L. 94-142?

ANSWERS: 1. (F), 2. (F), 3. (F), 4. (T), 5. (F), 6. (T), 7. (T), 8. (F), 9. (T), 10. (T)

ADDITIONAL RESOURCES

Books and Publications

A.A.C.T.E. (1978). *Beyond the mandate: The professional imperative: Educating professionals for educating the handicapped.* Washington, DC: American Association of Colleges for Teacher Education.

Grosenick, S., & Reynolds, M. (Eds.). (1978). *Teacher education: Renegotiating roles for mainstreaming.* Reston, VA: The Council for Exceptional Children.

Middleton, E., Morsink, C., & Cohen, S. (1979). Program graduates' perception of need for training in mainstreaming. *Exceptional Children, 45,* 256-71.

National Education Association. (1978). *A study report: Education for all handicapped children. Consensus, conflict, and challenge.* Washington, DC.

Rauth, M. (1978). *Mainstreaming: A river to nowhere or a promising current?* Washington, DC: American Federation of Teachers.

Schubert, M., Glick, H., & Bauer, D. (Not dated). *Least restrictive environment and handicapped students: Aids for the regular classroom teacher.* Dayton, OH: Wright State University.

Films (F) and Filmstrips (FS)

Approaches to Mainstreaming. Teaching Resources, 50 Pond Park Road, Hengham, MA 02043. Filmmakers Library, Inc., 133 East 58th St., New York, NY 10022. (F)

Introduction to P.L. 94-142. Council for Exceptional Children, 1920 Association Drive, Reston, VA 22091. (F)

Mainstreaming Series. Teaching Resources, 50 Pond Park Road, Hengham, MA 02043. (F)

I Am Not What You See: Being "Different" in America. Filmmakers Library, Inc., 133 East 58th St., New York, NY 10022. (F)

Ears to Hear: Teaching Deaf Children. Filmmakers Library, Inc., 133 East 58th St., New York, NY 10022. (F)

Pins and Needles: When Disability Strikes in the Prime. Filmmakers Library, Inc., 133 East 58th St., New York, NY 10022. (F)

The People You Never See. Filmmakers Library, Inc., 133 East 58th St., New York, NY 10022. (F)

To Live On. Filmmakers Library, Inc., 133 East 58th St., New York, NY 10022. (F)

More than Hugs and Kisses: Affective Education in a Mainstreamed Classroom. Filmmakers Library, Inc., 133 East 58th St., New York, NY 10022. (F)

Organizations

American Association of Colleges for Teacher Education, One Dupont Circle, Washington, DC 20036

American Federation of Teachers, Washington, DC

Council for Exceptional Children, 1920 Association Drive, Reston, VA 22091

National Education Association, Washington, DC

REFERENCES

Glick, H. M., & Schubert, M. (1981). Mainstreaming: An unmandated challenge. *Educational Leadership, 38,* 326-329.

Morsink, C. V. (1980). *P. L. 94-142 and guidelines for staff development in colleges of education: A generic view from the Dean's grants.* Unpublished manuscript, University of Kentucky.

Public Law 93-380 (1974). 93 Congress, second session, 93-380.

Public Law 94-142. Education for all handicapped children act of 1975. 94 Congress, November 29, 1975.

CHAPTER 14

NONRACIST EDUCATION

One of the most persistent problems in American society is that of racism. The United States has struggled with this concern for most of its existence. The problem has caused considerable expenditures to be made in material and human resources. While great strides have been made in combating the effects of racism, the problem remains.

Schools have been viewed as a major agency for the reduction of racist practices in America. It has been envisioned that through education and the schools, racism would be eradicated. Unfortunately, this has not been the case. Vestiges of racism remain in our society and its effects have ramifications for all of us.

EXPECTED OUTCOMES

This chapter will concentrate on problem of racism in education. By reading the material in this chapter you should be able to

1. explain the legal basis of nonracist education,

2. discuss the implications of the myth of the American Dream,

3. identify racist features in our language, and

4. list several strategies to overcome racism in schools.

At the end of the chapter you will find an assessment section. You can use this section to test your understanding of the material in the chapter. A section on materials and resources follows the assessment test. These materials may be used to help you in locating supplementary materials and resources.

LANDMARK DECISION

On May 17, 1954, the Supreme Court landmark decision, *Brown vs Board of Education,* changed permanently the course of education in the United States. The concept of separate but equal education was struck down.

Ramifications of the Court's decision is still being experienced after three decades.

Compensatory education was instituted as a means of addressing the problems of inequalities in backgrounds of nonwhite children. The failure of compensatory education has been noted elsewhere in this text. The following presentation sums up many of the impressions that compensatory and welfare programs have on their clients.

I'm tired of everything they try to do to help us. They send us those welfare checks, and with them comes the lady who peeks around every corner here and gives me those long lectures on how I should do everything...like her, of course. I want to tell her to go charge around and become a spy or one of those preachers who can find sin in a clean handkerchief. They take my kids to the Head Start thing and the first thing I hear is the boys' fingernails are dirty, they don't eat the proper food, and they don't use the right words, no one can make them out. It's just like that with the other kids. They try to take them to those museums and places and tell them how sorry life is at home and in the neighborhood and how they're no good and something needs to be done to make them better, make them like the rich ones, I guess. But the worse is, they just make me feel no good at all. They tell you they want to help you, but if you ask me, they want to make you into them and leave you without a cent of yourself to hang onto. I keep asking them, why don't they fix the country up so that people can work, instead of patching up with this and that and giving us a few dollars to keeps us from starving right to death. Why don't they get out of here and let us be and have our own lives? (**A Poor Woman's Letter,** *read by Gwen Morgan, Vice-chair of the Day Care Council of American, at the Ninth Annual Changing Family Conference)*

THE AMERICAN DREAM

The American Dream has always been a part of this country's mystique. An essential element of this dream is that material rewards are available to all who are willing to work for them. Perhaps, for every American Dream there has been an American nightmare. The economic crash of the twenties, and the limited resources of the eighties are examples of times that fostered considerable economic hardships for some, especially nonwhite members of society.

The failure of the American Dream is not so much that the concept is not correct as that people have associated the Dream almost exclusively with material resources. Rather, if the American Dream were rooted in justice and equality for all, the prospects of success would be higher. Thus, a chicken in every pot and a car in every garage, is not as important to the Dream as equity for all in the society's institutions. The real American Dream may be expressed in Martin Luther King, Jr.'s March on Washington Speech in 1963.

> I say to you today, my friends, that inspite the difficulties and the frustrations of the moment, I still have a dream. It is deeply rooted in the American Dream ... I have a dream that one day this nation will rise up and live out the meaning of its creed: "We hold these truths to be self-evident; that all men are created equal ... I have a dream that one day on the red hills of Georgia the sons of former slaves and the sons of former slave owners will be able to sit down at the table of brotherhood ... I have a dream that my four children will one day live in a nation where they will be judged not by the color of their skin but by the content of their character ... I have a dream ... that one day there in Alabama little Black boys and girls will be able to join hands with little white boys and girls as sisters and brothers. I have a dream today ... with this faith we will be able to hew out of the mountain of dispair a stone of hope. With this faith we will be able to transform this jangle of discord of our nation into a beautiful symphony of brotherhood.

The economic features of the American Dream cannot be realized for every citizen unless each American has equal access to his/her share. Since this has not been the case, frustrations and sometimes anger are inevitable results of those who are denied access.

Education is often thought to be the main vehicle for access to the material components of the American Dream. In many respects, high educational achievement was tantamount to economic success. In the past, "Get a good education and you will get a good job," was accurate. However, the economic woes of the eighties have severely limited the viability of the concept. Additionally, the public's satisfaction with American education has diminished dramatically during the past two decades. The National Commissioner's Report on Education of 1983 boldly stated that American education was at best mediocre.

Thus, if education were perceived as the only basic strategy to change racist practices in the United States, there is reason for gloom. However, while a more balanced view of education's role in eliminating racism in our society is warranted, this does not mean that the search for the elimination of elements in education that support racism should stop. Traces of institutional racism should be eliminated from our schools. While schools cannot eradicate racism from society without massive economic and social reformation in policies, education should do everything in its power to make schools as free from racism as possible.

A mark of maturity of this nation may be evidenced by the people's revelation that racism cannot be eradicated by schools alone. A more realistic view of what education is capable of doing is certainly welcomed. However, any role that education plays in the elimination of racist elements of our society will be major. Schools are one of the few institutions that incorporates essentially all members of society. Further, schools are operated by state and federal agencies, thus, they are bounded by legal aspects of racial practices.

The clash between the idealistic hope of this country, that all men (and women) are created equal, and the practical reality of society's structure has been evident for most of our 200 year history. Yet, the clashing of these two different aspects of our society have caused, at times, remarkable changes. The Brown court case, affirmative action, and civil rights laws are examples of changes that have taken place during our history.

Teacher's Role

A major concept of this text is that the classroom teacher is the core of effective human relations in teaching. The centrality of this concept cannot be overemphasized. However, some teachers, especially those that are white, have problems teaching nonwhite students. These problems often interfere with effective classroom teaching.

One problem that white educators have teaching nonwhite students is that of fear. The potential for making teaching mistakes is enhanced under the condition of fear. Exum (1979) stated that errors in judgment result from lack of information and fear. Apprehension of Black students is based on several factors. Some of these factors are listed in the following.

1. The disparity of common ground between students and teacher.

2. The different value systems of teacher and students.

3. The apprehension of demonstrating prejudice.

4. The fear of being able to understand Black dialect.

5. The fear of being able to handle, quickly and effectively, racial problems that occur in the classroom.

6. The threat of vulgar and profane language.

7. The fear of Black students downgrading themselves.

The insecurities that these fears create in teachers can be tremendous. Teachers react in predictable ways to reduce their fears. Unfortunately, their actions are not always effective. For example, many teachers, especially beginning ones, adopt an "I am your friend" posture. In an attempt to demonstrate their liberal attitudes, some teachers try to become pals with their nonwhite students. This strategy is rarely effective. In some cases, it encourages aggression and hostility in students.

It is not surprising that the next stage that fearful teachers go through is disillusionment. Exum (1979) claimed that teachers in this stage may become burned out, adopt a callous attitude, disparage students, or leave the profession with a bitter taste. The most effective approach, according to Exum (1979) is the humanism one. Teachers at this level assume a leadership role, maintain a sense of humor, exhibit high levels of enthusiasm and energy, and display a respect for the individual student. While discipline is maintained in the classroom, it is based on equity and firmness rather than capricious actions.

Students learn in this type of classroom. There is an increase in student self-esteem because mutual respect between student and teacher is the cornerstone of the classroom climate. A sound psychological basis is provided for growth. Perhaps, most important of all, students are exposed to adult models that demonstrate effective inaction in relationships. The power of this modeling can be far reaching since it is based on the worth and dignity of both the teacher and the students.

The skills that are necessary for developing a psychological basis of a relationship are the same as those outlined previously in chapters three and four. Empathy, genuineness, warmth, regard, and concreteness encourages the development of a facilitative relationship between teacher and student regardless of the racial composition of each. These skills transcend racial consideration and are valid for all groups (Higgins & Warner, 1975).

LANGUAGE AND CULTURE

The language we use when we talk about people, especially people different from ourselves, reveals a great deal about what we think and feel about them. Consider these commonly used terms, for example: race, ethnic group, and nationality. Most of us use each of these terms from time to time. But very few of us really know what each of these terms means and can distinguish among them or between them. Can two people be members of the same race, but different ethnic groups? Can people with the same nationality belong to different races and different ethnic groups? We will now explore definitions for the three questions and for some additional terms that are similar to them.

Race is a term that often is used very carelessly. People refer to "the Jewish race;" while there is no such thing. Many people believe that Northern Europeans belong to "the Nordic race;" still there is no such thing. We all hear about "the Black race;" the "yellow race," or the "white race." Again, there are no such things. Race is a word that scientists use for the convenience of classification. Even scientists disagree among themselves about what race means. In general, scientists use those classifications to separate human beings into three large classes. Members of each class usually have similar, superficial physical characteristics in common. These three major classes are Caucasoids, Negroids, and Mongoloids.

Caucasoids, originally from Europe, North Africa, and Southwest Asia, most members of this race have reddish white to olive brown skin and fine hair that ranges in color from light blond to dark brown. *Negroids,* originally from Africa, most members of this race have black or brown skin and very curly hair. *Mongoloids,* originally from Asia and the islands of the Pacific Ocean. Members of this race usually have yellow or brown skin and straight black hair. These three classes are very general. For example, there is a broad range within each class. There are Caucasoids who are dark-skinned and who are light skinned, Mongoloids who have yellow skin tones and who have red skin tones, and Negroids who are dark and who are light.

Racial intermixture has broken these distinctions even more. Interbreeding between races over the centuries has produced mixed races. That means that there are very few individuals who belong only to the Negroid, Mongoloid, or Caucasoid race. Individuals from each of these classes have mixed together to form numerous sub-classes. Chances are that you are a result of a blending of at least two or even all three of these races.

Physical similarities among races are far more significant than differences. General body build is the same in all races. All races have types

O, A, AB, and B blood. There is no such thing as "Negro blood," "White blood" or "Oriental blood."

It should be obvious from this discussion that the word *"race"* is not a very useful term for identifying the group to which someone belongs. When someone says that someone belongs to a certain "race," chances are that he/she means something else.

Other words that are used to designate differences in people which are often misunderstood are nationality and ethnic group. *Nationality* can be defined as a group of people who belong to or come from one country. When we ask about someone's nationality, we usually mean, "What country did your parents, grandparents, or great grandparents come from?" Nationality is a poor term to use because it can have two different meanings. Like the word "race," it is very general and easily misunderstood.

Ethnic group may be a better term to use than race because fewer people have preconceived assumptions about the term. Ethnic group refers to a group of people who have the same background and the same general beliefs. It describes a group of people who share a common cultural heritage, that is, the same language, religion, and customs. The term "ethnic group" has little to do with what someone looks like. It really refers to the way someone was reared, or the culture he/she has inherited. To a large extent we are all shaped by the environment in which we live. As children we learn from our environment the values, customs, beliefs, and attitudes that we carry with us to adulthood. The nature of that environment determines much of how we behave and relate to our family, our friends, and to individuals outside of our particular group. What is essential to remember is that this behavior is learned. It is not something with which we are born, and it can be modified by differences in environment.

It is important to note the differences between the terms race, nationality, and ethnic group, and to use them carefully. It is equally important to keep in mind the great range of differences among individual members of any race, ethnic group, or nationality.

Languages are full of symbolisms, color connotations, analogies, and similes which transmit dynamic messages. In many cultures white is associated with goodness and purity, while black with evil and death. Bad guys wear black—good guys wear white. Heroes ride white horses while villains ride black horses. We refer to the black sheep of the family, black and ominous clouds, calamitous events as in blackball or blacklist. We speak of "black as sin" and "pure as the driven (white) snow." White is superior or winners while black is inferior or losers. For example, when the Chicago White Sox lose the World Series they become the black sox. Superstitions and rituals also use colors to denote good and evil. It is bad luck for a black cat to run across one's path and white doves are featured in heavenly scenes or oftentimes to denote heaven.

RACISM IN THE MEDIA

The attitudes people have toward others are influenced to a great degree by their perceptions of the personal qualities of the other individual or group of individuals (Freedman, Carlsmith, & Sears, 1970). There are, however, other important factors which operate in the process of interpreting or making meaning out of what we hear and see. Cognitive information, past experiences, and the context of the sensory input (hearing and seeing) contribute to the perception of individuals.

One important and potent source of stimulation and cognitive information about others is television. Television is a source of information that influences the formation of attitudes toward minority groups through its characterization of them. Television also provides a context that freely mixes truth and reality. Ashmore and McConahoy (1975) suggested that media, especially television, perpetuates racial prejudice and stereotypic attitudes by their portrayals of and omission of facts about minority groups. They asserted that by emphasizing one type of behavior as characteristic, certain perceptions and attitudes among viewers were encouraged. In this study the behavior of Black characters and white characters on comedy programs was investigated to determine whether there were differences in the manner in which groups were portrayed. The existence of difference in the behavior of characters that are determined by racial feature would support the contention that differential attitudes of viewers are encouraged, since human actions are frequently interpreted as intrinsic to the person performing the actions or to the group with which the person holds membership. For example, if a woman viewed on television is engaged in many different activities and is overcome by the responsibility of completing all of the tasks required and breaks down and cries, then the viewer generalizes and comes to the conclusion that all women and weak and incompetent. Similarly, when Blacks are viewed as being happy in a situation where the Black character is unemployed and living in substandard housing, then the viewer generalizes and concludes that *all* Black people who are unemployed are or will be happy also.

Twenty-five or even fifteen years ago, Blacks were a rarity in television and the inclusion of a Negro actor or actress in drama or situation comedy in anything other than a menial servant's role was guaranteed to produce controversy, angry reaction from viewers, and possible sponsor withdrawal.

To fully understand the status of Blacks on television, it is important to review history. Despite television's position as the primary source of information for most people, it is a fairly new medium. One would think that because of its fairly new arrival on the media scene that it would be free of some of the traditional institutional racism that has permeated other forms of the media, such as newspapers and magazines.

Because of the civil rights movement in the South in the 1960s, television began to give serious attention to the condition of Blacks in this country. Many would credit television for helping to hasten passage of the civil rights legislation during that period by its dramatic coverage of the civil rights activities during the early 1960s (Patterson, 1984).

It was during this period in the aftermath of eruptions of the cities that the broadcast media like the print media, began to recruit minority journalists and management personnel. It was a major breakthrough, and for the first time, Blacks, though in small numbers, were a visible presence in the white media.

The importance of Black ownership is underscored by the poverty of Black programming by the major networks. Neither ABC, CBS, or NBC had, in the Spring of 1975, a program which concerned itself with the needs or history of the Black community, such undertakings were restricted to special one-time efforts, as the "Autobiography of Miss Jane Pittman," which was aired on CBS in 1974. This film was nominated for 9 Emmy awards and won 2 (Ploski & Marr, 1976). The paucity of Black produced programming also remains a problem. There is only one nationally televised Black public affairs program, the "Tony Brown Journal," which is owned and produced by Tony Brown, the former dean of the School of Communications at Howard University. Another national Black program, "For You Black Women," aimed at the female viewer continues on the air but "Go Tell It," a program which featured Benjamin Hooks, executive director of the National Association for the Advancement of Colored People, has been discontinued. Major network news programs also omit Blacks, especially programs of the question and answer variety where reporters interview political leaders. Black journalists rarely appear on CBS's "Face the Nation" or ABC's "Issues and Answers."

Blacks have, however, been given greater exposure as performers in such light entertainment programs as "Good Times" and the "Flip Wilson Show" and Blacks do appear more and more frequently in local news programming. The 1974 season brought about a new comedy series, "That's My Mama" which joined "Sanford and Son" on prime time television.

Although the number of Blacks and other minorities has increased on television since the 1960s, the proportions in which they appear are not representative of their proportions in the population in the United States.

Today, in this the enlightened age of civil rights, the barriers of race have been lowered and Blacks are gaining acceptance in television, Unfortunately, they are gaining acceptance as Blacks, not as human beings. That is, they are seldom shown as thinking, caring, breathing, feeling rounded characters with whom the audience can become involved emotionally. An important part of this problem is, of course, that television to a large extent mirrors American society, in which, despite substantial gains, the Black person is still viewed as playing only a limited role in society.

P. Jay Sidney, veteran Black actor who has appeared in more than 200 television dramas, took this position in the 1960s: "Negroes rarely get the opportunity to portray human beings on television. They are usually cast in the role of auxiliaries to white people. Their only reason for existence on the screen, is for the benefit of white people in the story."

Blacks in fact, are seen in a variety of dramatic roles on network programs. However, television's acceptance of Blacks parallels that of society at large. Blacks are most often cast as servants or entertainers.

Blacks, for example, are rarely involved in dramatic scenes which show America at play, be they at a restaurant, country club dances, or church social. Blacks are seldom cast as judges, airline pilots, ship captains, college presidents, cowboys, bank executives, salesmen, editors, or engineers. Blacks are generally accepted in television dramas as policemen, soldiers, teachers, detectives, or criminals.

Donald Bogle (1974) in his interpretive history of Blacks in American films classified the characters in which Blacks are cast as "Toms, Coons, Mulattoes, Mammies, and Bucks." Bogle derived these classifications by studying Blacks in film from the very beginning of the birth and growth of the movie industry.

The Tom is personified most in Harriet Beecher Stowe's Novel, *Uncle Tom's Cabin,* which included the tale of the good christian slave. Toms are always characters in films who are chased, harassed, hounded, flogged, enslaved, and insulted. They, however, always keep the faith and never turn against their white masters. They remain submissive, stoic, generous, selfless, and very kind. While white audiences find Toms endearing and heroes of sorts, Black audiences view the character role as weak and at best one who has sold out on his people.

The Coon appeared in a series of films presenting Blacks as amusement objects. The pickaninny was the first of the coon types to be found in films. Characters are usually children who are harmless, less intelligent creatures whose eyes popped,   whose hair stood on end with the least excitement, and whose antics were funny and pleasant. Examples of pickaninnies are Farina, Stymie, and Buckwheat from the still popular *Our Gang Series.* Another member of the coon family is the Uncle Remus. Uncle Remus is harmless and congenial and distinguishes himself by the naive and funny philosophy he takes of life and the manner in which he makes meaning out of what is happening to him. Remus' complacency with life and the cons's contentment has always been presented to indicate the Black man's satisfaction with the system and his limited place in it.

The mulatto is the third figure among Black characters on film. Mammy, the fourth type, is closely related to the comin coons and is usually relegated to their ranks. Mammy is distinguished by her sex and her powerful independence. She is usually big, fat, and cantankerous. Mammies, the fourth type, were often more dedicated to their jobs or mission, usually that of serving as washer-women (or the foreman in the big house or serving as surrogate mothers for white children insisting that they obey the rules of the house and insisted that they behave in ways so they would not be confused as being white trash. While the blatant stereotypic roles Blacks portray are not as many or as frequent now as they were in the early day of film, the subtle stereotypes nonetheless is still present on todays film. We only have to consider prime time television for evidence of this fact. A casual glance at a recent copy of the *TV Guide* reveals that during the 1983-84 season, there were 12 shows which featured Black characters on a regular basis. Half or six were situational comedies. Patterson (1984) when considering entertainment television explains that the accent on comedy, while seemingly harmless, has no counterbalance. The predominant image of Blacks on television remains that of buffoonery. For example, the work of the very talented actress Cicely Tyson in the "Marva Collins Story" must be balanced against "Beulah Land" in which Blacks were depicted as being enthralled by their slave state (both programs aired in 1981). While the blatant stereotypic roles Blacks portray are not as many or as frequent now as they were in the early days of film, the subtle stereotypes nonetheless is still present in todays film. We only have to consider prime time television for evidence of this fact.

Bogles (1974) designation of Toms, Coons, Mammie, and Bucks are still accurate for most television characters portrayed in current programming. Modern television characters can be grouped in three categories: servants, characters who exist in visible anonymity, and a new phenomenon which puts Black children in white families. Nell Carter of "Gimme a Break" is maid (Mammy) which takes care of a family. Quite infrequently she is written in with a tender moment substituting for the deceased mother for the young girls in the family. "Benson" while he has been promoted from the manager of the governor's mansion to Budget Director for the state, is placed in the kitchen more often than he is placed in his office. "Trapper John, M. D.," "Hill Street Blues," and "Love Boat" are examples of the second category. These characters are always portrayed at work but not one ever goes home after work to a family and home. "Webster," "Different Strokes," and "Facts of Life," to a lesser degree represent the third category.

Two shows have not been placed in categories, perhaps one reason it is difficult to label them is the fact that they are so unreal and unbelievable. "The Jeffersons" which have enjoyed unusual longevity, features a Black family with a strong willed maid and an interracial couple for the best friends. What is even more outrageous is the fact that

George, an egocentric Black man, earned a fortune in the dry cleaning business. The introduction of Polyester alone renders this virtually impossible. The second is equally unreal, "The 'A' Team." "The 'A' Team" is a group of Viet Nam renegade Robin Hoods who have among the group B. A.; Mr. T even in real life is unbelievable.

Current television when examined in the light of what it offers children in terms of Black involvement and Blacks influence on meaningful levels miss the mark of presenting Blacks on television in a positive image, negotiating the real world and pursuing the American dream.

Television continues to be a growth industry and its influence upon the way we live and think seems certain to grow even more in the future. What is not clear however is how it will affect our lives and our perception of ourselves and each other as we attempt to bridge the gap between the races and move forward a more equitable and just society.

The most casual review of Blacks and the media results in the conclusion that Blacks seem destined to be on an uphill struggle to reach representative status in the media as employees. Decision makers and television is indeed a powerful tool and seems destined to become even more powerful in the future. Joel Swerdlow, co-author of the book, *Remote Control: Television and the Manipulation of American Life* (Mankiewicz & Swerdlow, 1978) reported that young children, especially white suburban children who may have little contact with Blacks, believe that situational comedies on television accurately depict Blacks and other races even when this contradicts what their parents have taught them. Swerdlow further asserts that these findings about television and Blacks also generally hold true for Hispanics, native Americans, and other ethnic groups.

Anyone who doubts the powerful role that television plays in the lives of young children in the United States should consider the results of a poll conducted by the *World Almanac* and *Book of Facts.* It surveyed 2,000 eighth graders, many of whom were Black, who they regarded as their 30 top heroes, the person they admired most and wanted to be like when they grew up. The answers demonstrated conclusively that television and movies often have more influence over young children than their families, churches, and schools. At the top of the list were film stars such as Burt Reynolds, Richard Pryor, and Alan Alda. Others in the top 30 were Brooke Shields (4th), Bo Derek (7th), Sugar Ray Leonard (9th), Bill Cosby (6th), Magic Johnson (22nd), and Earl Campbell (24th). What should be most striking about these rankings to teachers and parents is the fact that there was not a single political, cultural, economic, or civil personality in the top 30. In fact there are only two professional groups represented among the thirty individuals which were athletes (3) and entertainers (27). Most would agree that none of the individuals mentioned above are "bad" people, but it is clearly alarming to think that over 2,000 eighth grade children (teenagers) would regard athletes and entertainers as the role models who they most admired and would most like to emulate. These findings support emerging belief that television among other things is a transmitter of culture, a custodian of traditions, and the creator of heroes, a role formerly held by our schools.

The minds of young children are sufficiently receptive to positive thinking which corrects erroneous conclusions and explanations, stereotypes, and negative impressions. The effects of positive experiences on the development of attitudes toward racial diversity has been clearly demonstrated by Campbell, Yarrow and Yarrow (1958), Litcher and Johnson (1969), and Best, Naylor, and Williams (1975) experiences that promote the acquisition of positive concepts of racial diversity must be provided in the early years. We believe that teachers have a vital responsibility and countless opportunities to assist children in making correct meanings about racial diversity even if the image of Blacks are distorted on television. Unless children are presented positive images and provided positive experiences they can become victims of indirect influences which can translate into rigid prejudices.

Effects of Television on Children

There is considerable controversy about whether mass media, especially television serve to reinforce or change preexisting ideas. This question had been studied especially in the context of commercial advertising. In the 1940s and 1950s, studies contradicted the long-held theory which suggested that people were easily swayed by persuasive messages in the media when it came to voting habits. According to earlier studies, voting behavior is most influenced by family and acquaintances, and voters select those political messages that reinforce preexisting beliefs. Later studies, those conducted in the 1960's and 1970's, have found that a voter may sometimes completely change his/her vote as a result of a political message. Thus far, the results of studies dealing with advertising are inconclusive. The question remains unanswered however about whether the effect of television serves to reinforce established ideas or contributes to one's changing idea about certain issues. If these questions are raised about the effects of television on adult viewers, then similar questions should be raised about children and television. In fact, the more compelling question should concern the effect of television on children. Television is one of the most widespread influences on todays youth. Recently, some of the most sophisticated crimes committed by youth were those for which the idea was gotten from popular television shows.

It is estimated that the average child will have watched 15,000 hours of television by the time he/she is 17. This represents more time than hours spent in school. In fact, television watching is only second to sleep in terms of time consumption (Rothenberg, 1977). In spite of the considerable study of the effect of television on children, the findings are inconsistent. Theories which have been advanced from the results of these studies suggest that television provides vicarious reinforcement that is imaginary. Participation is an activity that is rewarding for the characters on the screen and will reinforce this same type of behavior in a real-life situation. This does not imply a negative or positive value. Yet, when the activity is violent and promotes race stereotype, children cannot separate themselves from fantasy, this effect can be harmful.

Because children watch television for various reasons, ranging from entertainment to loneliness, they unknowingly can become involved in a process of observational learning; that is, they learn certain things by simply watching the behavior of characters on television.

Social learning theory teaches us that children learn many different things through observation and modeling, including skills, values, norms, roles, sex, and race stereotypes. What a child learns can be either positive or negative, depending on the content. Another important effect of television is that it often replaces parental influence and supplies role models for children and adolescents who have inadequate ones at home. The television set can become a substitute parent, a baby sitter, and a replacement for family interaction. This effect goes against the welfare of the individual.

The sociology effecting most Black children; broken homes, working mothers, single mothers, and lack of money for entertainment are such that television plays even more of an important role in the lives of Black children. Because of the lack of live role models in their families or communities, many Black children use television to find heroes, role models, and examples of successful Blacks. Current television programming projects an extreme image of Blacks. Blacks are almost never portrayed as individuals engaged in meaningful work who are making a significant contribution to society. Many, however, are cast in roles seldom found in the real world, except for that of servant or policeman. Teachers in their work with all children in the classroom can help to balance the sensational portrayal or otherwise stereotype roles of Blacks on television. While many Blacks can be seen by children who are athletes or entertainers, these in my view are sensational roles.

What is needed is teachers to point to Black citizens who are in the mainstream of American life and who are successful by traditional standards; those who are University presidents, scientists, lawyers, politicians, and so forth.

INSTITUTIONAL RACISM

When Blacks, or whites for that matter, complain about racial discrimination, recently referred to as "institutional racism," they do not refer to the overt acts of bigotry that are so vividly illustrated in the activities of either the KKK as an extreme example or the closed shops of many unions as a more moderate one. The racism that so clearly motivated the early slave traders to subjugate human beings to misery and indignity, and to rationalize any feelings of guilt by the sole consideration of profit, is not the contemporary white man's viewpoint, his guilt, or responsibility.

The difficulty that most people have in understanding the angry cry of institutional racism lies in the fact that they do not understand institutionalization. They assume, since most of the people they know or speak to do not appear to be overtly prejudiced, that the institutions they live and work in do not contain racist functions. They do not consider that because Black people have inadequate work situations, poor housing, little education, and little political power, there must be something inherently discriminating in the larger institutions that regulate social life. The structure of racism is infinitely more potent than the accumulated prejudices of the citizens who conduct the routine affairs of social organizations. Most individuals, for that matter, cannot even conceive of ways of restructuring these institutions given the most humane set of motivations.

Schools continue to maintain institutional racism by the very nature of the practices and policies instituted to guide the participation of students in school activities. Black children have always excelled in athletics and music programs in the schools. However, in many school districts, policies, and practices eliminate many Black children from participating in these activities. For example, some school districts require that boys who try out for junior high school football and varsity football are required to purchase their shoes and insurance in order to participate. In junior high school music programs, students are required to purchase or rent their instruments. Those who survive the junior high school program and are selected to participate in the high school program meet with even more barriers. One common practice in many school districts for example is the practice of requiring members of the marching band at high schools to attend a summer band camp. Many times these camps are residential for a full week and consequently very expensive to attend. This practice alone eliminates untold number of talented Black children from participating in the music programs in the schools.

While the previous examples relate primarily to economic considerations, there are also noneconomic practices which eliminates Blacks from participating in school activities. In some school districts, female students are required to have certain specific physical attributes to be considered for participation in certain school activities. For example, female students who try out for a spot on the cheerleader squad or for an opening among the majorettes are required to have shoulder-length hair. This practice automatically eliminates most Black girls from meeting a basic criteria while they may be otherwise well qualified in every other way. In many school districts these policies continue year after year unchanged and examined. Faculty advisors and activity leaders continue these practices many times without realizing the exclusionary in fact these practices bring to bear on Black students particularly those Black students whose families might not be financially able to foot the bill for their children's participation.

As an example, one school district has maintained the practice of sponsoring at the junior high school a trip to Washington, our nation's capital, for children at the end of the eighth grade year. The cost of the trip totals more than four hundred dollars for those who participate.

Needless to say the financial feature of this activity eliminates many children from participating both Black and white, yet it continues year after year.

Jarolimek (1981) explained that institutionalized racism consists of practices that have been legitimized by the social system or society and that systematically discriminates against members of specific groups. Practices that are legitimized are accepted as fair and good. Seldom are they questioned by others. Even those against whom the discrimination is directed accept these practices when they are given legitimacy. It is also important to understand that institutionalized racism systematically discriminates. This means, in other words, that it is not a random, idiosyncratic happening. Rather, it occurs regularly and consistently. It is directed against certain groups because members of those groups have particular characteristics or qualities.

Jarolimek provided other examples of institutionalized racism.

1. Imposing height requirements for certain jobs, such as those help by the police, fire fighters, bus drivers, and so forth. (This practice discriminates systematically against some Asian groups who tend to be physically short of stature.)

2. Instituting literacy requirements for voting. (This discriminates against Blacks and other ethnic minorities who are known to have lower literacy rates than the dominant group.)

3. Having high fees for filing for public office. (This practice discriminates against the low-income groups, many of whom are ethnic minorities.)

4. Associating certain groups with specific positions. (This stereotyping discriminates against easily identifiable persons, such as ethnic minorities, because traditionally they have been in low-status occupations.)

5. Using qualifying tests that require a high level of verbal behavior. (This discriminates against ethnic minorities.)

6. Zoning with segregated housing patterns. (This practice discriminates against individuals easily identified as members of certain groups, that is, visible minorities.)

7. Employing homogeneous grouping in classrooms. (This discriminates against ethnic minorities because it often results in their being in low-achieving groups.)

8. Implementing automation, technology, labor-reducing practices. (These absorb jobs of low-skilled persons, thus a high percentage of ethnic minorities.)

9. Specifying racial quotas. (These quotas foreclose opportunities beyond the stated quota regardless of availability of qualified personnel from disallowed groups.)

10. Developing curriculum content unrelated to the life of certain groups.

Estes (1978) described how one school system met the challenge of attempting to eliminate institutional racism. The article offers one example of accomplishments a school district can achieve when a court order to eliminate racism is accepted in a spirit of fairness for all children. When highlighting the process the school system used to study itself Estes explained:

> First of all, we had to try to get everyone to understand the meaning of institutional racism. In the schools it is covert and indirect, and oftentimes it is unconscious. It keeps certain people in inferior status not on the basis of color line but with institutional structures related to color.
>
> Perhaps an example will help explain my meaning. A girl's drill team regulation said that members' hair must be shoulder length. This would automatically exclude many Blacks, although no restriction is overtly placed on the race.
>
> Major decisions in institutions have traditionally been made by middle-class whites for the majority (which in many U.S. school districts consists of middle-class whites). The results has been that many nonmajority characteristics have not been taken into account, and minorities have become victims of institutional discrimination or racism. (pp. 186-7)

Some of these positive steps which resulted from the process instituted by this school district included increased participation of minority students in school activities, made changes in school board policies, developed an affirmative action plan, and increased the number of minorities holding top-level executive positions in the school district.

Estes concluded that affirmative action means becoming advocates of all children rather than adversaries of some. It means seeing all children as human resources to be developed to their greatest potential, and finally and most important, affirmative action means giving educators an opportunity to assert their professionalism in the interest of all children regardless to race, color, or creed.

INTEGRATION OR COMPENSATORY EDUCATION

Many educators agree that integration is a desirable goal. Achieving equitable educational opportunity for all America's children presents society and education with one of its most profoundly complex challenges. In the past thirty years we have seen a number of programs instituted in this country to redress past social injustices and to open the doors of education to those groups who have traditionally not enjoyed the advantages that a good education can provide, mainly, visible minorities, ethnic groups, and women.

Equalizing educational opportunity is a complicated process; it is made especially so in our society because of the fact that we are multisocioeconomic, multiracial, and multiethnic. Consequently, achieving educational equity becomes enmeshed in other volatile social problems such as racism, sexism, affirmative action, discrimination, reverse discrimination, and institutional racism. Legislative and judicial decisions relevant to any of these issues have consequences for educational opportunity. The reverse also is true. Accommodating the vocational aspirations of individuals and at the same time meeting the social needs of society in a nation as diverse as ours will probably never be achieved wholly to the satisfaction of everyone. It seems inevitable that there will always appear to be some measure of inequality to those least favored by the social systems.

The Principle of Equality

The principle of equality is introduced to us from those around us in our earliest childhood days. During play, young children are taught to be fair to others, to share, to be considerate. Those concepts are clearly related to equality. At a very young age in the elementary school we learn that the founding fathers who established this great nation endorsed the idea that "all men are created equal" and wrote this principle into that great document of freedom, the Declaration of Independence. This idea has since been reaffirmed countless numbers of times, most notably in Abraham Lincoln's Gettysburg Address, in which he proclaimed the nation as being "dedicated to the proposition that all men are created equal." In spite of all this rhetoric about equality, many persons would be hard put to provide a workable definition of it.

Compensatory Education

The concept of compensatory education grew out of the national concern for equal opportunity to education for all children. In the early 1950's developments in human relations lead to the realization that people were more alike than different, and if they are not more alike, then it is important to make them that way. Hence, compensatory education was based on a deficit theory of cultural development that emerged from the humanitarian concern over equality.

All programs designed to enhance the school success of the disadvantaged child are by definition based on a deficit theory of development. Something is missing in the child development pattern that is impeding his/her school achievement. Compensatory education is intended to shore up those deficiencies.

Compensatory education also places great faith in education as a means of achieving social reform. In 1964, President Lyndon B. Johnson signed into law the Economic Opportunity Act. This was his first shot fired in what was commonly referred to as President Johnson's "War on Poverty." Carnoy and Levin (1976) called attention to the role of education in this effort:

"if such a war was actually declared during this period, then education and training were its artillery."

The rationale for compensatory education is based on the principle that appropriate intervention is justified on the basis of the presence of learner deficiencies and that such intervention will produce the desired results. Thus, preschool programs were designed to give pupils a head start, thereby enabling disadvantaged pupils to enter first grade on an equal footing with their more advantaged classmates. Special training programs were developed to improve work skills of unemployed young adults. School busing was used to move ghetto children to more stimulating school environments in other neighborhoods. A policy of affirmative action was advanced by President Johnson in Executive Order 11246:

> Imagine a hundred yard dash in which one of the two runners has his legs shackled together. He has progressed 10 yards, while the unshackled runner has gone 50 yards. At that pint the judges decide that the race is unfair. How do they rectify the situation? Do they merely remove the shackles and allow the race to proceed? Then they could say that "equal opportunity now prevailed." But one of the runners would still be forty yards ahead of the other. Would it not be the better part of justice to allow the previously shackled runner to make up the forty yard gap; or to start the race all over again? That would be affirmative action toward equality. (1965)

Perhaps the fact that Mr. Johnson was at one time a teacher in Texas contributed to the prominent role that education played in the poverty programs in the 1960s. In spite of Mr. Johnson's efforts, however, full desegregation in many school districts has been slow in coming or at best cosmetic more than twenty years after Executive Order 11246. The fundamental strategy to promote equity for socioeconomically deprived children in schools has served not to result in equity but rather to further segregation. For example, in desegregated schools, ability grouping and tracking have been used to resegregate students within school buildings. A study of desegregation outcomes reported that most of the classes for "gifted" students, as well as the college preparatory classes, were composed of white students, while Black and other minority students were channeled into special education, compensatory education, remedial, or vocational courses (Green & Cohen, 1974).

Green, Parsons, and Thomas (1981) further concluded that minority students are overrepresented in compensatory education and remedial programs in desegregated schools. Many students placed in such programs remain in them for the rest of their school years and often find themselves unable to meet graduation requirements. In states that require competency-based tests for high school graduation, a disproportionate number of those failing the test have been minority students.

Another practice which has led to resegregate students within desegregated school systems is that of discriminatory disciplinary practices. While minority students comprise approximately 25% of the nation's school population, they make up 40% of all suspended and expelled students (National Advisory Committee on Black Higher Education and Black Universities and Colleges, 1979). Minority students are not only suspended more frequently, their suspensions are also for longer periods of time. Thus, these students lose time in school, drop out of school, or fail to meet graduation requirements; they enter the job market with few work skills, destined to join the overflowing ranks of the unemployed.

Affirmative Action

President John F. Kennedy was first to call for "affirmative steps" in an executive order issued in 1961. In essence, it called on contractors involved in federal projects to recruit and promote Blacks and other minority workers. But not until the 1964 Civil Rights Act came into full force did affirmative action became a reality. Under Title VI, discrimination was prohibited in education, and, under Title VII, it was barred in employment. The original intent of the legislation was to provide for equality of opportunity, not for racial balance or preferential treatment, although federal courts were authorized under Title VII to "order such affirmative action as may be appropriate."

Under Title IV of the Civil Rights Act of 1964, the Office of Education in the Department of Health, Education and Welfare was empowered to refuse federal financial assistance to any institutions and school districts that were not in compliance with Title VI, that is, were not meeting the guidelines having to do with the requirement that no person because of race, color, or national origin could be excluded from or denied the benefits of any program receiving federal financial support. For all practical purposes, this meant every public institution and school district in the country, because by 1965, when the law was actually implemented, most of them were receiving federal financial assistance in some form. The U.S. Office of Education was, therefore, in the very powerful position of (1) establishing guidelines under which institutions and school districts would meet the requirement of Title VI, (2) overseeing and determining whether or not units were in compliance, and (3) releasing or withholding federal assistance on the basis of its own interpretation of whether or not a unit was in compliance. This procedure was very important in enabling the federal government to enforce antidiscrimination legislation as well as eliminating segregation in schools. Under Title VI, if a parent filed a segregation complaint with the attorney general, that office could bring legal action against the offending school district to force compliance with desegregation regulations. In some instances, that action constituted more of a threat than did the possibility of loss of federal funding.

With the introduction of the affirmative action principle, a whole new set of legal and ethical considerations surfaced in dealing with the equal opportunity issues. Affirmative action in principle require that some active measures be instituted to rectify the effects of past injustices or inequities. Under this policy it is not enough to provide open admission or easy access to education. What is required is intervention that will compensate for prior inequalities in the social environment.

Many would argue that affirmative action guidelines require that which was formerly prohibited by law because these practices were considered discriminatory. Students, for example, could not be admitted to programs and men and women could not be employed on the basis of race, sex, religion, or national origin. President Johnson introduced the principle of affirmative action as a method of further reducing possibilities for discrimination. Perhaps Bell (1973) was correct when he asserted that affirmative action is a significant shift in public policy and as it has been implemented by federal guidelines since the 1960s has dealt more with increasing representation and less with reducing discrimination. Regardless of the critics, the spirit of affirmative action guidelines are still valid and legitimate today. Black communities throughout this country are populated with individuals who on a daily basis face barriers to equal opportunity in employment, housing, access to adequate medical care, and fair treatment under the law. Therefore, we need to continuously assess whether equality and/or equity is being attained in education. Affirmative action is not only the legal thing to do; it is the right thing to do.

Teachers and other school personnel need to be familiar with the various laws and regulations which prohibit race discrimination. A general knowledge of federal antidiscrimination requirements enables teachers to assist children in determining whether their rights have been violated and what to do and where to go for help if such has been the case. Teachers knowledgeable about these also can assist the school and/or school district in reducing and eliminating institutional racism, racists, and other discriminatory elements, practices, and policies.

EDUCATION, LAW, AND HUMAN RELATIONS

Most socialization is informal in the course of spontaneous interaction. However, institutions for deliberate socialization are a universal feature of a complex society. Today education is more important in size and scope than ever before in human history. For example, a century ago the educated person was economically unproductive; today productivity depends on wide distribution of specialized skills. Modern political systems too, call for mass education. Therefore, effective participation in a modern society requires heavy investment in our schools. Schools, like the broader process of socialization, has a dual significance. That is, each is person-centered and society-centered. Education enhances the capabilities of the individuals and contributes to their self-realization; at the same time, education does practical work for the social system. The need to balance these functions, personal and social, possess important issues for education.

Two important functions of education are the transmission of culture and promoting personal development. Personal development is promoted by the schools ability to develop skills and communicate perspectives that cannot readily be gained through other socializing experiences. In addition to providing intellectual discipline and the opportunity to learn specialized subject matters, the school is often a place of transition from a highly personal to a more impersonal world. Habits are learned, such as punctuality, that may be necessary in a time-conscious society. Schooling can have psychological costs as well as benefits. If the school prolongs dependency beyond maturity, instills feelings of inferiority, or exaggerates the worth of intellectuality, it may have negative effects on personal growth and well-being of students.

The school is also a major agency for transforming a heterogeneous and divided community into one bound together by a common language and sense of identity. In the United States, schools have carried a major share of the task of integrating millions of immigrants; and now schools have the obligation and responsibility to bring into the mainstream of American life many other millions who have been disadvantaged.

Like education, law is a major institution of social integration. Legal injunctions lend coherence, regularity, and acceptance to social norms and codes of conduct. Law sustains and encourages social organization by defining what individuals can rely on in the conduct of others. As a sensitive indicator of cultural values, law dictates what people should aspire to in the ordering of their affairs.

The legal system is an area of conflict, as well as a source of stability. Law is therefore, a public, institutionalized mechanism for resolving controversies. Its contribution to social integration is active, not passive.

Two major social functions of our legal system are to communicate moral standards and to facilitate cooperative action. When the law defines rights and responsibilities and backs up its definitions with the threat of coercion, it becomes in effect a powerful agency of communication. Every act of enforcement is at the same time an act of communication. For this reason, it is important that there be close coordination of legal purpose and legal administration. Fairness at a legal hearing may not offset the effects of discrimination and racism inherent in the denial of education opportunity or employment opportunities for Blacks.

The educational significance of law accounts for the reluctance to change laws that embody moral standards. For example, many people may question the wisdom of attempting to regulate hiring practices such as quotas, but they want to keep the law on the books as a public expression of what is right and proper. They fear that removal of affirmative action guidelines would be taken as public approval for discrimination in hiring on the basis of sex, race, or national origin. By the same token, proponent of new values may be content for awhile with a law that has "no teeth." The hope is that having the law on the books will educate the public to the new values, in part by drawing upon the reservoir of respect for law.

To facilitate cooperative action is a second function of law. In most human interaction, people have to accept the risk that others will not do what is expected of them. Being courteous, showing up for meetings, lending a hand to a neighbor, and many other expectations are important to orderly social life, but for the most part they receive no legal recognition. Some expectations, however, are formally recognized and can be the basis of claims of right. Such a claim, if it stems from a person's status as a human being or a citizen, is usually formulated as a basis of constitutional right. Other rights are created by the parties themselves, by exchanging enforceable promises in accordance with the law of contracts. The filing of legitimate expectations is the reliance function of law; without it the risks of cooperative action would be much increased.

A modern industrial society is especially dependent on legal protection of rights, because there is so much cooperation between strangers who cannot rely on Kinship ties or other informal social control for the protection of their interests.

Laws have been passed by state and federal legislators which have had significant impact of the composition of school populations. The net effect of these legislations was to change the composition of the student population. Mass education forced teachers to deal with students from a variety of social, economic, and cultural backgrounds.

The impact of racial segregation on education in the United States is well known. Racial policies discriminating against Blacks and other minorities have led to the creation of laws and statutes which instruct the public about what is right and proper in dealing with these minorities. While these recent laws directly affect and/or protect the rights of minorities, they were written and enforced as being the constitutional rights of all people in the United States.

Laws have been enacted which seem to assume that changing behavior would eventually change attitudes, beliefs, and prejudices. We only have to review just casually the history of laws and the public response to those laws to realize that attitudes cannot be legislated. For that matter behaviors cannot be legislated because the law is open to such liberal interpretation that the original intent and spirit of the law are lost when individuals who oppose the law make interpretations for their own conscience.

Constitutional laws are those laws which deal with relationships of individuals one to the other or institutions dealing with individuals. While important, values and beliefs are inherent in the laws and statutes which provide broad guidelines for human relations behaviors. Accompanying changes in attitudes and prejudices toward affected groups for whom laws protect have been slow in coming. One important reason for this fact is that one of the basic characteristics of human nature is to reject and resist change, especially when change involves new ways of behaving toward individuals different in many ways from ourselves.

The broad purpose of education is to facilitate the integration of a student's total personality. The process of education is the process of change. When we educate students, we help them develop their own unique personalities by bringing their ideas and feelings into communication with others.

When the purpose of education is combined with the social functions of law, that is, to communicate moral standards and to facilitate cooperative action, then marriage becomes a potent vehicle for producing a healthier society. A society wherein each of its members can truly have an equal opportunity to achieve the American dream.

Schools have a tremendously important role to perform in our culture. As institutions, each school represents a microcosm of the larger society. Within each school, the basic unit is the classroom, which is under the direction of a teacher. The individual teacher appears to be the most vital factor in the system; few would deny the importance of the influence a teacher may have on a student's behavior and personality development. Unfortunately, we have not always provided our teachers with the proper training in human relations that would help to ensure that teachers understood the values which are inherent in the constitution of the United States which protects the rights of all people. More importantly teachers also should understand and adopt a supportive attitude toward those programs, such as compensatory education and affirmative action, designed to bring Blacks and other minorities into the mainstream of society. If our schools are to eliminate racism and provide equal opportunity for all children them considerable attention must be given to training teachers in ways which will ensure that they develop the skills, attitudes, and values important in human relations for multicultural education.

We believe the model presented in Chapters 4 through 8 of this text is a most potent vehicle to bring teachers to a level of personal and professional functioning which would allow them to be fully responsive to all children regardless of race. When the skills of the human relations-problem solving model is incorporated into the repertoire of teacher behaviors, a healthy climate is established for all children. Social norms are created by the example set by teachers in their treatment of students and the conditions which increase prejudice are eliminated and the potential of educational equity is increased for all children.

SELF TEST, CHAPTER 14

1. Discuss the difference between racism and ethnocentrism and indicate the implications of each for public education.

2. Provide examples of institutional racism that prevail in schools and colleges.

3. How can the public school combat institutional racism?

4. Discuss social trends and conditions that encouraged legislative and judicial actions favoring distributive justice since 1950.

5. Explain how the desire for justice and equality has affected the role of the public schools.

6. What is the difference between schools being "integrated" as opposed to ones being "desegregated?" Which is easier to achieve? Why?

7. How might a school be legally desegregated and yet provide instruction on a racially segregated basis? Explain how and why such a set of circumstances could develop.

8. What are the social consequences of the practice of tracking in a comprehensive high school?

9. Explain the rationale of compensatory education.

10. How do you believe television contributes to the attitudes we hold toward Blacks. Explain the possible effects television may have on Black children.

11. How is racism depicted in language and what are some examples.

ADDITIONAL RESOURCES

Britton, G., & Lumpkin, M. A. (1977). *Consumer's guide to sex, race, and career bias in public school textbooks.* Corvallis, OR: Britton and Associates.

The crisis: A record of the worker races is the official organ of the National Association for the Advancement of Colored People. Brooklyn, NY: Crisis Publishing.

Colangelo, N., Foxley, C. H., & Dustin, D. (Eds.) (1979). *Multicultural nonsexist education.* Dubuque, IA: Kendall/Hunt Publishing.

Epps, E. G. (Ed.) (1974). *Cultural pluralism.* Berkeley, CA: McCutchan Publishing.

Novak, M. (1971). *The rise of the unmeltable ethnics.* New York: Macmillan.

Ploski, H. A., & Marr, W. (1976). *The Negro Almanac: A reference work on the Afro American.* New York: The Bellwether Company.

Scimecca, J. A. (1980). *Education and society, Part III.* New York: Holt, Rinehart and Winston.

REFERENCES

Ashmore, R. D., & McConahay, J. B. (1975). *Psychology and America's urban dilemmas.* New York: McGraw-Hill.

Bell, D. (1973). *The coming of post-industrial society.* New York: Basic Books.

Best, D. (1975). The modification of racial bias in pre-school children. *Journal of Experimental Psychology, 20,* 193-205.

Best, D., Naylor, A., & Williams, J. (1975). Extension of color bias research to young French and Italian children. *Journal of Cross-cultural Research, 6,* 390-495.

Bogle, D. (1974). *Tom Coons, mulattoes, mammies, & bucks: An interpretative history of Blacks in American films.* New York: Bantam Books.

Campbell, J., Yarrow, L., & Yarrow, M. (1958). The study of adaptation to a new social situation. *Journal of Social Issues, 14,* 3-59.

Carnoy, M., & Levin, H. M. (1976). *The limits of educational reform.* New York: David McKay Company.

Estes, N. (1979). On eliminating institutional racism. In N. Colangelo, C. H. Foxley, & D. Dustin (Eds.), *Multicultural nonsexist education: A human relations approach.* Dubuque, IA: Kindall/Hunt Publishing.

Exum, H. A. (1979). Human relations for Black students. In N. Colangelo, C. H. Foxley, & D Dustin (Eds.), *Multicultural nonsexist education: A human relations approach.* Dubuque, IA: Kindall/Hunt Publishing.

Freedman, J. L., Carlsmith, J. M., & Sears, D. O. (1970). *Social psychology.* Englewood Cliffs, N.J.: Prentice-Hall.

Green, R. L., Parsons, M. A., & Thomas, F. S. (1981). Desegregation: The unfinished agenda. *Educational Leadership, 38* (4), 282-286.

Green, R. L., & Cohen, W. J. (1974). Northern school desegregation: Educational, legal, and political issues. *Uses of the Sociology of Education.* Chicago: The National Society for the Study of Education, 83-91.

Higgins, E. B., & Warner, R. W. (1975). Research in counseling: Counseling Blacks. *The Personnel and Guidance Journal, 53,* 382-386.

Jarolimek, J. (1981). *The schools in contemporary society: An analysis of social currents, issues, and forces.* New York: MacMillan.

Lane, H. U. (Ed.) (1980). *World almanac and book of facts.* New York: Newspaper Enterprise Association, Inc.

Litcher, J., & Johnson, D. (1969). Changes in attitudes toward Negroes of white elementary school students after use of multi-ethnic readers. *Journal of Educational Psychology, 60,* 390-405.

Mankiewicz, F., & Swerdlow, J. (1978). *Remote control: Television and the manipulation of American life.* New York: Time Books.

National Advisory Committee on Black Higher Education and Black Universities and Colleges (1979). *Access of Black Americans to Higher Education: How Open Is the Door?* Washington, D.C.: U.S. Government Printing Office.

Patterson, P. (1984). Blacks and the media in the 1980's. *Ivy Leaf, 60* (4), 21-25.

Peters, B. L. (1968, January 20). What the Negro wants from TV. *TV Guide,* pp. 17-20.

Ploski, H. A., & Marr, W. (1976). *The Negro Almanac: A reference work on the Afro American.* New York: The Bellwether Company.

Rothenberg, M. (1977, February 21). What TV does to kids. *Newsweek,* pp. 63-70.

INDEX

A

Acculturation 257
Activities
  human relations training program 20
Adell, J 293
Adler, A 198, 208
Admissions 274-5
Advanced empathy 135
Advice dispenser 93
Affective education 302
Affirmative action 360, 364-5
Agreement
  mutual 35
Albas, C 234
Albas, D 234
Aldrich, C C 236
Alexander, T 218, 234
All children education 46, 319-39
  legal basis 320
Alternative
  balance sheet for 184-7
  best 177
  brainstorming 162-8
  determining viability 182-4
  feedback 50
  generating 42, 157-72
  grid 184
  leading 180-1
  ranking 183-7
  recording 165
  selecting 42-3, 173-90
  stage 42-3
  strategy 162-8
Altman, H A 2, 18, 29
Altneale, C 253, 270
American Association of Colleges for
  Teacher Education 246, 333
American Association of Colleges of
  Teacher Education 244
American Dream 343-6
American minorities
  sketches 252
Anti-Defamation League 28
Anxiety 136
Approach
  problem-solving 34-5
  systematic 175-7

Approach-approach
  conflict 216
Approach-avoidance
  conflict 216
Avoidance-avoidance
  conflict 216
Asbury, F R 29, 129
Ashmore, R D 349, 371
Asian American culture
  implications 262
Asian American students
  characteristics 265
Asian Americans 260-4
Asian Americans, attitudes toward
  Table 262
Asian family structure 262-3
Asian immigrants
  American history 260-1
Assumptions
  model 35-6
Atkinson, D R 87, 256, 257, 258, 259,
  265, 269, 270, 271
Attending
  nonverbal behavior 60
Attending behavior report
  Form 76-7
Attractiveness 183
Authority 35
Autonomous morality 220
  definition 220
Avila, D L 28, 128
Awareness components 44-6

B

Baker, S B 190
Balance sheet
  Table 179
Balance sheet grid, categories
  explanation 186
Bananaism 264
Bandura, A 217, 218, 235
Baptiste, H D 244, 269
Baptiste, M L 244, 269
Baron, R A 235

mediator 248
Culture comparison
  Table 255
Curricula
  academic 9
  affective 9
  hidden 248
Curriculum
  secondary 248

D

Danford, B 12, 29
Danish, S J 109, 128, 129
D'Arienzo, R V 12, 29
D'Augelli, A R 109, 128, 129
D'Augelli, J F 109, 128, 129, 190
Dawson, M E 256, 269
Decision making
  steps 228
  valuing process 228
Decision-making process
  class involvement 181
Declaration of Independence 362
Dell, P F 235
Denial, definition 145
Descriptions, feedback 50
Deutsch, M 215, 235
Developmental growth 300
Dimensions of learning
  psychological 314
Diminishing returns 187
Disciplinary approaches
  crisis-oriented 177
Disciplinary procedures
  by-products 177
Discouraged child 198
Discrepancies
  confrontation 141
Distortions 141
  confrontation 141
Distributive justice 223
Doing culture 70
Dollard, J 215, 217, 235
Drabman, R S 237
Due process procedures 328
Durkin, D 235
Dustin, D 2, 13, 28, 29, 57, 58, 128,
  269, 293, 295, 296, 371, 372

Dysfunctional conflict
  characteristics 215
D'Zurilla, T J 171, 190

E

Echo Hawk, M 253, 270
Economic Opportunity Act 362
Education 366-9
  all children 319-39
  compensatory 12-3, 362-4
  cultural pluralism 239-71
  functions 366
  multicultural 44-5
  nonracist 45-6
  nonsexist 45
  psychological 46
Educators, implications 259-60
Egan, G 2, 28, 29, 32, 46, 47, 58, 87,
  90, 108, 128, 129, 135, 140, 141,
  155, 160, 161, 163, 164, 166, 171,
  172, 177, 190, 196, 198, 199, 208,
  212, 235
  guidelines 112
Elementary and Secondary Act of 1965
  321
Elementary school
  environment 283-5
Emotional security, students 306
Emotionally disturbed child
  characteristics 328
Empathic response
  rating scales 105-7
Empathy 40, 41, 95-6
  advanced 135
  examples 137-8
  primary 135
  questions 136
  skills 96-7, 131
Elementary school
  environment 283-5
Emotional security
  students 306
Emotionally disturbed child
  characteristics 328
Empathic response
  rating scales 105-7
Empathy 40, 41, 95-6
  advanced 135

Genuine behavior, checklist 108-9
Genuineness 40
  skill 107-9
German, S C 290, 293, 295
Gettysburg Address 362
Gibbs, J 225, 226, 236
Glazer, N 240, 242, 243, 269, 424
Glick, H 323, 331, 332, 338, 339
Goals
  helpee 37
  helper 37
  human relations training 17-9, 24
  human relations training program 20
  students 306
Gold, M 269
Goldfried, M R 190
Goldstein, A 155
Gollnick, D M 244, 269
Gordon, T 2, 28, 29, 92, 128, 129, 133, 155
Graham, R 235
Grant, C A 248, 269
Green, R L 363, 372
Greer, M 234
Grid
  alternatives 184
Grimley, L K 237
Grosenick, S 338
Group approach 47
Group awareness
  minority 6
  multicultural 6
Grout, C 269
Guidelines
  factors 192
  feedback 49-51
  nonverbal behavior 67-9
  time frame 192
Gutierrez, F S 247, 269
Guttentag, M 293

H

Hague, W J 236
Hall, E T 71, 87, 88
Handicapped children
  categories 327
  working with 334-6
Hansen, J C 237
Harmin, J 227, 237

Hawle, I L 236
Hawley, R C 234, 236
Hearn, M T 128
Helpee 36
  goals 37
Helper 36, 37, 38
  goals 37
  skills 37
Helping process
  three-phase model 32
Hersh, R H 236
Heteronomous 225
Heteronomous morality 220
Hicks, T 286, 294, 296
Hidden curriculum 248
Higgins, E B 346, 372
Hines, S A 284, 295
Hoffman, L W 279, 295
Hoover, T O 236
Horan, H H 190
Horan, J J 90, 129, 162, 163, 167, 171, 172, 177, 190
Howe, L W 228, 234, 237
Hudson, G R 190
Human behavior
  students 307
Human interaction skills
  using 51-2
Human needs
  basic 213
Human relations 366-9
  behaviors 2
  definition 1
  five factors 5
  ideological basis 12-3
  procedures 2
  purpose 7
  research basis 13-4
  training 1-29
  training procedures 46-52
Human relations training 1-29
  communication behaviors 15
  components 24
  definition 2, 24
  delivery model 24
  Figure 15
  goals 17-9, 24
  ideological basis 13
  knowledge areas 14
  knowledge awareness areas 15
  model 14-7

V

Vacc, N A 87
Vague and concrete statements
    Table 110
Value
    definition 212
Value clarification 211, 212
    classroom 227, 229-232
Value development 300
Value system, functions 213
Values 183
    cannot escape 209-37
    changes 210
    characteristics 212
    differences 210
    impact 211-2
    statement 211-2
Values clarification, children
    goals and processes 227
Values conflict 215-7
    dysfunctional 215
    functional 215
Values systems
    native Americans 254
Valverde, L A 10, 252, 271
Verma, S 237
Voice, qualities 136

W

Wallace, W G 190
Walter, R P 29, 129
War on Poverty 362
Warner, R W 372
Webster, C L 113, 114, 128, 129
Weingartner, C 234
Wendt, J A 11, 29
Wheeler, J H 289, 296
White flight syndrome 243
Whiteman, J L 237
Williams, J V 288, 296, 355, 371
Winborn, B B 90, 129, 190
Wirtenberg, J 284, 288, 296
Wittmer, J P 2, 29, 87
Wolfing 72

Women
    changing roles 280
    health problem changes 282
    role changes 282
    role expectations 281
    working 280
Women movement 8, 279
Women's Educational Equity Act
    Program 57
Women's Educational Equity
    Communications Network 28
Work, C E 289, 296
Workability, determining
    checklist 161-2
Workable problems 159-62
    definitions 160-1

Y

Yarrow, L 355, 371
Yarrow, M 355, 371
Yellow peril menace 261

Z

Zangwill, I 241, 271
Zintz, M V 254, 271
Zucker, K B 237

John C. Moracco, Ph.D.
Associate Professor and
Program Coordinator
Counselor Education Department
Auburn University
Auburn, AL

Professor
Author
Counselor

Dr. John Moracco , Professor and Program Coordinator— School
Counseling, Counselor Education Department, Auburn University,
earned his Ph.D. at the University of Iowa, in the area of Counselor
Education and Educational Psychology. He has served at various
Universities including the American University of Beirut.

Publishing many articles, Dr. Moracco has contributed to profes-
sional journals including *Journal of Counseling Psychology, Journal of
Vocational Behavior, Counselor Education and Supervision, Applied
Behavioral Analysis, Journal of Experimental Education, Elementary
School Guidance and Counseling Journal,* and others.

Active in professional leadership roles Dr. Moracco served as editor
of the *Alabama Personnel and Guidance Journal;* editorial board
member of the *Elementary School Guidance and Counseling Journal;*
and *Measurement and Evaluation in Counseling and Development* President, Alabama Mental Health Counselors Association; member of
Association for Counselor Education and Supervision Training Program; and member of other state and regional associations. Currently,
he is editor of the *AMHCA News.*

Earl B. Higgins, Ed.D.

Assistant Vice President
for Academic Affairs
Auburn University
Auburn, AL

Professor
Author
Administrator
Counselor

Dr. Earl B. Higgins, Assistant Vice President for Academic Affairs at Auburn University, is a leading authority in counselor education, including the administration of human relations programs. He has taught and written extensively on counseling and human relations programs, has made presentations throughout the eastern United States, and has served as a consultant for more than a score of school systems, associations, and agencies in the Southeast. His work has been published in the major professional journals in his field and in an anthology on human relations counseling.

Dr. Higgins was named Assistant Vice President for Academic Affairs at Auburn University in 1984 after serving for a year as Academic Advisor to the President, with general administrative responsibilities for management of instructional programs of the University. A member of the Auburn faculty since 1974 and carrying the academic rank of associate professor of counselor education, Dr. Higgins holds the doctor of education degree in counselor education from Auburn. He also holds a bachelor of science degree from Claflin College in South Carolina and the masters of education degree from South Carolina State College.

He served from 1982-83 as an American Council on Education Fellow in Academic Administration and has won numerous other honors, including being named to *Personalities of the South, Personalities of America,* and *Outstanding Young Men of America.*